*Praise for Jonny Steinberg's*

# A MAN OF GOOD HOPE

"Beautifully recounted. . . . Personal without being intrusive, educational without being preachy, and absolutely worth reading."
—*Pittsburgh Post-Gazette*

"A tale of luck, hustle, survival, and determination, *A Man of Good Hope* is an extraordinary examination of what it means to be human."
—*BuzzFeed*

"What a brave, important book. Steinberg's writing is so human, so humane, and so honest. . . . Steinberg stands shoulder to shoulder with other great writers who have also made sensible and visible so much that might otherwise remain insensible and invisible out of the political and human tragedies all too common in Africa—Michela Wrong, Ryszard Kapuściński, and Ishmael Beah. Steinberg's central question is one for all of us: What does it mean to live a 'fully human life' and whom among us has either the courage or the luck to live that life?"
—Alexandra Fuller, author of *Don't Let's Go to the Dogs Tonight*

"[*A Man of Good Hope*] tells one man's extraordinary and moving story, revealing the reality of life at the bottom of the world's worst pile."
—*The Times* (London)

"A masterpiece. Steinberg has illuminated a modern African odyssey to brilliant effect."    —Martin Meredith, author of *The State of Africa*

"Only through Steinberg's adroit persistence—he knows when to probe and pry and when to retreat when Asad seems nettled by constant questioning—can the account of Asad's remarkable, almost miraculous life journey emerge."    —*Minneapolis Star Tribune*

"South African journalist Steinberg vividly recounts one Somali man's experience of diaspora, resulting in a book that is part biography and part contemporary history. . . . Steinberg's thoughtful approach and Asad's attitude of droll resilience make for a tale that any reader can appreciate." —*Publishers Weekly*

"Painstaking and humane." —*Irish Examiner*

"Weaves together the many personas of a man whose story is at once unique and an archetypal example of an all-too-large collective. For truly capturing the power of dreams and the resilience of human nature, this book deserves a wide audience." —*Kirkus Reviews*

"Intuitively gentle writer patiently and thoughtfully teases out the memories of a young Somali man, Asad Abdullahi, a 'boy kicked through life like a stone.' . . . [Steinberg's] caring, questioning prose illuminates how, after all Asad has endured and all he remembers, he can still be a man who carries hope with him. A remarkable story, skillfully etched." —*Booklist*

Jonny Steinberg

# A MAN OF GOOD HOPE

Jonny Steinberg was born and bred in South Africa. He is the author of the critically acclaimed *Sizwe's Test* (also published under the title *Three Letter Plague*), as well as *Midlands* and *The Number*, both of which won South Africa's premier non-fiction literary award, the Sunday Times Alan Paton Award. Steinberg was also a recipient of one of the inaugural Windham Campbell Prizes. He teaches African Studies at Oxford University.

# A MAN OF GOOD HOPE

# A MAN OF GOOD HOPE

Jonny Steinberg

VINTAGE BOOKS
A Division of Penguin Random House LLC
New York

The Library of Congress has cataloged the Knopf edition as follows:
Steinberg, Jonny.
A man of good hope / by Jonny Steinberg.—First edition.
pages   cm
1. Abdullahi, Asad.   2. Somalia—Biography.   3. Refugees—Somalia.   4. Somalis—South
Africa—Biography.   5. Somalis—United States—Biography.   I. Title.
CT2208.A23S74 2014   967.7305'3092—dc23   [B]   2013046388

**Vintage Books Trade Paperback ISBN: 978-0-8041-7104-5**
**eBook ISBN: 978-0-385-35273-4**

*Book design by Soonyoung Kwon*
*Cartography by Mapping Specialists*

www.vintagebooks.com

Printed in the United States of America
10   9   8   7   6   5   4   3   2   1

*For two teachers*
*Sen Schonken and Peter Hudson*

# Contents

# Preface

Asad Abdullahi sits opposite me at a table in the Company Gardens. Around us, elderly white men are playing chess.

My notebook is open on the table, my pen in my hand. I am asking Asad about the Kaaraan district of Mogadishu, where he spent the first eight or so years of his life. He says he remembers so little.

"It doesn't matter," I say. "Instead of trying to remember, just tell me what comes into your head when you think of Mogadishu."

The oddest thought comes to me. He is wearing a body-hugging yellow hoodie and skinny blue jeans, and, in this tight attire, he seems not just tall and thin, but elongated. Each part of him—his nose, his cheeks, his palms and his fingers, his torso—appears to have been ever so caringly stretched. The result is elegant.

It occurs to me that he is sitting at Cape Town's point of origin. The gardens around us were planted 358 years ago, almost to the day. Here is Asad, on very old ground, while he himself is so new and so decidedly unwelcome.

In his slender fingers is a twig. I think he found it while we were strolling up from the library. Now he snaps it in half and draws it to his nose.

His eyebrows rise with surprise. He smells it again.

"Amazing," he says. "From the moment I saw it lying on the ground, I knew what the smell would remind me of."

And he begins to tell me how he made ink. He was seven years old, he thinks, a student at a madrassa, preparing the charcoal mixture into which he would dip his pen in order to copy out the Koran. To bind the ink, he says, you need the sap of the *agreeg* tree. You snap open a branch and with pinched fingers tease out the juice, allowing it to drip into the charcoal and water. While stirring the mixture, you absentmindedly put your fingers to your nose. You breathe in deeply. Ah!

The smile on his face is wistful and intense, and I think I have an inkling of where he has gone.

He knows that I am still here, that, at the table next to us, men are playing chess. But he is also elsewhere, and he is savoring it, for he understands that it can last only a few seconds. He has reeled back more than twenty years. With the twig he has found in the Company Gardens, he is reliving a forgotten high, for it is clear from the expression on his face that the sap of the *agreeg* is narcotic.

I feel a whim rising. I know that if I think about it, even for a moment, I will find a reason to back off, so I do not think about it. A man who idly snaps open a twig and is transported back so vividly, so powerfully, to another world is a man about whom I ought to write a book.

Several weeks earlier, I had driven out to his shack for breakfast. My diary records the day as September 24, 2010, a public holiday in South Africa. I was accompanied by Pearlie Joubert, a journalist, who had introduced us. I had had an idea for a very different book. I had asked Pearlie to introduce me to people who had fled Cape Town in the wake of South Africa's surge of violence against foreign nationals in May 2008. I had wanted to compare this episode to events that had happened fifty years earlier.

Asad came out to greet us wearing a turquoise *macawi* knotted around his waist and dropping to his ankles. Pearlie had told me that he was twenty-seven years old. He seemed more than that to me, perhaps because I associated the *macawi* with middle age.

The shack into which he invited us was covered everywhere in folds of delicate cloth. A dozen or so of them hung from the ceiling at the edge of his bed, screening it from the rest of the room. The tin walls, too, were coated in cloth, their colors dark and muted—maroons and deep greens. They dimmed the room, as if dusk were falling and nobody had turned on the lights. It was with a start that I noticed his wife. She was on a stool in the corner, her chubby face staring out from a head shawl that covered most of her cheeks.

Asad invited us to sit, then crouched over a Bunsen burner. He would make us a Somali breakfast, he announced: pancakes. The dough was at his side in a plastic bowl, and the pan on the stove sizzled with strips of meat and onions and peppers.

Asad lives in Blikkiesdorp—Tin Can Town, in English. It has been described as Cape Town's asshole, the muscle through which the city shits out the parts it does not want. Built by the city in 2007, it consists of sixteen hundred identical one-room structures laid out in sixteen identical square blocks. Erected to house people removed from homes they occupied illegally, it is a dump in which the city's evicted are mixed together. More than thirty kilometers from the center of Cape Town, it is separated from the city's economic heartland by a long and expensive taxi ride. It is the ultimate ghetto, its residents hemmed in by distance, by poverty, and by their own personal histories.

In early 2010, the city and the United Nations High Commissioner for Refugees decided, in their collective wisdom, to place thirty-four Somali and Congolese families in Blikkiesdorp. All had had to flee their homes in May 2008 with South African mobs at their heels. Each had spent the better part of the previous two years in makeshift refugee camps, too afraid to enter Cape Town again. Blikkiesdorp was the site of their reintegration. They could live rent-free in one-room shacks surrounded by the city's outcasts, people who could only hate them.

Two months before I meet Asad, a rumor spread through Blikkiesdorp. It was the day before the end of the soccer World Cup, held triumphantly on South African soil. Blikkiesdorp, the rumor went, would celebrate by killing its foreigners. That evening, a crowd assembled outside Asad's shack and began to hurl rocks at its tin walls. Asad phoned Pearlie, who seems to know everyone in Cape Town, including somebody in the higher echelons of the police. A detachment of public-order police rushed to the scene.

Over breakfast, Asad told us how he was making a living.

He headed each morning to Mitchells Plain Town Centre, about ten kilometers away, a retail hub in Cape Town's largest township, taken over by Somali traders. He would hang around until he found somebody who needed a driver—to pick up stock from one of Cape Town's wholesale stores, to take some people to another town, whatever. For a fee, Asad offered to drive.

He said that it was unsustainable, that he was a trader, a businessman, that if he were to live he must open a trading store here in Blikkiesdorp, that it was just a question of raising the capital.

This was not idle talk. I would buy his time over the following weeks. He was to guide me through the Somali zones of the city, take me to its hostels and its restaurants and introduce me to its businessmen. He would broker meetings with people who had fled various parts of the city in May 2008. With his help, I would write a history of Somalis' experiences of a famous episode of violence. I would be paying him seven thousand rand for his time, precisely the amount of capital he needed to open a trading store.

Sitting in his shack, eating the breakfast he had prepared, it occurred to me that our transaction might make his life considerably more dangerous than it was now.

"You want to run a cash business in this place," I said. "What will stop your neighbors from shooting you and making off with your day's takings?"

He smiled. Not just with his eyes but with his whole mouth. His teeth were brilliant white and perfectly ordered.

"It is not for the gangsters to decide when I die," he replied. "When you are still in the womb, Allah has decided the course of your whole life."

He beamed at me mischievously. I had the feeling that he had told a private joke.


A week after meeting him in the Company Gardens, I go to Blikkiesdorp to see him. He has cut a hole in one of his tin walls and covered it with wire mesh. Behind it is a stool and, behind that, ceiling-high shelves filled with cigarettes and crisps and tinned food and bags of mealie-meal.

I do not share with him at first what I am hoping for. I begin going to see him in Blikkiesdorp every second or third day. We sit on his bed and talk for an hour or so. Then I leave.

At the end of one of these visits, I ask whether he would consider the prospect of my writing a book about his life. I tell him that, were he to agree, I would ask for a lot of his time—two mornings a week, say, maybe for as long as a year. I would travel to the places he has lived—or at least to those to which travel is possible—and would try to find people who once knew him. I wish to see the houses in which he slept and to walk the streets he walked. When the book is published, I say, I will offer him 25 percent of the royalties; I give him a sense of the sort of sum this would probably turn out to be. I tell him not to answer me now, but to give it some thought.

As I drive back to Cape Town on the N2 motorway, my feelings are mixed. I am excited. Back at the University of Cape Town, I will not even stop in at my office; I will go straight to the library and take out four or five of the most reputable books on Somalia, and I will bury myself in them. I also feel uneasy. This is not the first time I am to write an intimate history of a person much poorer than me. Trading money for access to a poor person's private world is fraught with discomfort. And yet, what I produce, in the end, is a commercial product, and the prospect that I alone earn the money is distasteful.

On previous occasions, I had tried to have it both ways. I solicited the cooperation of a subject without offering him money, his motives for agreeing invariably complicated and often opaque. We would work together for a long period. I would show him drafts of the manuscript that was to be published. And then, once I secured his consent without payment, I offered him a portion of royalties.

I am tired of working in this way. I have grown leery of the condescension, of the concealment, of the authority I have conferred upon myself to drip-feed the full extent of the transaction. And so what I offer to Asad up front is a commodity, the proceeds of which we will split. It seems much cleaner and more honest.

And yet this hardly solves all. The money I paid him to start his business has freed him to talk to me; one cannot ask a man who scrounges daily for work to take off two days a week to sift through his memories. And the promise of royalties will no doubt see his commitment through to the end of the project, no matter how deeply into his private life I dig. I have not found a way of writing the books I do without exercising power.

In the end, our project brings a discomfort much more immediate and unanticipated.

It begins with the question of what is to happen to Asad's new shop during the hours he spends with me. His wife can work the counter while he and I talk, but she knows little English and no Xhosa or Afrikaans, and so Asad, increasingly adept at all three, must be on hand. Sometimes I accompany him to Mitchells Plain Town Centre or to Bellville, or to a chore he must do in the center of town. But, on the whole, we must conduct our interviews in shouting distance of his business.

At first, we meet in his shack. I sit on the edge of his bed, and he on a plastic chair. But he is uncomfortable with the arrangement. He fiddles incessantly with his hands. At the slightest sound outside, he cocks his head and listens. An hour into our second interview, he has had enough; he tells me briskly that we cannot meet in his shack any longer and insists that we move to my car.

And so, day after day, that is where we meet. I sit in the driver's seat, he sits in the passenger seat, my notebook passing between us as I record his testimony in shorthand and he draws pictures of the scenes he describes. I am parked parallel to his shack, no more than a meter or two from the mesh-covered hole through which his wife serves his customers. Each person who comes to buy from him brushes against my car door.

He tells me that he wants it this way because his shack is too small. But it isn't. It is a perfectly comfortable space in which to talk, far more convivial, in fact, than a car. I wonder what his real reasons are and why he wishes to keep them concealed.

It comes to me slowly, as our time together stretches into a rhythm, and as the rhythm begins to emit meaning. More bluntly, it comes to me once I imbibe the bizarreness and the perversity of our meetings.

I am a citizen of my country, and the many strangers around me are aware of this. One of them might choose to shoot a bullet into my head, but he knows that a machinery will kick into motion, and people will come looking for him. I and those around me are in an orbit together. We are all aware of the rules.

Asad does not move within this orbit. He stands outside of it, for the rules do not apply to him. His shop fills with cash every day, and he knows that his neighbors know that were somebody to shoot him in the head and take his money the machinery of state would stutter reflexively into motion and then grind to a halt. I come to see that this knowledge shapes his life. In his every decision, the imperative to be free tussles with the imperative to be safe. On his shoulders rests the incessant burden of dodging his own murder.

It is our third week together. We are sitting in my car, talking.

"Turn on the ignition," he says.

I look at him. A moment ago he was deep in childhood memory, his head bowed, his hand running habitually over the dashboard. Now he is sitting bolt upright, and his eyes are fixed on my rearview mirror.

I turn around.

"Don't," he says. "Just start the ignition."

I obey. Then I adjust my side mirror to see what he sees. A couple of hundred meters back, three young men, their hoodies low over their eyebrows, are walking toward us.

I am not afraid. I am certain that they will soon turn left or right and head down another street. They are simply three Blikkiesdorp residents going about their business. After all, everyone under a certain age wears a hoodie. Asad's lies neatly folded among the clothes in his shack.

We wait.

I begin to feel Asad's fear.

As if it is a virus, as if it jumped off him and sank into my skin and is now coursing through my veins.

This moment is so very productive. While a part of him is in my blood, I can understand. I know why he insists on meeting in my car. More important, I know the calculations he made when he allowed me into his life.

"You get scared every time I visit," I say.

"Yes," he replies, his eyes still fixed on the men behind us.

"You worry that a white man in a good car attracts men with guns, that you and your family are much more unsafe when I am around."

"I worry about that so much," he says.

"You insist that we meet in the mornings because that is when gangsters sleep."

"That's right."

"And you want to meet in the car so that you can see danger coming."

"In the shack," he replies, "you can see nothing. The first you see of them is the gun in your face."

By now, the three young men have walked right past us, and we are watching their backs as they disappear.

I turn off the engine and pick up my pen and notebook. I do not want to tell him what else I think I now know. Saying it out loud would be dangerous; would force us to examine our arrangement in its naked perversity; would make it hard for us to continue.

I am imagining the calculations he has made. He very much wants to hang on to me, for I am like Pearlie, a person from the other side, a person who travels within the orbit of law. Who knows when he may need such a person to come to his aid? Perhaps tonight.

But to keep our acquaintance he must sit for hours alongside me and remember his past. Otherwise, I will lose interest and disappear. And he must do this remembering in the vicinity of his home and family, for he cannot wander from his new business so often and for so long. Yet the routine of my recurring presence, he believes, is bound to attract men with guns.

And so he juggles. He draws close the parts of me that bring safety while diluting, as best he can, the parts that bring danger.

Hence, my car. Between October 2010 and September 2011 we spend many hours there. While his internal eye peers into his childhood, the eyes on either side of his nose scan the street.

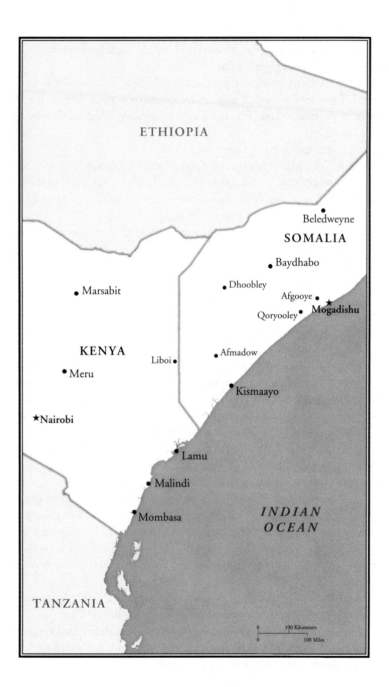

# PART I

# Somalia to Kenya

# *Mogadishu*

In describing his childhood there is really only one place for Asad to begin. It was early one morning; he is not sure of the day, but the month was January 1991. This he understands from collective memory; nobody who knows Mogadishu, the capital city of Somalia, is unaware of what happened that month.

He believes that he was eight years old. Whether he knew before that he was Daarood and that others were not is irretrievable now, but he certainly came to know it on that day.

In January 1991, militias began to attack the northern parts of Mogadishu. The men in these militias were Hawiye, and they wanted to overthrow the government of President Mohamed Siad Barre, who was Daarood.

"The militias were based in the countryside outside the city," Asad tells me. "They controlled the north of the country. They would come into Mogadishu to attack and regroup, attack and regroup, in waves.

"They came at night, and their target was all Daarood men. As far as they were concerned, Daarood men were government men. So, at night, the Daarood would leave their homes and gather together in government buildings for protection. They would leave women and children and the elderly at home. In Islam, one does not kill civilians—that means women, children, boys under fifteen, and the very old. Daytime, the men came back to see their wives."

Asad's father was sleeping away at nights, coming home during the day. Then one morning he did not come back. Or the next, or the next. It had been five days.

"When I look back now, I see that if I had been more focused on my mother, I would have been aware. There were three women staying in the house. I see now that my mother was hiding them. She must have discovered that some neighbors who were not friends had seen these three women. She must have known that she was going to get finger-pointed. I can see that now. Back then, I could not grasp that a person as solid as a parent could feel fear.

"I woke in the morning and found my mother pressed up against the front door, staring through the cracks. I came up next to her and looked too. There were five militiamen on our property. They were moving around the yard. I had no fear. I wanted to look at them closer, not through cracks. I tried to open the door. My mother grabbed me and pulled me to her. I was right up against her leg. I still did not share her fear. I find myself thinking now: Where were my brothers and sisters? I don't remember. In my mind it is just me and my mother. We were watching the militiamen. Three of them came up to the door and knocked very hard. My mother did not want to let them in.

"They pushed against the door and she pushed back. Then they started kicking, thumping the door. My mother pushed herself heavily against it. The door started breaking. I saw a pair of hands come through. They tore a hole out of the door, big enough for a person to climb through. My mother just stood there, as if there was still a door to push against. Still, she held me to her leg. The first militiaman just stared at her. She stared back. Then the second militiaman pushed the first one out of the way and shot my mother in the chest."

I wonder what the militiamen did when they entered the house. Did they slaughter the women hiding there? For how long did they remain? How much time elapsed between their departure and the arrival of the first friendly adults, for between those two moments the children were, I presume, alone with their mother's corpse. What did they make of it? What happened to their world during those minutes or hours?

Each time these questions find their way to the tip of my tongue, they stop and turn around, and I swallow them back down. I do not have the courage. I simply record what comes from his mouth.

And so I know only that he spent one further night at his parents' home and that the following day his aunt—the wife of his father's brother—whisked the five children across the city to her house. Later that evening, Asad's uncle appeared, the first adult male Daarood he had seen in days. He does not recall for how long he and his siblings stayed there. "When I say 'a few days,'" he advises me, "that could mean anything from two nights to two weeks. In any case, after some time, we split up. Rahma and I went with my uncle. The other children went with my aunt. We walked out of Mogadishu and kept walking. I think that that was the last day it was possible for Daarood people to sleep in Mogadishu."

As I picture Asad heading farther from home, I think, more than anything else, not of what he left behind but of what he took with him. He would never again be firmly moored to any particular adult, to any family. He would become a child whose connections to others would dissolve and re-form and disappear again. And yet he says with certainty that on his great journey through childhood and across the African continent he took his mother.

He has no memory of her face, or of the sound of her voice: her place inside him is more ambient than that, more powerful. It is indistinguishable from his sense of himself, of why he is a man who works hard and is kind and finds things funny; indeed, why he is the sort of man who can share such memories and keep his composure.

"If there is such a thing as a best mother, mine was it," he says. "My father was working all the time. It was she who was with us twenty-four hours a day. She was very, very kind. I do not remember her raising her voice or beating us. I remember calmness and gentleness. I remember that she enjoyed being with us. If we were naughty, she would tell us that our punishment would come when our father got home. But then, in the evenings, she would protect us from our father.

"I last saw her at such a young age. The way she taught me, although I grew up an orphan, I still feel that what she was I am today. I did not lose her despite her death. I am not sure that words can describe what I am trying to tell you. I mean that by the time I was seven, she had already made me."

I press him to attach these feelings to particular memories of her. He thinks silently for a long time.

"Her hair was very beautiful," he finally offers. "Some women had many plaits. My mother did not. She parted her hair in the middle into two long plaits that went halfway down her back. We children played with her hair, sometimes all of us at the same time. I remember my hand touching my sister Khadra's hand while we both played with our mother's

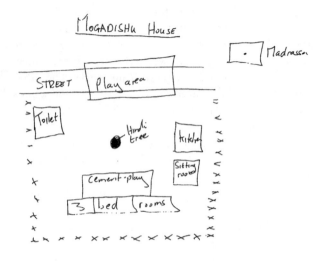

hair. Khadra's skin was so sticky, my mother's hair so smooth. I remember taking Khadra's hand away and running my cheek across the smoothness of my mother's hair."

When I ask him to describe his home in Mogadishu, he smiles and says he remembers each detail. But as soon as he begins talking, he stumbles and, in frustration, grabs my notebook and begins to draw.

He mumbles softly as he works, his cadences patient and singsongy, as if he is taking a small child through an exercise. Then he puts the notebook back in my lap. "Aha," he says.

As I examine the geography of his first eight years, he points a finger to the very center of his drawing, the colored-in dot representing the *hindi* tree.

"It reminds me of my brothers and sisters," he tells me. "When the *hindi* tree is big, it grows tall and wide, and everyone sits under it. But ours was still small, so the only people interested in it were the ones who did not mind the sun—the children."

He closes his eyes and tells me that he is picturing his siblings one by one, each under the *hindi* tree, each wrapped up in his own game. I ask him to describe them to me. "My older sister is Khadra," he says. "She was much whiter than us. She was almost like you. And her eyes were not like my black eyes. She had the eyes of a goat. The color was *quruurax,* like glass: not black or brown, not red, but like glass."

And then he describes his other siblings—his younger sister, Rahma, and his brothers, AbdiFaseeh and HasanAbshir—and I am startled as I listen, for he remembers them all, it seems, by their teeth.

"Hasan Abshir's were red," he says. "Khadra's were red with white dots. Mine are long and straight and very white. And yet we had the same mother and father. It is strange."

He curls his upper lip right up to the base of his nostrils and taps the nail of his index finger against his front teeth. Like his hands, they are long and well shaped.

I store this oddity in my notebook, not quite sure what to make of it. It is only later, after several weeks of conversation, that I come to understand what he invests in his teeth—they are his most vital connection to his father.

Asad refers to him as Aabbo, "Dad" in Somali. His memories of Aabbo take two forms.

The first is a medley of recollections, some of them images, others just disembodied ideas. Aabbo left early in the morning and returned very late, after the children had eaten dinner. In the first sequence in the medley, the children are summoned to the living room in the evening where their father receives them in the manner of a patriarch, quizzing each child about his or her day "top to bottom," Asad says, like a stern inquisitor.

Aabbo was often away. "He traded somewhere in the Arab world," Asad recalls, somewhere on the other side of the Gulf of Aden. On some days Asad says he does not remember what his father traded; on others he talks about animal skins bought from the nomads who came into Mogadishu, and sold on to Arabs in Yemen or Saudi Arabia or Dubai. He remembers that his father was once arrested and jailed in connection with his work—something to do with taxes or duties.

"My memories of this are not concrete," he says. "It is just a piece of knowledge that floats in my head. I don't remember the adults talking about it. I don't remember whether they were worried. Maybe they were worried; the regime could keep you locked up a long time."

Asad's other memory of his father takes the form of a single, vivid image. It was early evening. Asad heard footfalls in the yard. He stepped outside to find his father standing there, a bag over his shoulder. He had been away, somewhere, on business; Asad had not been expecting him. "Aabbo," he said.

In reply, his father put down his bag, flashed the broadest smile, and opened his arms. Asad ran to him and found himself lifted up to his father's face. They were so close that their noses almost touched. He inhaled Aabbo's breath; it was fresh, it smelled of a sweet herb. He observed the pores in the skin of his father's cheeks above his thin beard: they glistened; the skin was a little oily. But what remains with him most vividly is the smiling mouth into which he stared: the wide, pink tongue; the teeth so long and so perfectly shaped they seemed like narrow ivory tombstones.

"I have his teeth," Asad tells me. "When I look in the mirror and examine them, I think of the evening I looked into his mouth."

I think of Asad examining the smiles of the many Somalis he has met on his journey; he is judging his distance from them by what he sees in their mouths.

And then there is the madrassa. It was quite literally across the road from his home, as he remembers it. The journey from his front gate to his classroom took less than a minute.

That the making of ink is his most cherished memory of school is no surprise, for the rest, it seems, was not very nice. He remembers his teacher Dahir by his ceaseless voice and by his thrashing stick. Dahir had been reciting both books of the Koran for so long that he could shout passages of the Holy Book in rotation to twenty students at a time, each student at a different place in the text.

That is what Asad remembers. He clutched the handle of his *loox* in one hand, his pen in the other, and waited his turn. His cup of ink lay ready at his feet. The sound of Dahir's voice, hurling holy passages at one student after the next, would grow closer. Then it was Asad's turn. Dahir would shout; Asad would write on his *loox*. He kept his writing small, for if both sides of the *loox* were full before his passage was complete, he would have to try to remember the remainder of the passage by the sound of Dahir's voice.

As soon as Dahir moved on, Asad would begin to memorize what he had just written, for the clock was ticking; in the late afternoon, he would have to wash the ink off his *loox* with a damp clod of grass. The follow-

$|\,0\;0\;\times$

- hold with left hand when writing
- Stand (stands on legs when you wash it.)

ing morning, he recited what he had learned to Dahir. How much Asad failed to recall determined how heavily Dahir beat him.

Asad was six when he started at the madrassa. Learning both books of the Koran was meant to take another six years. He should have begun learning other subjects when he was twelve, like the Latin alphabet so that he could write Somali, then geography, history, and mathematics.

On the morning he describes the madrassa, I drive away from Blik-kiesdorp thinking of what he has said, and I see his mother and the learning of the Koran as opposite poles of his childhood. His time with her was what he lived for, it seems, while his time at school was so cold and drab. Then I blink and think again, and now I see that mother and madrassa share something important. They were the two pieces of Moga-dishu Asad took with him into exile. His mother he felt inside him all the time. As for the learning of the Koran: wherever he went, no matter how far or how strange, somebody was always starting a madrassa. Wherever he found himself, the Holy Book would open in front of him until he knew the whole thing by heart, as he does now, and as do the one hun-dred sixty or so Somali souls who bed down each night in Blikkiesdorp, each of them many years from home.

# *Flight*

Led by Asad's uncle, the party of fleeing Abdullahis made its way to Afgooye, a town thirty-one kilometers west of Mogadishu. Thousands upon thousands of people filled the town center, all of them in flight from the capital city, all of them Daarood, all discussing in which direction to go next. Here Asad learned not just that adult fear has a place in this world but that it can fill up the world. News was spreading that the militias were on the heels of the refugees, that they did not want able-bodied men to leave alive, that they had mortars and cannons and machine guns.

Asad remembers, above all, in Afgooye, his uncle flinging an arm around a truck driver whom he had come across on the street. There was something furtive in this gesture, as if his arm did not quite belong on the strange man's shoulder, as if he were trying something out. Although his uncle's face remained hard and blank, his excitement was betrayed in his dancing eyes. He had struck gold. For the truck in front of which the driver stood was from a fleet of what Asad still remembers today as "special trucks," special because they were run by clansmen, by Ali-Yusuf people. In normal times, they carried produce from the fertile river valleys of southern Somalia to Mogadishu. Now they were a passage to safety for anybody who could trace his ancestry nine generations to a forebear called AliYusuf.

On the back of the AliYusuf man's truck, the family moved from town to town. Asad names them one after the other, marking each on a map that lies between us. His marks stretch farther and farther south on the highway between Mogadishu and the Kenyan border. Were one to have a bird's-eye view, he says, and take in the whole, one would see a squirming snake of Daarood people. Most were on foot. Some, like the Abdullahis, were crammed into trucks. Asad concentrated above all on his uncle's face, for its expression was a weather vane telling him how things were among the adults. He recalls his uncle carrying a plucked chicken like it was his own nakedness, as if he were clutching in his arms a deeply private piece of himself. Then his uncle sat and hunched his shoulders and cut pieces from the chicken while the family assembled around him, a jealous and shameful gathering. It was only now, Asad says, perhaps as long as two or three weeks after witnessing his mother's murder, that he imbibed quite how much had changed. To see a strong, tall patriarch of a man cutting up a chicken like a guilty thief—he was truly in a foreign world now.

He points to a place on the map: Qoryooley. It is no more than a speck, about a quarter of the way from Mogadishu to the Kenyan border.

For some reason Asad no longer recalls, they were at this point separated from the AliYusuf fleet for a while; the driver of the truck was a stranger. Asad's uncle supervised the boarding of the vehicle. He gave his son, a fifteen-year-old boy called Abdi, a foot lift onto the truck. Then he passed his bag to Abdi, who put it down beside him and reached out his arms to receive whatever his father was going to pass him next. The rest of the family party was somewhere behind Uncle, waiting for their turn to board. Uncle picked Asad up and handed him to Abdi. There was a brief exchange, when the weight of the airborne Asad was transferred from his uncle's to his cousin's arms. At precisely this moment, the whistling of a handheld mortar arched over the scene, and everyone froze and looked up. The roadside exploded, throwing clumps of earth and rock into the air, and the truck rocked and tilted. And then Asad heard the truck's engine screech, and he was moving, still in his cousin's arms, the two of them thrown against the people next to them. Asad swiveled around in time to see his vanishing uncle turn his back, his attention now on those of his family who remained with him on the ground. Asad turned again and looked into Abdi's eyes; they were glazed over as if covered in a treacly liquid.

Something momentous can happen to a person we barely know, yet we will understand intuitively what he is going through simply because we, too, are human. But there are also moments in a person's life one will never understand if one does not know something about his world. Asad turned his face from Abdi's to take one last glance at his uncle's receding figure. Then he faced front and stared ahead. What lay before him was human, to be sure, but it was also distinctively Somali.

How best to describe this? Here is one way. Were I asked to name my forebears I could immediately rattle off the names of my parents and grandparents. With some mental effort, I could also tell you the names of some of my great-grandparents. Beyond them, I know almost nothing.

This is not so for Asad. From a very young age, he, along with all the other children with whom he attended madrassa, knew by heart the names of the last dozen generations of male ancestors on his father's side. It was the recital of these names, rather than a place on a map, or the site of a grave, that informed Asad who he was.

Speeding away from his uncle in a truck full of strangers, Asad was at risk of losing his connection to a lineage. It is an enormously complicated one; which part of it he invokes depends upon the situation at hand. When he counts back two generations, to his grandfather, Asad is an Abdullahi and is united to a handful of people who have the same paternal grandfather. When he counts back nine generations, he is an AliYusuf and regards everyone who can trace his lineage to the same AliYusuf as a clansman. These people are more distant than Abdullahis, and, Asad will come to learn, far less useful. But they are clansmen of a sort, nonetheless. Counting back fifteen generations, he is Mohammed Zubeyr. About twenty generations back, he is Abdille. Some two dozen generations back, Asad is Ogadeni, along with hundreds of thousands of others. Finally, somewhere in the mists of time, about thirty-five generations back, Asad, along with more than a million other people, is Daarood and thus a member of one of the Somalis' six great clan families. The others are Hawiye, Isaaq, Dir, Digil, and Rahanwiin.

He draws for me a skeletal image of Somali society, filling in the details of his own lineage while leaving the rest of the Daarood, as well as the other five clan families, peering down a blank page.


What, practically, do these lineages mean? That is probably the most contested question one can ask about Somalia. There was a time, certainly until Somali independence in 1960, when they were one of the bases of contractual and civil law.

The border between myth and actual evidence is by no means clear here. But in its ideal form, the story would go like this. Sometime in the past, all AliYusuf families sent representatives to a meeting to thrash out a treaty. They decided how cases should be adjudicated in the event that one AliYusuf kills, injures, steals from, or defames another. They agreed to a scale of punishment. Should the guilty party refuse to pay compensation, they licensed AliYusuf elders to tie him to a tree and threaten to kill his livestock.

They also agreed on what each family should contribute or receive in the event that an AliYusuf does wrong to, or is wronged by, a person from another group. This payment was called *diya*. The compensation for a man's life was, in principle, a hundred camels, a woman's life fifty camels. At the meeting at which their contract was settled, the AliYusuf would have determined how many camels the immediate family of an AliYusuf murderer pay the aggrieved party and how many camels the AliYusuf as a whole contribute.

Once the contract was concluded, it would have become a source of unwritten law, recognized in principle by all Somali elders.

Asad insists that *diya* is still operative. Were he to injure another Somali here in Cape Town, he tells me, the aggrieved one's family would seek compensation from the AliYusuf of Cape Town. But I am not so sure. As Asad tells me more about his life, and as I watch the way he organizes his affairs, the place of *diya* becomes more ethereal.

In any event, lineage is hardly all that there is to say about Somalia. To suggest so would be scandalous. Somalis have always come together in ways that transcend or ignore clans. There have been religious sects and great nationalist movements. In the cultivating villages of southern Somalia, people who have lived alongside one another for generations are bound to one another by *diya* agreements, no matter their respective clans. And clans themselves are by no means seamless; there are many internal divisions, some of them related to race.

When Somalia acquired independence in 1960, a great modernizing project to abolish clans and replace them with citizens ensued. The civil servants who ran the administration in Mogadishu were not permitted to mention their clans when they introduced themselves to one another. They were not meant to be patrons gathering power and goodies for their kin in the hinterland—they were building a single nation.

But clans remain a life force in politics, and new words were invented to describe them. In the late 1960s, civil servants simply began referring to their "ex-clans." And so an awkward culture evolved, one that alluded to the presence of ghosts in the corridors of power, describing a civil service that lived in double time, a piece of it in the past, another in a future yet to be realized.

After Mohamed Siad Barre came to power in 1969, he banned talk of ex-clans; they could no longer be referred to at all, even by another name. And yet, in his three decades in power, Siad Barre came to rule through a network whose members were drawn predominantly from three Daarood subclans. The Somali project to abolish clans had thus turned them into cancers; politics had now become a world in which things could not be called by their names, where people were forbidden from speaking in a language that described how power was actually wielded.

By the time Asad was born in the mid-1980s, there was civil war in northern Somalia, many miles away from the still-peaceful Mogadishu. It was as close to a clan war as Somalia had experienced in generations, for to be Isaaq or Hawiye was to be cut off from one's own nation-state, to be shut out in the cold.

The five men who pounded on Asad's mother's door that morning in January 1991 had walked into a capital city that no longer made any pretense to be theirs. It was, for them, a source of power and wealth that had been captured by an enemy. Their task was to rout the city's power holders, to force them to turn on their heels and flee, to leave them so wounded as to be unable to come back and fight.

In January and February 1991, clan allegiances were probably sharper and more poisonous than ever before in Somali history. What it might mean to be cut off from one's lineage, as had just happened to Asad, was hard to know.

Precisely what it was Asad left behind as the truck sped away is something about which he would often change his mind. That he was an Abdullahi and an AliYusuf would disappear from his life for years on end; there are, he would discover, many ways of being Somali other than through one's clan. And then, without warning, his lineage would burst back into his life and shape his fate. When it did so, he would feel that he had been asleep for years, reeling further and further from himself.

There and then, on that truck, Asad and Abdi were two minors without family. They were headed south toward Kismayo, the last Somali city before the Kenyan border, in a vehicle commanded by people with no immediate interest in their fate.

On the second night, they stopped at a town called Afmadow. In each previous town, the refugees had settled into mutually wary groups, and everything had felt brittle and on edge. Here, there were people in control. Some of the men in charge were government soldiers. Others were clearly not. The memory of them brings forth fragmentary images from Mogadishu: Asad recalls important men striding through government buildings. These buildings were unlike any others in Mogadishu. He remembers them by their very tall arches; he remembers walking beneath an arch and looking up. The men here in Afmadow, he registered, moved with the same long and purposeful strides as the ones in the government buildings.

For the first time, Asad was asked two questions that would be repeated to him again and again over the following twenty years: Who is your father? What is your clan?

He grabbed these questions gratefully, as if they were gifts of milk and bread. "Abdullahi Hirsi," he replied. "AliYusuf." These men would know what to do with such information. Perhaps they would lead him to uncles or other family; perhaps Aabbo himself was here.

Asad and Abdi were assigned places to rest for the night. They bedded down side by side. Many other bodies surrounded them. Asad enters the head of his young self, drifting off to sleep in a strange city on an evening in February 1991, and he thinks he knows what the young Asad saw. He rose up above the mishmash of bodies and found a cord running from each, just where the buttocks meet the back. These cords all raced away in one direction, many dozens of them, toward Mogadishu, where each made its way to the home in which its owner belonged. Asad's cord snaked into the house he had sketched for me and found its way to the parental bedroom where it wrapped itself with hunger around his sleeping mother.

When he woke, it was daylight. People were walking about. It seemed that much time had passed. He turned to his cousin to find that Abdi was not there. He remembers wandering from adult to adult, asking each if he had seen his cousin. And then his memory blanks. He does not recall how he found out that during the night the important men who reminded him of the government buildings had recruited Abdi into a militia, that they were conscripting every boy fifteen years or older to fight.

## *Yindy*

The stack of names Asad had offered when first asked—his own name, that of his father, his lineage, his clan—entered the great circuit of information that traveled through the ranks of Afmadow's refugees. It was as if Asad's lineage was being poured through a sieve so that the grit of thicker, closer attachments would get caught in the netting.

At some point during this process of sifting, Asad was led by the hand through a market in the very center of the city and deposited into the hands of a woman he did not recognize. He had been told that she was family, close family, and that she would look after him. He remembers well his first sight of her. She sat on a low stool, legs apart, stirring a large pot of tea. Her name was Yindy. As with his siblings, Asad describes her in the first instance by her teeth.

"They were damaged," he says. "I had never seen teeth like these before. They were black, as if they were bruised. As if somebody had beaten her in the mouth. What I remember is that they were darker than the skin on her face. She was very pale, and also very short."

It was early evening. Yindy, it appeared, was serving customers. They sat on plastic chairs at the roadside and drank her tea and spoke to one another. Much later, Yindy opened a large black pot and began serving them food. Asad remembers thinking that Yindy resembled her pot: short and squat on legs that barely raised her from the ground.

This drinking of tea and eating and talking seemed to Asad to go on forever. Several times, he drifted off and found himself hurtling through the night toward Mogadishu, only to be startled back to Afmadow by a shout or a laugh. He seemed to have entered a world that did not sleep, where people drank tea through the small hours instead of going home to families.

Eventually, he grew so tired that he crawled under a plastic chair and slept, the voices of Yindy's patrons filtering through his dreams. He was woken, gently, by the morning call to prayer and by the shuffling of many feet. He climbed out from under his chair to discover that the patrons were all gone, their place taken by several middle-aged women who were moving about among the pots and brewing tea. Yindy chatted with them for a while and then led Asad away.

At first, he did not realize that they had arrived at Yindy's home, for it did not seem a private space at all. It was a two-room shelter made of wood and zinc and mud. In front of it stood a small yard that opened onto the street. The room in which Yindy put him to sleep was so close to the people walking by, it felt as if a hand could reach in at any time and snatch him away.

He does not recall whether it was Yindy or someone else who explained it to him, but she was a close relative, the daughter of Asad's father's sister.

"She had walked by herself all the way from Mogadishu," Asad recalls. "I am not sure what her family situation was, only that she was divorced and that her husband's family was not helping her. She was alone and in trouble. She got by running a cafeteria, cooking, and selling tea. She worked very, very hard and each day had just enough to eat."

Yindy was not quite alone. Asad had entered a world of women. There were about half a dozen of them, as he recalls, and they shared the cafeteria in shifts. Each day, Yindy would leave her home for work at five or six o'clock in the evening and would begin to make tea and food. She would work through the night. In the morning, at first prayers, other women would take over, and Yindy would go home to rest. She seldom slept in one of her two rooms. Instead, she would make herself a bed in what Somalis call the *balbalo*. Each Somali household has one, some two or three. It is a wall-less shed—four poles holding up a thatched roof— and stands in the family yard. When the temperature reaches a hundred or so degrees it is too hot to be indoors or in the sunlight, and people live in the shade of their *balbalo*.

Lying there under her thatched roof during the daylight hours, Yindy was practically on the street, her only shield from passersby a large barrel that lay on its side across the width of the *balbalo;* Asad wondered how she managed to sleep. But sleep Yindy did, without stirring, sometimes until as late as two or three o'clock in the afternoon.

Asad was forbidden to leave the yard while Yindy rested. The world outside was deadly, she kept warning. It was no place for a child.

"She was not wrong," Asad recalls. "Everyone was shooting. Two people would start arguing in the street. One would shoot the other. Ogadeni shooting Ogadeni. Refugee shooting refugee. And there were constant rumors that the Hawiye were going to attack. And so there was this nervousness, this fear, that tomorrow the world is going to fall on everyone's head, so maybe it is better not to care so much about anyone today."

Yindy's yard became the whole of Asad's world. There were the two rooms, each insufferably hot and dark; there was the yard, barely large enough for him to pace; and there was the sleeping Yindy in her *balbalo*. Sometimes, he would enter the *balbalo* and watch her diaphragm expand and contract until the rhythms hypnotized him and the street outside disintegrated. He would find enormous relief in this movement of her body; he had no idea why.

He was left with his thoughts, and these, recurrently, were of his house in Mogadishu, of his mother, his father, of his life. His memories, he found, took the form of several images—some of his mother, others of siblings, others of the *hindi* tree, some of the madrassa. They would come to him in sequence and reel over and over before his eyes, the order in which they appeared always the same. It was so unreal, the recurring sequence; it struck him that, already, after just a few weeks, he was losing his memory of his life. For these spooling images did not seem to involve him: they were images from another world.

On some evenings, he accompanied Yindy to the cafeteria, where he would sit and listen to the adults talk and thus get some sense of what was happening. It was here that people kept discussing an imminent Hawiye attack and exchanged stories about refugees shooting one another in the streets of Afmadow. They discussed, too, whatever news or rumor they had received from Mogadishu. These discussions fell together into one big stew of talk so that Afmadow and Mogadishu, the past and the present, bubbled and cooked.

In Mogadishu, it seemed, the Daarood people who had not left had been sucked into a hole of butchering and slaughter, and he wondered whether his father had escaped or whether he was among the dead. He heard, too, at the cafeteria, that the Hawiye militias had taken the towns on the Kismayo highway one by one, and as the names spilled off the tongues of Yindy's customers, he recognized each as a town he had passed through. Until, finally, someone among Yindy's customers mentioned the town of Qoryooley, where Asad had been separated from his family. The Daarood in this town and the others, people said, were "hostages." Although it was not a word he had heard before, he soon knew what it meant, for the people were saying that the hostages were like slaves and that those believed to have worked for the Somali government were being tortured, some of them killed.


How long had he been in Afmadow when it happened? He is not sure. He thinks maybe a month. It was late morning on an especially hot day. Yindy was asleep in the *balbalo*. Asad, a child with no use for shade, even when the sun pelted down, was lying on his stomach on a concrete slab between the house and the *balbalo*. Half awake, half asleep, his ear flat against the slab, he was roused by a thumping and pounding that seemed to emanate from the ground. He raised his head in time to watch a woman hurdle his prostrate body and make for the house. She pulled unsuccessfully at the door; it was locked. Then she jumped over Asad once more and ran to the entrance of the *balbalo*, kicked aside the barrel that served as its door, and went inside.

A man ran into the yard from the street and skidded to a halt. Only once he was past Asad and standing in the mouth of the *balbalo* did Asad notice that in one of his hands was a pistol, its barrel pointing at the ground. The man lifted his gun, turned his face away, and fired twice into the *balbalo*. In that instant, Asad recalls, he was struck by the oddity of the man looking away. Why shoot at all if you do not direct your eyes at your target? What is the point?

From the *balbalo* came a volley of cries. Although he had never heard Yindy cry like that before, Asad nonetheless recognized them as hers. The man turned on his heels and ran. Asad pursued him, primarily to get away from the noise Yindy was making. He recalls sprinting through the crowded streets of Afmadow, screaming, for all he was worth, "You have killed Yindy! You have killed Yindy!"

And then he was surrounded by adults, and he was crying, and they were leading him back to his house. A crowd had already gathered. Yindy lay in the *balbalo* sweating, delirious, cursing under her breath. She had been shot square in the shin, and the wound was deep and wide and gruesome. Chipped bone and blood and raw flesh: things, Asad thought, the world had no right to see.

Later that day, he learned that the man and woman who had run into Yindy's yard were brother and sister. The woman had just announced that she was pregnant. She was also unmarried. Her brother had picked up a gun and chased her through the streets in pursuit of his family's stolen honor.

Asad scoffs as he tells the story.

"Somali men," he says. "Shooting an innocent woman in the leg to get back this thing called honor, a thing you cannot even see, let alone eat or drink."

He will do that again several times: he examines things Somali from a distance and shakes his head in disbelief. At other times, though, *he* is the dishonored man, and he warns that no deterrent is frightening enough to stop him from snapping a South African's neck.

His memory clouds. He no longer distinguishes the hours from the days. What he does recall becomes very abstract. He remembers one network of people fading and another coming into focus. The cafeteria women disappeared. Their alliance was not one designed for emergencies. Their mutual business was survival, and a woman down did not help at all. The network that appeared, as if from nowhere, was kin: Yindy's father's kin. Asad had not seen any of them around when Yindy was well. He did not know that they existed. It was a matter of life and death that drew them. From deep within the lives of the refugees, it seemed, a set of unwritten rules of conduct was rising, rules that nobody had thought out or said aloud but that took shape around each new moment. The prospect of Yindy's death had summoned them from nowhere. They arrived and took control.

There was no doctor to be found, and so the search became one for antibiotics. Some were located, and they were duly fed to Yindy at intervals, but it was not long before she had swallowed them all. And so another search was convened. It was said that in the countryside around Afmadow were nomads. They had never had Western medicine, but they had always had deep wounds, and so they would know what to do.

Some days after Yindy was shot, an old man appeared and took command of the patient. He stank something terrible, a stale, fetid smell that made Asad want to retch. His bag was made from the same cloth as the clothes he was wearing. Such were the ways of the nomads, people who made all their possessions from the same material and who knew nothing of baths and soap.

The old man unfolded his bag until it was a flat square laid out on the ground. It had many different compartments. From one of them he took a knife, from another several sticks. From a third emerged a long piece of rope. He put a flame to the knife and held it there a moment or two. Then he ran it down each side of Yindy's damaged leg, leaving two long stripes of bright red blood.

There were as many as half a dozen people around her body, and all Asad could see of her were her legs. It dawned on him that these people were waiting; they were waiting until Yindy's pain was so great that they would have to press her down. Would it take six people to keep Yindy still? Is that how badly this old man was going to hurt her?

As if on cue, the old man instructed everyone to hold Yindy tight. His voice was high-pitched like a bird's, but nonetheless commanding. He lifted Yindy's leg a little, took her toe in his hand, and pulled it hard. She screamed.

"It was very cruel," Asad recalls. "He was handling her roughly. He was not treating her like an injured person. I could not see her face, but her cries were terrible, terrible. The old man was trying everything. He massaged her leg. He tapped it with his stick. Eventually, he put a piece of cardboard on either side of her calf, then put a stick up against each piece of cardboard. Then he bound the whole thing together with ropes."

He instructed that nobody touch the contraption until he returned. He folded up his bag, tucked it under his arm, and walked briskly into the street. He did not say when he would be back. Asad stared at the material that the old man had left on Yindy's leg—the cardboard, the sticks, the rope. In the things that the nomad left behind were traces of his smell. Now Yindy would be stuck with it. Whenever she breathed, she would take into her nose and mouth the memory of this awful man.

The tone of Asad's voice brings into my car the anger his younger self had felt. He was a boy from Mogadishu, an urban boy; between himself and those who lived in the countryside he wanted to draw a bold line. And yet, among the memories he took with him from Mogadishu was a fragment from a family poem. He does not remember it well. It went something like this: "We were tired of wandering, wandering, wandering. And so we settled. We settled in one place to farm. It was a place called Fadhadhi."

"The poem refers to my grandfather's time," Asad tells me. "It was my grandfather Abdullahi who settled at this place called Fadhadhi. He was the first member of the family who was not a nomad. He was therefore the beginning, the beginning of what we are now."

"Where is Fadhadhi?" I ask.

"I have no idea. But I know that if I go there one day I will find family. Maybe not Abdullahi or AliYusuf people. Maybe they will be family on the maternal side. But Fadhadhi, wherever it is, is our place."

And so two nomadic worlds lived side by side in his head. In one of them was the history of his family. In the other was a stupid and barbaric man who arrived in Afmadow with his cloth bag and caused Yindy to cry out in pain.

The old nomad came back unannounced about a month later with more cardboard, more sticks, and more rope. He cut the contraption off Yindy's leg and examined the wound, which was swollen and yellow. Then he placed a hand on either side of the wound and squeezed, and Yindy shrieked with all her might, and the yellowy liquid that had been discoloring her leg oozed to the surface and dripped off the sides of her calf. The old man replaced the contraption with another just like it and promptly left, his patient shedding tears of sheer agony.

As he tells the story of the old man's second visit, Asad's voice becomes testy again, and he begins speaking immediately of his and Yindy's departure from Afmadow, as if the two events occurred on the same day. There was fighting very close to the city. He does not know what it was about or whom it was between. The refugees began to move out. It was very rapid. One day, the rhythm of the city's movement was as it had always been. The next, there were boxes everywhere and trucks and people shouting at one another. By evening, Yindy's street was almost empty.

Yindy was put on a truck. Asad was given a large canvas bag and told to pack into it whatever would fit. He recalls wandering through Yindy's tiny house, folding cloth and clothing and putting them in the bag. He selected two of the pots Yindy used to make her customers' tea. He grabbed two cups. Then he took a last look at the yard and the *balbalo,* the place in which he had spent almost every waking moment of the last two, three, perhaps four months: the precise length of his stay in Afmadow is lost forever. Then he climbed into the truck and sat, Yindy by his one side, the canvas bag at his feet.

. . .

The truck journey, he recalls, lasted one very long day. By evening, they were in the town of Dhoobley. It was dark when they arrived. Yindy was unloaded from the truck, and they slept that night on the side of the road. Asad assumed that things would change the next day, that some accommodation had been made for the refugees. But as morning became afternoon, he realized that this was it. In Afmadow, the refugees had been integrated into the town center and lived under solid roofs and behind gates. Here, they were simply dumped on a sparsely wooded piece of land, side by side. The people around them were complete strangers. It dawned on Asad that Yindy's father's family was gone. He had assumed that they were on another truck, that he and Yindy would be reunited with them at their destination. Just as Yindy's injury had conjured them from nowhere, so the flight from Afmadow had caused them to vanish.

Yindy was placed under a tree with a blanket suspended in the branches above her head. Asad took out the assortment of things he had put in the canvas bag: the pots, the cups, the clothes. And that is how he and Yindy remained for the next few days. Around them, their neighbors were building makeshift homes. Once or twice a day, they would bring food. Otherwise, they left the injured woman and her child alone, under the stars, sheltered only by the blanket.

It was perhaps on day four or five—he is not sure—that, without warning, several neighbors descended upon Yindy and began building a house around her where she lay on the ground.

"It was a nomadic house," he recalls. "Holes were dug in the shape of a circle. Thick sticks were placed in the holes. The sticks were then bent over, all coming together at the top, closing. Rolled wire and rope, made from trees, was then spun around the structure. Then an entrance was made. The whole thing took maybe two days."

Their work done, the neighbors retreated, and now it was just Yindy and Asad and their house. For the first time since she was shot, they were alone together, an invalid and a small boy. It fell to Asad to look after her.

"I cared for her twenty-four hours," Asad tells me. "The wound in her leg oozed pus, and I cleaned it. She started to stink, I washed her. She got her period and bled, I cleaned her." He cocks his head, so that his face is turned from me. "I was a small boy," he says quietly.

Then he turns to face me again and smiles, his mild embarrassment gone. He lifts his buttocks off my car seat and pats one of them.

"She could not go to the toilet. I wiped her."

I try to press him on what it felt like to discover her body in this way. Indeed, if there is anything I want him to relive it is this nursing. But he recoils from the intimacy. "We became like brother and sister in Dhoobley," he simply says.

It was one thing cleaning Yindy's body, quite another feeding her. For once they had erected the house, the neighbors stopped bringing food. Yet another of those unwritten rules of collective flight was taking shape: How much does one sacrifice to help an invalid who will never get well and care for herself? When does one cut ties and watch her sink or swim?

Each day, Asad went out to forage. He would cross into Kenya at the border post and hang around the soldiers until they gave him food. There was also an NGO setting up a base, and he would sometimes get cooked meals and water there. He would bring everything back to Yindy.

"I got to be so close to her during this time," he says. "I would get home from the other side of the border, and from the minute I walked in I knew what she was feeling: either she was worried about me because I had been gone so long; or her leg had been very painful and she had been sitting with this pain for a long time; or she had wet herself because she could not wait for me to get back; or there had been no pain and she had been lying there dreaming about nice things, about better times, maybe. All this I knew the moment I walked in."

Their time in Dhoobley turned out to be brief, far briefer than in Afmadow. For one evening word went around that the fighting was coming into town, and everybody began packing hurriedly. The neighbors came back, this time to carry Yindy out of her house and to take her across the border into Kenya, to a town called Liboi.

## *Liboi*

Liboi is a border town in the dust lands of the North Eastern Province of Kenya. Before the Somali war, it was home to some ten thousand people, the majority of them Somali speakers, the remainder an assortment of Kenyan military and civilian personnel. Many made a living, in one way or another, from the steady traffic of people and things that crossed the border post with Somalia.

When war broke out, people from across southern Somalia fled toward Liboi. Asad was one of countless numbers who massed on the Somali side of the border and waited. Realizing that the tide could not be turned and that its borders would have to open, a doubtful and ambivalent Kenyan government invited the United Nations High Commissioner for Refugees (UNHCR) to hastily establish a refugee camp outside Liboi. Two nongovernmental organizations, Doctors Without Borders and CARE International, were contracted to hurry in to provide medicine and food.

When the camp at Liboi opened, people teamed across the border. In no time, the camp's population grew to more than forty thousand. And so the UNHCR set up another camp in a nearby town called Ifo, then another outside a town called Dagahaley, then a fourth camp at Hagadera. Collectively, they became known as the Dadaab camps, the name of the district in which they fell. Among them, they came to shelter about one hundred sixty thousand people.

Liboi is closed now and is thus perhaps the least well known of the four camps. But when one goes back to the reports written about it in the early 1990s, it feels as if one is reading in dry officialese a description of hell.

Water was perpetually in short supply. At one time during Asad's stay there, it was reported that refugees were dying at a rate of more than a hundred a month, many of them children under the age of five, many of them of thirst. Food, too, was scarce. Although each family was given a ration card, there was never enough to go around. Each family would send a member to queue at midnight to wait for a ration distribution that began at six o'clock the following morning.

If the UNHCR did not distribute enough food and water, neither did it provide adequate security for the thousands of strangers who had been thrown together. Report after report speaks of an epidemic of rape in Liboi and other camps. Some say that clan divisions determined who raped whom; others that when Bantu Somalis began arriving at Liboi in October 1992, their women were raped as punishment for coming to take scarce rations. Other reports complain that the UNHCR turned a blind eye to the obvious fact that the camp was awash with firearms. The popping of gunfire would ring in the night, it was said, and continue at regular intervals until morning. Anything was possible, it seems, no matter how diabolical, for whoever could gather sufficient force.

It is interesting to compare the reports of nongovernmental organizations and international newspapers with the memory of somebody who was a child there. It is not that Asad's recollections of Liboi contradict the official documentation. He confirms everything I have read. His presiding memory of Yindy during this time was her pervasive fear, especially at night, when the most terrible fate might befall one. But in the Liboi preserved in Asad's mind, these deprivations and anxieties are a background hum. He has instead taken with him from that time something else entirely.


Very early, perhaps on the day Yindy and Asad came to Liboi, a white woman who worked for Doctors Without Borders noticed the short, crippled woman and her young child. Yindy was taken away to the military hospital—Asad does not remember for how long—and when she returned her leg had shrunk back to its normal size, and it no longer oozed yellow pus.

Asad smiles at the memory of the white woman. It is, in part, a smile of gentle self-rebuke, for he tells me that he remembers neither her name nor her nationality.

"When I think of her," he says, "the only word that comes to my mind is *gaal.*" In Somali, *gaal* means "white person." "Whenever she came to our place, I would know long before she arrived, because a group of children would run up to me saying, 'Your *gaal* is coming, your *gaal* is coming.'"

Arranging for Yindy's medical care was the first of many things Asad's *gaal* did. She had a large *balbalo* built for Yindy, while the other refugees had only tents. A pipe was extended under the ground to provide water to the *balbalo,* when the other refugees had to form long lines at the water pump. Fresh food was brought to Yindy twice a week; the other refugees had to queue for their dry rations for six hours each day.

It was certainly a blessing, albeit a mixed one. Whether Asad could have kept foraging for himself and Yindy indefinitely, as he had during their time on the Somali side of the border, is doubtful. It is quite possible that the nameless *gaal* saved Asad's and Yindy's lives. And yet, their special treatment marked them: their piped water and fresh food made them objects of envy; their *balbalo* was an advertisement that they were just a disabled woman and a child and were thus defenseless. As sunset approached, Yindy's fear would rise. She was terrified of the night, and her terror, Asad recalls, did not abate for all of the two years that they lived in Liboi.

Not long after they arrived, Yindy sent a very reluctant Asad off to a madrassa that had been established just a two-minute walk from their tent. To his dismay, he was trapped there each day from eight o'clock in the morning until four in the afternoon, another tyrant barking reams of holy text into his ears.

"The method was not the same as in Mogadishu," Asad says. "There was no *loox,* no ink. We would all sit, and the teacher would come to each of us in turn. He would shout a passage out from the Koran once, then pause for a few moments, then shout it again. You would have to repeat it. He would count the mistakes you made and then beat you once for every mistake."

Asad loathed school, but he also clung to it gratefully, for it marked him as a boy who was not an idiot.

"I do not remember when they began arriving," he says, "but at some point, nomadic children from the countryside started coming into Liboi. You would get much-older children, people already well into their teens, who could not read Arabic or Somali or anything else, and who therefore could not go to school. These people were a laughingstock. We called them *reer baadiye*—'from the bush.' Nobody wanted to be *reer baadiye*, and so children learned from other children how to read to save their dignity."

The educational institutions that emerged at Liboi were a riot of fragments. Asad went to a makeshift madrassa that had no writing materials. But many of the kids he played with in the early evenings received a very different education. Into the vacuum left by the absence of schools in the camp stepped a host of entrepreneurs. Two men who claimed to have been math teachers in Mogadishu established classes to teach children basic arithmetic. Soon after that, piles of material arrived from UNICEF: alphabet books, storybooks, exercise books. Camp leaders assigned refugees who had lived clerical lives back home to use these books to teach.

"The majority of the children around me understood the Latin alphabet and could read basic Somali," Asad tells me. "So I was somewhere between an educated child and *reer baadiye*. I had to make distance between myself and *reer baadiye*. It was a question of pride and shame. Whatever material was going around, I would look at, I would ask questions.

"It was not just me. It was a thing between children. A young child would ask an older child, a child a foot taller than him, 'What is two times two?' The question would be asked with arrogance. It was like a challenge to a fight. If the older child could not answer, he was *reer baadiye*."

It was thus that Asad, along with many other Liboi children, educated himself. He left Liboi in 1993 with basic numeracy and a capacity to recite the Latin alphabet. Soon, he would acquire the ability to put to paper any conversation he had conducted in his mother tongue. His grammar was shocking, his punctuation rudimentary. His phonetic spelling and oratory phrasing made the language he wrote a territory of its own, quite distinct from that of standard written Somali. But he could read and write, after a fashion; he could add and subtract, and he could multiply. These were the anvils and chisels with which he would fashion the rest of his life.

He learned something else at Liboi. In Mogadishu, the languages he knew were the Arabic of the madrassa and the Somali of the world. It had never crossed his mind that there might be other tongues. The first time he walked across the border post at Liboi to forage for himself and Yindy, he heard Kenyan soldiers talking to one another in Swahili. The shock was so great that the ground rushed up to meet his eyes. And when the soldiers spoke to him in their simple, practical Somali, he at first did not understand what they were saying. The moment he returned to Yindy in Dhoobley he asked her what it was he had heard, and she laughed and explained to him that here and now across this world human beings were chattering away in dozens upon dozens of languages.

In the camp at Liboi, there was the Somali of the refugees, the Swahili of the Kenyans, and the languages of those who staffed the UNHCR and the nongovernmental organizations. There was French and German and Danish. But more important than all the others combined was English, for that was the language in which the camp was run, and those who ran the camp knew not a jot of Somali. To learn English was thus to become useful to those with power.

The race to learn English began the day the camp opened its doors. All sorts of English schools appeared; the nongovernmental organizations provided them with blackboards, chalk, and learning materials. Refugees paid good money to send their children there. Perhaps people sensed even then, in the earliest days of the war, that the damage being wrought on their country was immense and that they would have to learn the skills of an exile. Among the reasons Asad so hated his madrassa was the knowledge, as he sat there listening to the endless recitations, that across the camp other people were learning a language that would take them upward.

"Two groups of people at Liboi spoke English," Asad recalls. "The first was those who got jobs with the NGOs. They considered themselves the elite of the camp. They would speak English and French among themselves, in front of everyone else, to show that they were superior. The second group were the people who went to the private schools. They would also flaunt their English, practicing with each other in the middle of the camp. In loud voices, they would say: 'How are you?' 'Where do you come from?' 'It is unusually hot today.'"

I ask Asad why Yindy did not send him to a school that taught English, hoping, in this manner, to learn something of her thinking.

"I don't know," he replies. "Some children went to madrassas, some to English schools, some to the mathematics schools. I think maybe it was just chance."

It is not the first time I ask Asad a question designed to elicit something about Yindy. She and Asad were so viscerally close, the bonds between them made of pain and blood. And yet, when he speaks of her, a lifeless being spills from his tongue. His love for his mother he can conjure from a brief description of the plaits that run down her back. His father he brings to life in the recollection of a single embrace. Yindy, by contrast, is a mere corpse.

Once, driving through Bellville Town Centre, the streets around us thick with Somalis, we see a short, squat woman sitting on a low stool stirring a pot of stew. Her clothes are dirty and threadbare, her skin an unhealthy gray. When she looks up, her eyes are vacant, as if she has removed her spirit from the world.

"She is in trouble," Asad says quietly. "You can see. She must have no family. We should give something. We should eat her stew."

"When you feel pity for her," I ask, "are you thinking of Yindy?"

He turns from me, looks straight ahead, and smiles without pleasure.

"I hate Yindy," he says softly. "I do not have a place in my heart for her."

We sit there in silence, watching the street life about us. A man comes to buy stew from the woman on the stool. She dishes his portion into a polystyrene bowl. It is no secret that memory is not very reliable. But here is a special case. For more than two years, Yindy and Asad relied upon each other in body and spirit. He must surely have loved her. And yet what happened subsequently has turned her to poison.

"One night," Asad says quietly, apropos of nothing, "people broke into our place. They stood over us discussing whether to rape Yindy. Some said she was too crippled to rape. Others said, no, she was still rapeable. In the end, they left with the raw food the NGOs had brought us and then went to our neighbor's place and raped her instead."

He begins talking of other things, and it seems from his rapid and rehearsed diction that the memory of that night is gone, that what he really keeps of that moment are the words with which he tells the tale.


At some time in 1993, Yindy told Asad that she had qualified for resettlement to America. It had happened, in some way or other, through an uncle who lived there. She had to report immediately to a temporary waiting center called Lang'ata. It was near Nairobi.

Asad remembers the conversation vividly. They were sitting under the shelter of the *balbalo,* each in a plastic chair provided by the kind *gaal.* Yindy said that she would have to go to America without Asad at first but that he would not have to wait long before he could come, too. Once she had settled there, she said, she could *responsa* him and he could join her.

Neither of them knew what this new word *responsa* might mean, only that it was drawn from the great stock of legal and other concepts that lubricated the world of the UNHCR and America. Yindy also told Asad that America had the finest schools in the world, and colleges, where people studied to become doctors and lawyers and engineers. She told him that he was her son, that he was very clever, and that in America he would have the opportunity to become someone great.

Yindy left him in the care of the neighbor who had been raped in her stead. She instructed him to stop attending school, to stop playing with other children, to leave the house only when accompanied by the neighbor. She said that she would find him a home in Nairobi, where he would live while he waited to leave for America. There were many AliYusuf in Nairobi, she said. She would find him somewhere safe.

When I ask Asad to recall his time in Liboi after Yindy's departure, he shrugs. He speaks instead of the end of this period. Yindy had called for him to come. She had sent him a ticket for the Ziafania Express, the intercity bus service. He bid Liboi farewell and boarded the bus. Although he was to travel alone, the conductor, who had been given instructions and money to care for him, bought him food whenever the bus stopped.

It was a very long journey, about twenty-four hours. He wondered what would happen if Yindy had the time of the bus's arrival wrong and nobody was waiting on the other side. "Nairobi" was a name to which he could not pin an image. As much as he tried, he could not fathom what he might find.

In the end, the first person he saw when he stepped off the bus was Yindy. She was standing in a circle with several other ladies and a boy. Asad was struck for the first time since Afmadow by how short she was; even the boy, who was no more than nine or ten years old, was taller than her. He wondered how such a stubby woman had survived so momentous a journey.

Asad remembers that the boy wanted to talk to him but that he felt tired and, in ways that confused him, a little upset. Yindy took his hand, and together they boarded another bus, this one to Lang'ata. She led him to her refugee tent and put him to bed.

"I was very dizzy," he recalls. "Everything was upside down. The sun seemed to set where it should be rising. At night, lying down, it felt like the ground was moving. When I woke up, the door was not in the same place I remembered it. Maybe this was because of all the movement on the bus."

"In English," I say to him, "the word that describes what you were feeling is 'disoriented.'"

"Disoriented," he repeats slowly. He files it, along with the countless English, Swahili, and Amharic words he has learned this way, and I can see from the expression on his face that he will not forget; he is attaching the word to a mental image of this conversation, and, when the occasion arises, he will use it himself.

"The Somali word for that feeling," he says, "is *salal.*"

## *Islii*

On Asad's second day at Lang'ata, Yindy told him of a neighborhood in Nairobi called Islii. It was not a refugee camp, she said, just a part of the city, but it was nonetheless full of Somalis who had escaped the war. They lived in houses and buildings like other people. The moment she had settled at Lang'ata, she told him, she went to Islii in search of family. There were many AliYusuf people there. She had made contact with one of them, a man by the name of Ahmad Noor Galal. He told her to bring the boy Asad to Nairobi; he was the one who had paid for Asad's bus ticket and had given the conductor money to feed him along the journey.

In a matter-of-fact tone, Yindy told Asad that he would be staying with his new uncle, and she made sure to say in the same breath that it would be temporary. She did not know how long it would take until she could *responsa* Asad and bring him to America, but she promised that it would be soon.

He said nothing. Yindy's words swirled around his head as if caught in a gust and then flew out and up into the sky above Nairobi.

Asad stayed in Lang'ata one more night. The next morning he and Yindy took a bus to this place called Islii and made their way through the streets. And then they were standing outside a house that belonged to the AliYusuf man called Ahmad Noor Galal, and they were speaking with him. Ahmad Noor Galal had a wide girth. He stood in front of his house with his hands on his hips. He also had two children, a boy and a girl, both about Asad's age; Asad remembers them hovering with interest somewhere in the background.

"Yindy began speaking about me to my uncle right in front of me," Asad recalls. " 'The boy is clever. The boy is polite. He is a wonderful boy who looked after me when I could not walk.'

"My new uncle cut her off. 'Say no more. He is my son. That is the beginning and the end of the matter.' Then he turned to me and said, 'I invite you. Be a part of my family.' "

Asad and Yindy slept that night in the house of Ahmad Noor Galal. The family asked them many questions about the two years that had passed since they had left Mogadishu and, in return, offered stories of their own. The family's route to Islii had not been easy; it had been lubricated, it seemed, by forms of inventiveness Asad strained to grasp. During the course of the evening, the conversation sketched a great map of what had happened to the AliYusuf since the outbreak of war. It seemed that they had exploded into countless shards, and that the task of gathering them all together again was hopeless. Asad's father's name did not come up until late in the evening.

"Alas," Ahmad Noor Galal said, "we have heard nothing of him. But there are many possible reasons for the silence. He could turn up here in Islii any day."

"Did you ever meet him?" Asad plucked up the courage to ask.

"No," he replied. "There are so many AliYusuf men one only hears about but never meets."

The following morning, Yindy prepared to return to Lang'ata alone.

"No, I am coming with you," Asad said.

It was not a question. It was a demand.

A distraction was found. Asad was sent on an errand with his new stepbrother and -sister. When they returned, Yindy was gone.

He does not have a final image of her. Instead, he has a series of numbers.

"Yindy either flew on 09-03-1993 or on 03-09-1993. It is one of the two. I don't remember which."

"Why do you remember the date in that particular way?" I ask. "Did you see it written down like that somewhere?"

"I don't remember where I saw it," he replies. "I just remember the numbers."

When Asad first mentions Islii, I ask him to spell it.

"*I-s-l-i-i,*" he says.

That evening I begin reading about Somalis in Nairobi and immediately come across a place called Eastleigh.

Islii. Eastleigh.

I discover later that all Somalis say and spell it this way. I will come to see what they have done to the English name of the neighborhood as an analogue for what they have done to the neighborhood itself.

"Islii was dirty back then," Asad says. "It rains a lot in Nairobi. There was no tar on the streets, no bricks on the pavements. There was a lot of mud. And there was nobody to come and take the rubbish. The place stank. It was overcrowded with Somalis, at that stage, all Daaroods. They were streaming in, more every day. But the kiosks and the shops were all run by Kenyans. The Somalis were not yet the businesspeople they are in Islii today.

"There is the Ring Road around the whole of Nairobi. Islii is just outside the Ring Road. People would watch the taxis and buses going to the rest of the city. But they were not for us. Most Somalis stayed in Islii the whole time.

"Although Kenyans ran the kiosks," Asad continues, "Somalis ran the lodges. They were overcrowded with families and with children. Sometimes there was more than one family in a room. There was the Hotel Taleh, Morion Lodge, Alfalaah Hotel, Garissa Lodge. They were full of wives and children. In general, each hotel was occupied by a different clan. The Hotel Taleh was full of AliYusuf people. Most had nothing to do. They would sit all day and talk and talk and talk about other AliYusuf people and where they might be."

Unlike most Somalis in Eastleigh, Ahmad Noor Galal had a steady, well-paid job. There was no need for his family to squeeze into a hotel room. They rented a house all their own. They ate three square meals a day. Their clothes were new.

For Asad, this was, on the face of it, manna from heaven. A house, a family, a patriarch who put meat on the table: just a week earlier, it had been doubtful that Asad would ever again be exposed to such precious normalcy. But his new home also had its politics.

"My uncle was very nice," Asad recalls, "but it was clear from the beginning that his wife was uncomfortable with a strange child in the house. Us three children would play inside and make a mess. My aunt would shout at us, punish us. The children would say, No, Asad did it. She would immediately take their side. Soon, it became the way of the house. If there's a problem, the children automatically point my way:

Asad did it. I was very, very lonely, my brother. More lonely than if there had been nobody else there."

Sometimes, Asad would take refuge with his uncle, who whiled away many an afternoon in the yard at the back of his house chewing khat, which Somalis call *mira,* and talking to friends. Asad would sit a few paces away, the back of his head against the wall. He would close his eyes and listen to the men's voices. They spoke of Mogadishu with such exquisite and gentle nostalgia that Asad would sometimes find himself weeping. He did not always follow what the men were saying. But as the sounds of their voices washed over him they became the voices of his own father and *his* friends; and if he closed his eyes for long enough, his mother was there, too, somewhere in the background, cooking the men dinner.

Ahmad Noor Galal was often away. He had a job with CARE International, for which he drove a supply truck between Nairobi and the Dadaab refugee camps. He would head off before daybreak for northeastern Kenya and not return for days. While he was gone, there were only enemies in the house.

Asad began to drift. He would wander from the house after breakfast, skip lunch, and not return until the sun was setting. Staring at the tips of his bare toes, trying as hard as he might to imagine the American world in which Yindy now lived, he walked through Eastleigh street by street.

Looking back, Asad thinks that at this time his thoughts of his mother took on a new intensity. The image of her two thick plaits, the feeling of her smooth hair passing through the webs of his open fingers: he associates that image with the beginning of his time in Eastleigh. He believes that this was when he installed the feeling of her inside him, permanently, such that, whatever he did and wherever he went, he took with him a mother's love.

One afternoon, during his daily wanderings, Asad came across a group of Somali men leaning against a wall chewing *mira.* He is not sure why he chose to linger. Cautiously, he picked a spot close to them and crouched on his haunches. They eyed him lazily and then returned to their conversation. He drew a little closer to them and, finally, pushed his back against the wall, closed his eyes, and listened. He sat there a long time. The sun slanted, the street became fuller and noisier; still, nobody chased him away.

When night fell, the men retired indoors, and Asad followed behind. They laughed at his precociousness and cuffed the back of his head and asked his name, but they did not shoo him out. A woman served food. Once the men were eating, she called Asad over, handed him a bowl, and invited him to fill it.

Sometime during the course of the evening, there was a rap on the door. Somebody answered it, and Asad heard urgent voices; he recognized one of them as that of Ahmad Noor Galal. He had been searching the length and breadth of Eastleigh for Asad and now called him in a firm and angry voice. Asad walked past the men he had befriended as if through a gauntlet, his cheeks burning with shame.

He followed Galal through the streets of Eastleigh, his head bowed. He trembled when he thought of the beating he would receive once they were home. Still some distance from the house, Galal suddenly stopped and turned. Instead of striking Asad, he knelt on one knee. He put his hand on Asad's shoulder and asked him quietly what was wrong. It was such a gentle, sensitive gesture, this tall man lowering himself to put his face so close to Asad's. Willing himself not to burst into tears, Asad was mute.

And then, with the wind of Galal's breath brushing his cheeks, something silent and unpleasant passed between them. Asad knows now, if he did not then, that it was the chill of a new estrangement. They walked home together in silence. Dimly, but palpably enough, Asad understood that in that moment Galal had given up. He had weighed the costs of forcing his wife to accept Asad, and he had calculated that it was too high a price to pay.

"The family ate breakfast together every morning," Asad tells me. "When it was finished, everyone was responsible for washing their own plate. One morning, the other two children did not wash their dishes. They put their dirty plates in the washing bowl and went out to play. At lunchtime, my aunt sees these dirty dishes, and she starts to shout at me. Automatically at me. I tell her I have already washed my plate. She gets even angrier. For lying, she says, I must wash the whole family's plates."

Asad imagined himself cleaning the dishes his lying stepsiblings had dirtied, and the humiliation of it flooded his cheeks and his head. He picked up a dish and threw it as hard as he could at Galal's wife. He aimed for the bridge of her nose, but instead struck her square on the shoulder. The plate rebounded onto a wall and shattered.

Asad ran outside, his aunt close on his heels. When he had crossed the street, he stopped, armed himself with a handful of stones, and turned.

"We stood like that for a long time," Asad recalls. "Me on one side of the street, the family on the other. Whenever one of them took a step toward me, I threw a stone. My uncle was out back eating *mira* with some friends. Somebody went to call him. I ran. My aim was to go to the furthest place in Islii, to get somewhere they couldn't find me."

It was by chance that Asad's route took him past the house where the men had sat eating *mira*. There was just one man there now, and Asad stopped, walked up to him, and stared. The man chuckled and invited Asad to sit.

"What's with you?" he asked. "What's wrong at home?"

They sat together in silence for a long time. Finally, when the man got up to go, Asad followed. They walked several blocks before entering a hotel. The man's room was on the second floor. Bare and simple, it had a single bed and a few possessions. The man told Asad that his name was Bashir.

He cut Asad a thick slice of bread and poured him a glass of milk.

"When you are finished eating," Bashir said, "you must go home."

Asad shook his head.

"Okay," Bashir bargained. "You stay here. I will go and speak to your family. I will smooth everything. Then you will come."

"No," Asad said.

The stalemate was only broken when Asad drifted off to sleep. At some point, he felt himself being lifted and carried. Then he was gently settled on the bed. He woke during the night to find Bashir in the bed beside him.

The next time he woke it was morning. Bashir was dressed.

"I am leaving," he said. "I will not chase you out now, but when I return this evening you must not be here. You must go to your family."

Asad left about an hour later, but not for home. During the course of the previous three months, he had come to know several Somali children. He went to the house of one of them, sat down, and settled in. At nightfall, the adults of the household told him to go home. He refused and was allowed to spend the night. The following day, he visited another child and did the same there.

"Four nights in a row I spent in different homes," he tells me. "Now, my story is out. The women talk among themselves. They bitch about my foster mother. 'How can that woman . . . ? The child has nobody. Who does she think she is . . . ?'

"The story is now reaching Galal and his wife. It is becoming embarrassing for them. So I am caught. But I am not taken back to Galal's house. A meeting is held among the AliYusuf elders. It is decided that I will live in the Hotel Taleh. The whole hotel is full of AliYusuf. Two floors. Wherever you go, families, full, full, full, mattresses in the corridor. Everyone offered me food. Everyone knew my story. I became friends to all the children. I slept in a different bed in the hotel every night."

The AliYusuf allowed for this situation on the grounds that it was temporary. Sooner or later, Yindy would call for Asad to come to America. Or his father would turn up unannounced in Eastleigh. That was the thinking. In the end, Asad would live this way in the Hotel Taleh for more than two years.

That Asad spent so long in Eastleigh without ever learning its English name says a great deal, not only about his time there but about Eastleigh itself. Throughout its history, since long before Somalis came to live in its houses, Eastleigh was one of those twilight zones one encounters in great colonial cities. It was set a safe distance from the districts in which white expatriates lived, and white people seldom went there. Yet neither did it house black workers. The people who first settled in Eastleigh were largely Asian. They owned property there, but often had no title deeds, only verbal agreements and shared knowledge. They traded, but much of their trade was off the books. It was a place where business is transacted under the eye of legal officers but is nonetheless not regulated by law, where the rules are unwritten and the nature of commerce is a little opaque.

Somalis began to settle there in small numbers long after the British left, sometime in the 1970s. By then, most of the original Asian occupants had abandoned Eastleigh for more secluded suburbs, and the Somalis' landlords were generally Kikuyu businessmen. It was a natural place for undocumented immigrants to settle, for one could do business and trade or work for another without too many questions asked, a place where one could figure out a modus vivendi with the agents of the law.

When the Somali civil war broke out in 1991, the number of Somalis in Eastleigh soon swelled. The footing they established in Nairobi was precarious. Kenya had accepted Somali refugees with great reluctance. Their legal status was kept ambiguous, partly because of bureaucratic inertia, partly because ambiguity leaves all options open. Somali refugees who lived in camps were legitimate, while those who made their way to places like Eastleigh lived in a zone somewhere between illegality and unofficial acceptance.

Among Asad's most vivid memories of Eastleigh is the role Somali children played in mediating between their parents and the police.

"The children ran around all day," Asad tells me, "and they would come home with Swahili phrases. They would learn from the talk around the kiosks, from the Kenyan children, from the taxi drivers. The children realized that this was very useful, to speak a language their parents did not, so it became a thing among them that they must know Swahili."

Somali children learned Swahili in order to keep secrets from their parents. But in the end, their new language was put to other uses, too. Periodically, large groups of police would descend on Eastleigh, move at leisure through the streets, and arrest anyone and everyone they saw.

"You would have these bunches of fifteen chained Somalis out on the streets," Asad says. "Then the negotiations begin. The police only allowed the children to interpret: if anyone else tried to interpret, they would be arrested. You pay; they let you go. You don't pay; you go to the police cells. To get out of the police cells, you pay much more. Everyone paid at some point. That was the only route out. You pay. You go back to Islii.

"But we children always had this special role. The police arrest some-one: people say, 'Call the kids.'"

Now much has changed. When Asad passed through Eastleigh in 2004, after an absence of almost a decade, he could barely believe what he saw.

"There was so much money in Islii," he says, "Somali money. There were paved streets, beautiful new shopping centers, buildings much taller than any that had been there before."

In this twilight world, with one foot in and the other outside the law, Somalis had established a transnational banking system, a network of global trade links, and a marketplace for all sorts of commerce. Many of its residents remained dirt poor, living off others or on cheap, informal work. But alongside them were Somalis who had grown rich. By 2004, Eastleigh's Somalis were purchasing electronic and white goods and fresh food so much more cheaply than anyone else in Nairobi that they were wholesaling to the rest of the city. Eastleigh had become the center of Nairobi's consumer-goods economy, despite remaining all but invisible in the city's deeds office.

. . .

But back then, Somalis were new and barely had a foothold in the city. "The Hotel Taleh was full of people with no work," Asad recalls. "Most Somalis had no jobs, no businesses, they knew nobody. Everyone would get up every morning and hunt. And there was no school for the children to go to. So we would also get up and hunt. The adults and children of Islii all hunting together."

How Asad feels about his years at the Hotel Taleh depends on his mood. When he is feeling light, he remembers the joy of being unencumbered.

"It became a free life," he says. "If something is good, I do it. If something is not good, I don't do it. In the mornings, I would go out with the other kiddies who lived at the hotel. We would visit this one and that one. We would go and fight with the Kenyan kids. There was an old lady who only came out of her house once a day. We would throw stones on her roof to force her to come outside. Sometimes, we would sleep wherever we happened to be when night fell. We'd walk back to the hotel for breakfast the next morning.

"Inside the hotel, every room was mine. I would sleep with a different family every night. I would eat with a different family every mealtime. I was the orphan AliYusuf boy. Because I belonged to everybody, I belonged to nobody."

But on days when he is not feeling so good, his memories of this time are taut and anxious.

Early one morning, for instance, before the adults had emerged from their rooms, Asad picked up a stone and hurled it at an unwitting boy. He does not remember now what provoked him, but he does recall the trajectory of the stone. The moment it left his hand, the world around him paused, for he knew that he had thrown too hard and too straight. The stone slammed into the top of the boy's cheekbone, just below the eye, and when the world unfroze, the boy was lying on the ground, and the left side of his face was streaked with blood.

Somebody ran to wake the boy's father, an important AliYusuf man at the Hotel Taleh, and word went around among the children that he would catch Asad and drag him to his room and thrash him.

Asad bolted. Once he was across the street, he looked back at the Hotel Taleh, picked up an assortment of stones, and waited. Then he dropped his stones and ran.

"There is a bus that goes around and around Nairobi's Ring Road," Asad says. "It is free for children. I jumped on the bus. It was overloaded like you can't believe. I went around and around Nairobi three times before I got off."

The spot he chose was miles from Eastleigh. He wandered away from the Ring Road, into Nairobi's central business district, and walked and watched for hours.

"It was becoming dark. I heard this loud, pumping music coming closer and closer from behind me. It was a minibus taxi, full of people. They stop. One of them puts his head out of the window and talks to me in Swahili.

" 'Small boy, where are you going?'

" 'Islii.'

"They all laughed, the whole taxi. 'We are not going to Islii. We are going the opposite way.'

"But they took me to Islii anyhow. On the journey, questions, questions, questions. 'Why you wander so far? You want to be a Kenyan? You looking for a nice young Kenyan girl?' They did not charge me. They dropped me far from the hotel, the other end of Islii."

Asad walked home very slowly. He had half a mind to turn around and bolt again, but he had just come from Nairobi with his tail between his legs, and he did not have the stomach for another defeat, especially now that the sun had set. He thought of taking refuge elsewhere in Eastleigh, but there was no such thing. Everyone knew him as the AliYusuf orphan boy. The whole place was a conveyer belt that would deliver him to the Hotel Taleh.

"When I got to the hotel, there were these guys outside chewing *mira*.

" 'Asad, why did you hurt that boy?'

" 'It was a mistake.'

" 'His dad is going to beat you.'

" 'No.'

"They hid me in their room, and I slept there that night."

In the morning, when he braved the hotel corridors, one of the first people he saw was the boy he had hurt.

"His eye was very bad. I said I was sorry. I said I didn't mean it. And his father did not beat me, but after that everyone kept their children away from me."

.   .   .

"The most senior AliYusuf at the hotel," Asad tells me, "was a man named Mohamed Sheikh Abdi. He complained that there were no schools good enough for his children in the whole of Nairobi. So he found a Muslim boarding school in a town far away, still in Kenya, but on the border with Tanzania. When he enrolled his children there, he said, 'Asad is going, too. One day, his father will come, and he will expect to greet a child with an education.' Other AliYusuf men with money also sent their children. My old stepbrother, Galal's child, he went, too, and also one of Galal's brothers. Mohamed Sheikh Abdi took us personally in a hired minibus."

Asad no longer recalls how many times he escaped from the school and returned to Eastleigh. He thinks three, maybe four.

"In Kenya," he says, "if you wear a school uniform, you can hitch a lift. Anyone will stop for you. On the journey down, I knew that I would soon be coming back the other way. I did not want to go to school. I think that that first time, I was there maybe a week." He stops speaking to let out a long giggle. "The adults at the Hotel Taleh think they have gotten ridden of Asad. One morning they wake up and there he is, leading the little ones through the streets."

I press him on what school was like, on why it was so intolerable. He shrugs.

"I was too wild for the other children. I was either hurting them or upsetting them. This was a very proper school, a strict boarding school for Muslim Kenyan children to learn Arabic. The teachers did not tolerate my wildness. I felt bored. The teachers shouted too much. I would come up to other children to ask them questions in the middle of a class, when you are meant to be quietly listening to the teacher. I would take other children away to skip class with me. Mohamed Sheikh Abdi kept sending me back, but I never lasted. I think the longest was maybe three weeks."

There was one Eastleigh ritual that did turn the crazy orphan boy into a solemn child. Every now and again, a Ogadeni would arrive in Eastleigh having escaped from a part of southern Somalia controlled by enemies. News of each arrival would crisscross the neighborhood in minutes. The following morning, after the newcomer had been given a chance to eat and rest, people would begin queueing at the door where he or she was staying. Everyone had been cut off from family. Everyone was hungry for information.

Each time, Asad would go and listen. And each time he would convince himself that he was about to hear news of his father. He did learn about other people. His uncle, for instance, in whose care he had fled Mogadishu, had been captured by enemy forces in the town of Qoryooley, taken back to Mogadishu, and tortured. It was said that he had lost an eye while in enemy hands but had escaped and was safe now, somewhere in Ethiopia. And Asad's cousin Abdi, into whose arms he had just been transferred when the mortar exploded, had been killed in battle.

About his father, he heard nothing.

In his mind, always, he believed that he was living in an unfortunate interval from which he would soon be delivered. Either his father would appear and sweep him away. Or Yindy would call for him.

# PART II

# Ethiopia

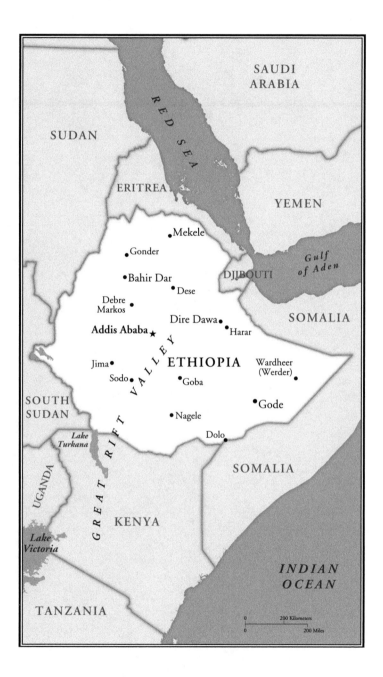

# To Addis and Dire Dawa

Yindy did call for him, but not in the manner he had imagined. The way he saw it in his mind, an air ticket would appear; he did not know from where. In the Hotel Taleh, it would pass from one AliYusuf hand to the next, each person who touched it imagining in his own private way the land to which this thin piece of cardboard was to take Asad. Then Mohamed Sheikh Abdi would hire a minibus to take him to the airport and fill it with well-wishers, adults and children alike. They would wave and cheer and take photographs as he walked away from Kenya and into the tube of an airplane. Of the journey itself he had no notion at all; he knew only that Yindy would be waiting on the other side to lead him into a new life.

It was not that simple. Yindy's proposal was an awkward one. She was able to *responsa* a dozen people to join her in America. Among them were her mother—who was also Asad's father's sister—her father, and several of their relatives. They were all in Dire Dawa, a town in Ethiopia many hundreds of miles from Nairobi, waiting for their applications to be processed. Asad must go to them, Yindy said. It was only from there that he could get the documents to go to America.

The AliYusuf elders held long discussions about these people waiting in Dire Dawa. Who were they, precisely? There were close blood family among them, to be sure: Asad's paternal aunt. But she was part of her husband's family now, and while he was Ogadeni, he was not AliYusuf; the ties were thus thin. And so the question arose: Do we send this lone AliYusuf boy far away into the care of a man we don't know? What if

Asad's father should come to Islii to collect him? He must stay with his people.

In the beginning, that was the majority opinion. But as the discussions with Yindy continued, perspectives changed. What if his father never arrives? What if he is an orphan? Can we deny him the opportunity of a life in America for the sake of a father who is quite possibly dead? Life is for the living; one does not wait for ghosts.

Once, Asad himself spoke to Yindy on the phone. Her voice sounded surprisingly close, as if she might walk into the Hotel Taleh at any moment. But her manner was stiff and nervous: Your uncles are thinking, she said. You must do whatever they decide.

As the weeks passed, Asad grew increasingly certain that the elders would tell him that he was going to Ethiopia. And as his certainty grew, so his relation to the world around him began to change.

"Something funny happened with me. I became quiet. I didn't drift far from Islii. I stopped leading the other kiddies to trouble."

He was, he now realizes, preserving himself for America, for he was no longer merely a lost boy but an asset, a person in whom much was to be invested.

"I had this picture in my mind of Yindy waiting at the airport. But there is no Asad on the airplane. He is buried back in Kenya. This wonderful future with a university education and everything never happens because Asad is no longer there."

When the AliYusuf elders finally told him that he was going to Ethiopia, Asad had long known it in his bones. The moment was nonetheless enormous. He walked out of the hotel, and the people in the streets appeared to be moving much slower than usual. The sun itself seemed to have frozen in the middle of the sky. He traced a long circuit around the Hotel Taleh, his path taking him right to the other side of Islii, and, although it seemed that hours had passed, when he returned it remained early afternoon.

In the period that followed, the movement of time seemed almost to cease. "I couldn't believe how long it took for a day to pass," Asad recalls. "Something that happened just yesterday seemed like it happened last year. When it was a week left to go, I didn't think I could last that long."

Asad left Nairobi one scorching afternoon on the back of a truck. He believes that it was November 1995 and that he was eleven or twelve years old, but he cannot be sure. He had with him a small bag containing three or four changes of clothes, a Koran, and a dozen or so snapshots taken in various parts of Nairobi. I have three of them with me now; when I met Asad, they were the last of his photographs that remained in his possession.

His minder was a kindly woman named Haliimo. He does not recall now who she was or why she was making the journey. He remembers that she had a round, padded face and that she spoke to him softly and with care; she was someone who knew how to be with children.

The lorry took them to Mandera, a city wedged into the northeastern corner of Kenya, the Ethiopian border directly to the north, the Somali border to the east. In Mandera, they transferred to a donkey cart, which for many miles tracked the southern bank of a brown river. Finally, they crossed the water in a boat.

There were men in uniform on the other side who spoke a language Asad had never heard before. When Haliimo told them that neither she nor Asad had documents, they demanded the two travelers' bags and emptied them onto the riverbank. Instinctively, Asad got to his knees, picked his Koran out of the mud, and clutched it to his chest. The soldiers wanted to see it; they pointed at it and spoke about it, and then one of them made to prize open Asad's arms. He turned his back and clutched his book tighter.

"Koran! Koran!" Asad heard somebody explain to the soldiers. From behind his back came quiet murmuring, then a brief chuckle. Then the voices of the soldiers receded. Haliimo took Asad's Koran from him and tucked it back into his bag. Then she took his hand and led him into Ethiopia.

They stayed for two days in a small town just a few kilometers from the border, and on their third evening climbed onto another lorry. It drove through the night and into the dawn, and by noon it was chuntering up a mountain pass that appeared to Asad to take them into a different world. Mist and cloud formed around them, and the air was wet, sometimes with drizzle, sometimes just with fog. In the midst of this new world, a town appeared. The people neither walked nor drove cars; everyone moved about on horseback. They spoke several languages; one resembled the sounds he had heard from the tongues of the border soldiers; the others were unlike anything he had heard before.

They were delayed there for a week—Asad has no idea why—and throughout those seven days, the rain did not cease, and Asad did not see the sun. Finally, they were moving again, this time on a bus. It took them to Addis Ababa, the capital city of Ethiopia.

The moment Asad begins describing Addis, the pitch of his voice changes. He speaks with urgency, with surprise; he has brushed aside subsequent experience, it seems, and is reinhabiting first impressions.

"This was an interesting place, brother," he tells me. "It was very, very interesting. It was cool, not just in the weather, but in the feeling it left inside you. The doors were all closed. The streets were empty. There was no noise. No hurry. No exhaustion. A city full of people, but all of them behind walls. This was a very different place. From way, way back they did things very differently from us."

Haliimo and Asad were there less than a week. Their hosts were family of Haliimo's, Somalis who had lived in Addis many years. The block on which they stayed was inhabited entirely by Somalis, but from the end of the block onward, the city was a foreign place. Asad had strict instructions not to wander. Each day, he would walk to the end of the little island of Somali life and watch the silent streets beyond, where the scarcity of people and the quietness of those few who did pass never ceased to amaze him. On his fourth or fifth day it came to him as an epiphany: the streets here felt so different because they were used differently; they were a means of getting from one place to another, and that was all. He marveled at his discovery. He contrasted it with Islii, where everyone lived their lives in public spaces. And he wondered what it was that caused some people to live one way and others another.

His last memory of the streets of Addis Ababa was of a long bag-laden walk, right through the center of the city, to the bus that would take him and Haliimo the final five hundred kilometers of their journey to Dire Dawa. He, too, now, was using the streets only to get from A to B, and he allowed himself an idle fantasy, imagining himself to be an Ethiopian boy.

"Dire Dawa is a very beautiful city, brother," Asad tells me. "We lived in a neighborhood called Hafad. There are trees everywhere, and they throw their shadows from one side of the street to the other, so you are always walking in the shade. And on each street, under the biggest tree, there is table soccer. I lived there from the end of 1995 until somewhere near the end of 1996; I think that I played table soccer every day. And when I say every day, brother, I mean *all day* every day."

More than sixteen years later, in the first week of April 2012, I arrive in Dire Dawa, my aim to find whatever traces remain of the footprint Asad has left there. I check into my Dire Dawa hotel and walk into the street clutching a map. Unable to make head or tail of it, I slip it into my pocket and decide to get utterly lost.

I find myself on a long, straight road lined with trees I do not recognize. There are cobbles underfoot, and the trees cast shade from one side of the street to the other, just as Asad has described. I will only discover the next day that, quite by chance, the neighborhood through which I am wandering is Hafad, the very place Asad had lived. I am quite literally walking in his footsteps.

It is no wonder that Asad was so struck by the appearance of Hafad. The people who designed it had in mind a neighborhood in Toulouse or Marseille. Dire Dawa was born in 1902 as a railway town linking southern and eastern Ethiopia to the port of Djibouti in the north, and the French company that won the concession to build the railway was also given a ninety-nine-year lease on half the town. It put down a grid of wide avenues, some of them bisected by ornamented pedestrian walkways. In the middle of the larger intersections were traffic circles filled with landscaped flowerbeds. But the town's French population of engineers and other personnel was never large enough to occupy all the land the company had leased, and so many of these lovely streets stood empty for years.

Three or four blocks into my stroll, under the shade of a hefty tree, a group of boys is playing table soccer. I watch them from a discreet distance until one of them comes to me and offers to shake my hand. He tells me that his name is David and invites me to play. I smile at him broadly, considering whether to explain that he is, to my eyes, an incarnation of a boy who once lived here, and whom I have brought with me in my thoughts.

I wonder whether Asad chooses to begin the story of his time in Dire Dawa with the streets and the trees and the table soccer because the most obvious beginning, his arrival, is so rude an introduction.

His first taste of the city was not the placid streets of Hafad but the central bus station, a place whose order and design were beyond his grasp. People moved fast, with purpose and in great numbers. They wore strange clothes, their jabber was unintelligible, and their facial expressions told you little about what was inside them. From her hesitation, it was plain to Asad that Haliimo, too, was out of her depth. The first two people she approached ignored her, just walked on in their distracted busyness, as if acknowledging this lost and confused woman could only bring bother. But the third took a great interest. He was tall and very thin and wore wire-framed spectacles, and he bent low to hear what Haliimo was saying and nodded and pointed a long finger into the distance. He led them through the crowds and onto a busy street, and the next thing Asad knew he and Haliimo were on the back of a donkey cart.

At the intersection where they stopped, everyone was Somali. There were restaurants and loud music. For the first time since Islii, Asad was on a street that smelled and sounded like home, his mother tongue bouncing from one mouth to the next, the world a hive of shouting and laughing. And yet, when Haliimo hailed a stranger and told him the name of the family they were looking for, the man frowned in confusion. And so did the next stranger, and the next. There were many, many Somalis in this city, it seemed. Soon, a congregation had assembled at the roadside to tackle the matter of Haliimo's family. Young children were sent to summon people from the other end of the city. The summoned ones came hours later, but they, too, shook their heads in puzzlement and offered advice of their own. Haliimo and Asad spent the night under the stars, covered by a thin blanket, in the yard of a Somali family that had taken pity on them. It was only on the afternoon of his second day in Dire Dawa that Asad was finally led to Yindy's family's house in Hafad—his home for the better part of the next year.

His memory narrows. The streets and their sounds disappear from his story, making way for just one face and one voice—that of Yindy's father.

"He was standing at the front door," Asad recalls, "watching our taxi approach his house. He was holding himself straight and stiff, with his hands at his sides, like a soldier. He watched us get out of the car, watched us take our bags. As I walked toward him, he stared at me with a scowl on his face, like I was a piece of shit about to come into his house and make it smelly. I felt cold when he looked at me."

Asad folds his arm behind his head and touches the back of his neck. "I felt his look here. He turned away from me and started talking to the person next to him. 'Yindy is too concerned with the AliYusuf.' He said it like I could not hear him, just because I was a child. My pressure went very high. I had just met him, and already I hated him. I targeted him.

From that day forward, I showed him no respect. He would address me, and I would turn my back."

I try to tease more memories from Asad. Who were the other members of the family party? What were their names? Were they a nuclear family or members of disparate families joined together by the fact that Yindy had summoned them? Each time Asad tries to answer my questions, his tongue thickens.

"I slept in a room with three other children," he tells me. "They took their example from the old man and treated me like I was invisible. If I tried to talk to them, they'd shout at me to go away. I would wake up in the morning and eat breakfast with the family, and then I would disappear for the whole day. I would miss lunch. I would return to them only when the sun was setting. I did not want to be with them. I felt like a dog to whom the family throws scraps."

And so his days were spent around the soccer table on the street, his refuge from his home. Here, he began to learn something of the city in which he now lived.

"There were two main groups in Dire Dawa," he tells me, "the Oromo and the Somali. Both thought that the city was theirs, and they fought each other for it. This fight would sometimes come to the table soccer. People would be playing together for hours and hours, Oromo alongside Somali, and then there would be a dispute over a goal, and, all of a sudden, it is Oromos on one side, Somalis on the other. The feeling in the air is not nice, and the fight is about much more than table soccer.

"Also, it was not always so nice being young around the soccer table. Sometimes, I would skip breakfast with Yindy's family and go and play as soon as I woke up, early, early. Then, it is only boys playing. But as the sun gets higher, the older ones come to play, and they do not think it is very dignified to wait for young boys, so they throw you out of the queue. And I must wait until they are finished playing. Sometimes it is the whole day, and the sun is already going down by the time I am on the table again.

"The way it worked, you would hold the table until you lose. Sometimes, if I won too many in a row, and the people around became frustrated, they would just push me off the table, and I would try to fight my way back. I would throw stones at the people playing. They would abandon their game and come after me to give me a hiding. I would go home with a bleeding mouth or with the dirt of the street stuck to the side of my head.

"Sometimes, the older ones would play for money, and that's when things became very tense. That is when it would turn into Oromo versus Somali."

Asad came to see these daily pilgrimages to the soccer table as the circuits in a holding pattern. This was merely an unexpected delay in his journey between Islii and America. For as long as it lasted, he would wake in the morning and make his way to the table; the days would tick away, one after the other, until, finally, word would come that they would be joining Yindy.

Yet if this was the shell of the story Asad wrapped around himself, there was also a stick of doubt tapping away at it, and the echoes of this tapping at times caused him to panic. The family did not once discuss their American plans in front of Asad, nor did it come to his attention that the family had been summoned to an interview with American officials. At times he wondered whether they were going through the process behind his back. He was desperate to speak to Yindy, the only person in this world he was sure had his interests at heart. He knew that her father was in touch with her; every now and again, he would hear the old man speaking to her on the phone. Once, Yindy asked explicitly to talk to Asad. He knows that this was so because he heard the old man quickly swallow the words "Asad is not here" and "No, he is fine" before hastily changing the subject.

At times, Asad woke with a shudder in the night at the prospect that secret plans were being hatched to leave him in this strange city.

Then there was Yindy's mother, Asad's father's own sister, his flesh and blood. Her name was Hawo. Asad would often feel her eyes upon him, turn around, look at her closely, and see that he had been occupying her thoughts. He could see, too, that these thoughts were troubled. He would stare at the flesh on her forearms and at the dry, crusty points of her elbows. He would marvel at the fact that his own father, whose image in his mind was now more and more reduced to a mouthful of teeth, had watched those very same forearms and elbows when they belonged to a small girl. His family was right here in front of him in the form of Hawo, quite literally close enough to touch, and yet it was also as elusive as ever.

"When the AliYusuf at the Hotel Taleh decided it was okay to send me to Ethiopia after all, they said to themselves: Maybe we are not sure about this America thing, maybe it won't happen after all. But we can be sure that we are sending the boy to family. So we know that he will be okay.

"They were wrong about that. The only family I had there was a woman, and females have no rights, no freedom. They are somebody's sister or mother or daughter. They are nothing in themselves. Hawo wanted to help me. She liked me. She worried about me. But she didn't have the power."

When they were alone, they would talk.

"Where is my dad?" Asad recalls asking her.

"I don't know," Hawo replied.

"I think maybe he is here in Ethiopia," Asad said. "All the time I was in Islii, many hostages came from Somalia, and none of them had news about him. I think he left early on for Ethiopia."

"Ethiopia is a huge country," Hawo said. "If he came, it would be to a particular place, a place called Qorahay. That is where the Abdullahis are from."

If it seemed strange to him that his forebears hailed from Ethiopia, rather than from somewhere in Somalia, he did not dwell upon it for long.

"How far is Qorahay from here?" he recalls asking.

"It is not so far, maybe three hundred kilometers."

As he sat next to Hawo, his mind raced. He imagined waking at dawn the next morning, hurrying to the soccer table, holding the game for long enough to win money for a bus ticket, making his way to the central bus station, and going to Qorahay. Could it really be so hard? When he and Haliimo arrived here in Dire Dawa they knew nothing but the clan names of the people they sought. Why could he not do the same in this place called Qorahay? He imagined himself getting off the bus and shaking at the sleeve of the first respectable-looking person he found. "I am looking for my father," he would tell them. "His name is Hirsi. His father's name was Abdullahi. His lineage is AliYusuf of the subclan of the Mohammed Zubeyr."

There on the street in Qorahay, the people would scratch their beards and murmur among themselves and instruct young children to fetch this one and that one, and eventually—who knows?—Asad's father would appear in the distance, walking slowly, perhaps even shuffling (maybe he sustained injuries after the attack on Mogadishu?), but nonetheless moving palpably closer to the Qorahay bus station.

As the weeks passed, the vision grew fainter. What remained was the name, Qorahay, chiseled into his memory, along with the many, many other names—Qoryooley, Afmadow, Liboi, Islii—that Asad had acquired since his flight from Mogadishu more than five years earlier.

# Ogaden

Sometime in 1996—probably August or September—Asad was told that he and the family would leave Dire Dawa for good in four days' time. Nobody told him why they were leaving, or whether the move had anything to do with their American plans. And, but for its name—Wardheer in Somali, Werder in Amharic—they told him nothing of the place they were going. He did not even know in which direction one went to get to Wardheer.

The family and its possessions were loaded onto the back of a truck before dawn one morning. By the time the sun rose, they were driving through a desert landscape. It stayed precisely the same, just dry sand and scrawny bush and rock, for mile upon mile upon mile, until the sun went down and the truck stopped in a small village and they slept. They rose early the following morning and drove through more desert, arriving at their destination at around noon.

Everybody in this place called Wardheer was Ogadeni; the town was in Ethiopia, but it was really Somali. Even the currency people used was Somali in the center of the town, Ethiopian on the outskirts, and Asad wondered how one knew where the Somali currency zone ended and the Ethiopian zone began. There were many money changers, and they were always calculating and recalculating the rate of exchange; it was changing all the time, every hour, sometimes even more often.

He now knew for certain that something was horribly wrong. There were no American officials here to quiz them on whether Yindy was their relative. There was no airport from which a flight might take off and fly to America. They were deep in the desert. This place was full of *reer baadiye,* nomadic people who walked in from the bush, stinking and ignorant. It was the opposite of America.

There was a new, starker quality to his estrangement from the family. The moment they left Dire Dawa, in fact, he had felt a fresh coldness emanating from them. Even Hawo, who still looked at him fondly and with worry, stiffened when he tried to speak with her about the future. It was clear that she had been instructed to say nothing.

Asad now spent even more time away from the family than he had in Dire Dawa. He would leave at sunrise, carrying his breakfast in his hand, and return late at night to find that a plate of food had been left out for him. He was a ghost now; the boldest sign of his presence in the household was the food in his stomach.

To show me how he spent his days and evenings away from Yindy's family, he takes my notebook from my hands once again and begins to sketch Wardheer.

"It is a beautiful town," he says, as he draws, "but there is too much sand. It is thick and soft. When you walk, you get tired after just a moment or two. So nobody walks. Everyone sits for a long, long time.

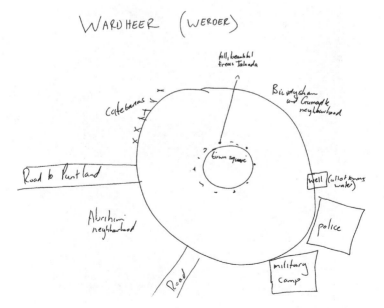

"The town center is shaped in a circle," he says, tapping his sketch with his fingernail. "There is an inner circle in the middle surrounded by tall, beautiful trees. And in the very center there is one tree, much bigger than all the rest. It is called the *tala'ada.*

"Then there is the outer circle. Between it and the inner circle, the sand is very, very thick. You think it looks easy to walk on. You learn soon that it isn't. At the edge of the outer circle are all the cafeterias. That is where the whole town comes to drink tea and coffee and to eat and to discuss. And because it is shaped like a circle, everyone can see everyone. So the people sit there drinking their tea and they watch.

"Beyond the circle are the houses where the people live. And all the people live in their lineages, so one section is one lineage, another section is a second lineage, and so on. Even from this drawing," he says, patting the page, "you can see that it is beautiful. All these people sitting around the edge of a huge circle drinking and eating and talking; and, in the circle, all these trees."

I could not visit Wardheer on my trip to East Africa, for the Ethiopian military does not permit a foreigner to wander that far into the Somali region. I look for photographs on the Internet. The only ones there, it seems, are taken from satellites. This is the one that best describes Asad's circle:

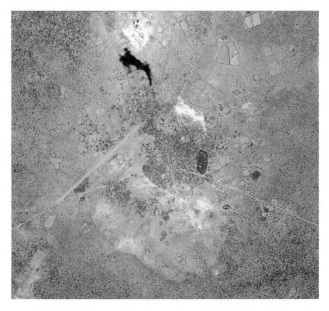

In the time before Yindy's family left, Asad would spend most evenings in the town circle, watching. What he noticed, above all, was that this place was very poor, far poorer than anything he had seen since his days in the refugee camp at Liboi.

"There were two sorts of people," Asad tells me, "the ones who would sit in the cafeterias drinking and eating, and the ones who would sit a short distance away and watch. Nobody would openly beg. That was too disgraceful. But there was an indirect way of begging. At the call to prayer, the people eating and drinking would get up and go to the mosque to pray. After they had finished praying, the poor ones would enter the mosque. The cafeteria customers will have left some coins for them."

How did Asad come to know that Yindy's family would move from Wardheer without him? He is not sure. Perhaps it was simply implicit. Several months had passed since their arrival in Wardheer, maybe as many as six, and the family began to pack their belongings. Nothing was said to Asad. He simply knew that he was not going along. That's how he thinks it happened; he is not sure.

He recalls helping them carry their belongings out of the house. He understood that the moment they left he would lose his home, for the place was rented, and new tenants were moving in. His only visible expression of protest, he recalls, was to refuse to help them carry their possessions from outside the house to the truck. He remained indoors, staring into space, wondering what on earth he was going to do.

When the area around the front of the house fell silent, he took it that they had collected the last of their possessions and were gone. He left the house and walked in the direction of where the truck had stood. The sand through which he walked was very hot; the heat coursed through his legs and up his torso and into his head. He was on fire with anger, with sheer rage. He was also deeply afraid.

Sitting in my car, all these years later, he still marvels at what happened to him.

"They just left me in Wardheer. I had nowhere to stay, no one to look after me. I was twelve or thirteen years old. They thought that in Islii I had been a wild boy who could sleep anywhere. But it is not true. I was in a known place. Other kids could give me money. The Hotel Taleh was a roof over my head. Here I was truly alone. I was full of worry. What will happen to me? The only people I knew were in Islii. How can a twelve-year-old get himself from Wardheer to Islii? It was not possible."

In the time before the family left, Asad began to notice a group of three boys at the town circle. They were always there, day in and day out, and he found the sight of them funny, for the first was tall and thin, the second short and fat, and the third kind of in between. Something else about them struck him: although they seemed unconnected to any adults, they carried themselves with confidence, as if they knew where they belonged. But where did they belong? Toward the end of the evening, as the circle was emptying, they would vanish; where to, Asad was not sure.

Now, on his first evening alone, he approached the tall, scrawny one.

"Where do you go to at night?" he asked.

The thin one looked him up and down. The way Asad remembers it, the boy had a stick lodged in the side of his mouth, and he chewed on it thoughtfully while Asad spoke.

"My people have left Wardheer," Asad continued. "The house in which I have always slept now belongs to other people."

The thin boy looked over Asad's shoulder, somewhere in the distance; Asad thought that he was about to walk away.

"Wait for us to finish working," he said, "and we will show you."

Asad waited a long time. It was not until the cafeteria workers were packing away their plastic chairs that the tall boy went to the other two and the three of them whispered and looked at Asad. Then one of them signaled for him to come. They led him around the back of a cafeteria. Tucked into a corner, under an awning, were three long pieces of cardboard.

"These are our beds," the tall one said. "Find yourself something to sleep on."

"That was my first night without Yindy's family," Asad tells me. "The second night, we slept on a street corner a little way back from the circle. On the third night, we slept in a mosque. That is how it goes. You sleep in a cafeteria for a few nights, until the owner chases you away, and then you find somewhere else to sleep."

During the day, the boys worked. There were two ways of earning money. The first was to scour the town for plastic bags and, once one had a few, to take them to the market beyond the edge of the circle where men buy *mira* to chew. You watch a man buy his *mira* and then offer to sell him a plastic bag so that he can carry his purchase home.

The second was more lucrative, but far more difficult. Each cafeteria on the town circle kept its water in a four-hundred-liter barrel. Wardheer was very hot, Asad says, the hottest place he has ever lived, and the restaurant owners would bury these huge barrels in the ground, just the top half sticking out, for water stored in direct sunlight would be too hot to drink. On a busy day, a cafeteria would have to replenish its container several times.

That is how the three boys earned a living. The town had but one source of water, a well at the edge of the circle, just off the main road leading into Wardheer.

"The soft sand makes water very hard to transport," Asad says. "You cannot use a wheelbarrow, for instance. And so, when a cafeteria needs water, the waiter gives you a sixty-liter drum. You carry it to the well. There is always a very long queue. You wait your turn, fill the drum, and then you close the cap very tight. The drum is much too heavy to carry. You kick it back to the cafeteria. You call the waiter, and he picks up the drum and empties it into the barrel; he is much stronger than you are. Then he brings you another empty drum. While you are bringing back the second drum, they have already finished the water from the first. The restaurants paid one hundred Somali shillings a barrel. That is enough to buy a cup of tea or a glass of milk. What was more important was the leftover food the cook would give you when you brought water for him. Sometimes, he didn't want to give it to you. Then you had spent half the day kicking a barrel for nothing."

At first, Asad could not get any work. Nobody in town knew him as a water carrier, and thus nobody came to him. And he was shy. But in the absence of work, he was going hungry. On the first evening, one of the three boys left Asad a few morsels of his dinner. On the second, one of them gave him a few shillings with which to buy a glass of camel milk. He could not live off their largesse. By the end of the third day he was so ravenously hungry that he could not sleep. They were in a mosque that night. He got up and walked around the empty building and ground his teeth, imagining that he was chewing food.

On the fourth morning, the boys went their separate ways, as they always did. They would work alone during the day, each looking for his own packets and kicking his heavy barrel across the sand; they would only come together again well into the evening, once the restaurants stopped calling for more water. Asad picked a cafeteria and went inside, and when a waiter came to chase him away, Asad pushed out his chest and announced that he was here to carry water. The waiter shouted that he had no need for thin little boys and told Asad if he did not get out from under his feet, he would kick him into the sand.

Asad turned his back and left and sat down on the hot sand and felt the sun throbbing on his head and allowed the sand to run through his fingers. He steeled himself to stand up and try another waiter, but before he could get to his feet, something large and heavy hit him on the very top of his head. The thud echoed along the walls of his skull, and he reeled backward. The waiter who had just turfed him into the sand was walking away from him. A sixty-liter barrel lay at his side. He had just been asked to fetch water.

And so it began. By the time the sun went down he had done four or five trips to the well and his stomach was full and he was so sore and so tired that he could barely stand.

That is how he remembers some days. Other days, he says that the work was impossibly hard; for the first week or two, he was quite sure that he could not keep it up and that he was destined to die. When he woke in the mornings, his weariness was so profound he was not certain whether he could rise, let alone kick another barrel of water through the soft sand. Lying there one morning, he felt his breathing grow awry. For a moment, he wondered whether some invisible creature was sitting on his stomach, until it dawned on him that his own panic had seized his diaphragm and contorted it into a clench. He truly did not know whether he could survive this life. And if he could not, if he fell very ill, he wondered whether anyone would care enough to nurse him.

Sitting in my car, he ducks his chin and brushes the back of his hand over his chest and down his stomach. "I became very thin," he says. "I have never become fat again."

I glance down at the parts of his body his hand has shown, and, momentarily, I glimpse his form through his eyes. He is indeed lean, but he is also broad-shouldered and tall, and I have always understood his body as a badge of elegance. For him, I now realize, it is a legacy of hardship, a mold in which his life experiences have found form.

Aside from those who gave him work, he avoided contact with adults, for they asked questions. "I told some truths and some lies," Asad recalls.

"An adult would come up to me in the street and ask why I was alone. I would shrug. He would ask my lineage. I would answer truthfully: Reer Abdullahi. But when he asked where my family was, I would say they were all in Somalia. I am not sure why I lied. Sometimes I would say, It is none of your business, and walk away."

As for the boys, Asad warms whenever he speaks of them. It is the in-between one whom he remembers most vividly, the boy who was neither short nor tall, neither thin nor fat. His name was Khadar.

"We called him Zena," Asad tells me, "which means 'news' in Amharic. He was a spy, always picking up information and taking it to other people, even though nobody forced him to. It is just something he enjoyed doing. The other two were Abdi, the short one, and Tube, the tall one. I have no memory of us fighting. Well, we would have small fights, as children do. But never anything serious. We sometimes lent each other money. We cared about each other. Even long after I stopped staying with them, I would come and find them, I would do things for them."

I ask Asad what sorts of news Zena brought to the boys from the world of adults, and my question is not innocent. The more I read about the places where Asad lived as a child, the more astonished I become. Asad is telling me his story with a child's innocence, questions of history and of politics all but invisible. Through my reading, I discover that he was living in the midst of something of a catastrophe. I ask Asad about the news Zena brought from the world of adults because I know that the town circle in Wardheer had been the scene of a massacre just two years before Asad arrived. The Ethiopian army accused the town's leading families of harboring Somali rebels; it took its revenge by dragging several dozen of Wardheer's most prominent residents into the circle and executing them in front of their peers.

For several days I try to prompt this information from Asad without suggesting it myself, but nothing is forthcoming. Eventually, I ask him if he did not hear of the killings that occurred before he arrived.

"Yes, you are right," he says. "In 1994, the army killed a lot of people in the town center, nearly a hundred, I think. The rebels were in town. The army tried to catch the president of the rebels. The town defended him. People were talking about it when I got there. The kids I was sleeping with were witnesses. They would say the names of people. They would show where and how they were killed."

Beyond that, he has nothing to say, not how he felt about it then, nor how he feels about it now. It is something I have brought in; it does not arise from the feelings his memories evoke.

I imagine Zena and Tube and Asad in the town circle in the dead of night. Zena and Tube lead Asad to a spot in the inner circle and point to it and tell him that it is the ground on which the head of Reer Abrahim was killed. Zena takes Tube by the throat and enacts the scene. The rest of the town is still. In all of Wardheer, there are just three people awake, three street kids, and they are replaying the town's great trauma.

I wonder about the countless events that do not come into a person's head when he is telling his life story to a chronicler. Is it simply a question of chance? Had we not been in Blikkiesdorp, but elsewhere, in some Somali settlement in an American city, for instance, would Asad's recollections of Wardheer have triggered very different memories? Would the reenactment of the massacre have taken center stage? Or does it simply lie untouched, out of reach, on the deep ocean bed of his inner world?

# Dire Dawa, 2012

I was walking past Dire Dawa's railway station on a Saturday afternoon in April 2012 when the heavens opened. Solid sheets of water slammed down onto the street and onto the backs and the heads of passersby. People scattered, their shirts clinging heavily to their shoulders and chests, goose bumps welling up on their necks and arms.

I scurried onto the veranda of the large café opposite the railway station. Already it was filling with wet bodies and hot breath, all of us refugees from the torrent. After an initial flurry—furniture being rearranged, waiters weaving their way through the crowds in response to the deluge of new orders—the café calmed. We sat there, about a hundred of us, staring at the rain. The noise of the storm drowned the sounds of conversation, so that it seemed we were sitting in silence. A lovely feeling descended upon me: the rhythm of the rain outside, the protection of the shelter within, the many faces looking out; for a while, the gathering felt almost religious, as if we were paying homage to a force much larger than us.

As I sat there, my mind played an odd trick. I wondered whether people had huddled together in this very space thirty-five years earlier, in 1977, when the skies over Dire Dawa were filled, not with rain, but with fighter jets, the Somali air force's Russian MiGs in battle against the Ethiopian military's F-16s. I have tried to find out how badly the city was damaged during the war and how many of its civilians lost their lives, but the documentation I have found skates over these questions. What I do know is that the city was under siege for several months and that the crux of the battle was for air supremacy. Relations between Dire Dawa's residents could only have been tense, for while most of them wished desperately for the Ethiopian forces to successfully defend the city, some wanted the Somalis to overrun it.

When I think of the fighter jets that battled overhead, I think also—indeed, primarily—of Asad and how to tell his story. The war may have been fought seven or so years before his birth, and Dire Dawa may have been a place utterly foreign to him, but the 1977 war is nonetheless central to his tale.

Were the world to stand vertically, south at the bottom, north at the top, Dire Dawa would look down onto the vast arid plains of the Ogaden, otherwise known as the Somali region of Ethiopia, the territory into which Yindy's family took Asad when they moved from Dire Dawa to Wardheer. He didn't know it, but on that journey into Ethiopia's Somali region, Asad traveled across the ground on which his family had lived for generations and from which they had recently fled.

Nomadic Somali pastoralists, among them Asad's forebears, have lived on these plains since the sixteenth century and have formed the majority of the Ogaden's population ever since. Why this Somali-speaking land did not become part of Somalia when the country acquired independence is a long tale of treachery and deceit, one that Ogadeni nationalists like to tell over and again. The Somali-speaking territories controlled by the British and the Italians joined to form the independent state of Somalia in 1960. But the Ogaden was excluded, remaining under the control of Ethiopia, as were the Somali clans of northern Kenya. From the first, the new Somali state agitated without success to redraw its borders to incorporate all Somalis. That the country was incomplete, an amputated limb in Kenya and another in Ethiopia, became Somali nationalism's great clarion call.

Hawo told Asad that if his father had fled Somalia, it would have been to a place called Qorahay, for that is where the AliYusuf were from. Qorahay is a region of the Ogaden. It is not far from Wardheer. The Ali-Yusuf thus understand themselves to be at the center of the great drama of Somalia's thwarted nationalism, a part of the limb severed from the motherland. Fate placed them within the borders of the vast, complicated colossus of the Ethiopian empire, one whose subjects spoke no

fewer than eighty languages and whose rulers were Christian and conducted their official business in the foreign language of Amharic.

In 1974, Ethiopia's imperial regime was overthrown in a coup and
replaced by a military junta. Several hundred of the regime's top officials
were executed, and the emperor himself, Haile Selassie, was imprisoned
and soon died. In the times of instability that followed, it seemed that
the Ethiopian state might fall apart, for nationalist demands for succession arose throughout its borderlands: from Eritreans and Tigrayans in
the north; from the Afar in the northeast; from Oromo people, who were
dispersed throughout Ethiopia; and, of course, from the Somalis in the
southeast.

Taking advantage of this uncertain moment, the Somali government
began supporting a guerrilla campaign in the Ogaden and then launched
a full-fledged invasion in July 1977. Backed by a local population that
overwhelmingly supported it, the invading Somali forces were very soon
in control of the Ogaden. Flush with confidence, and more than a little
greedy, they marched on beyond the Ogaden and attacked Dire Dawa
and the ancient city of Harar. This was an altogether more risky business, for the majority of the civilian population here was not Somali,
and, to many, the invading army was a foreign foe. Moreover, with Dire
Dawa up for grabs, the stakes for Ethiopia now became existential, for
the railway line that the French built connected the entire southern and
eastern economy of Ethiopia to the port of Djibouti and, thus, to the
world. Were Dire Dawa and Harar to fall, Addis Ababa itself would lose
its lifeblood.

Why a war is won or lost is always a matter of debate. The Somalis
did not anticipate that their invasion would stir feelings of loyalty to the
new Ethiopian regime among millions of people, who fought very bravely
to defend their cities. As important, perhaps, were decisions made many
thousands of miles away. Somalia's Cold War backer, the Soviet Union,
switched sides in the middle of the war. The Somalis found themselves
fighting thousands of Cuban soldiers and an army buttressed by endless
new supplies of Soviet matériel; the very same Soviet advisers who just
weeks earlier were crafting Somali strategy were now devising plans to
rout the Somali military.

By March 1978, the war was over, Somalia's armed forces in hasty
retreat. But for the Somali-speaking people of the Ogaden, the trauma
was only beginning. Precisely what transpired between the Ethiopian

military and Ogadeni civilians in the aftermath of the Somali defeat has never been recorded except in the Ogadeni memories that have become folklore. But it was pretty devastating. An estimated eight hundred thousand people fled the Ogaden for Somalia. Many were slaughtered. If the fictional reconstructions of the Somali novelist Nuruddin Farah are accurate, entire families were killed, the inhabitants of entire villages cut down, on suspicion of having supported the enemy. Any Ogadeni who was educated, or who had wielded political power, fled for his life. By the early 1980s, the population of the Ogaden had halved.

Although he does not know it, Asad's parents were among the eight hundred thousand who fled. This information is new to me. I learned it just a week before I came to Dire Dawa. After much searching, I had found an Abdullahi in London who grew up with Asad's father. He was a cabdriver in White City. As we sat in his living room on a Saturday afternoon drinking tea, he relayed what he remembered of Asad's parents' wedding. It was a garrulous, colorful affair, he said. To my surprise, he mentioned in passing that it had taken place in a village called Marsin in the Qorahay region of the Ogaden.

"The wedding was not in Mogadishu?" I asked.

He shook his head. Hirsi Abdullahi grew up in Marsin. He and Asad's mother fled the Ogaden shortly after they were married. This was in March 1978, in the aftermath of the Ogadeni war.

And then the man, whose name was Sheikh Hussein, described his own flight from Qorahay in 1978. He spoke of his years in a refugee camp in southern Somalia and of his perilous journey back into the Ogaden to retrieve a sister who had been stranded there. He described what it was like to be a refugee in Somalia—they were treated like leeches, he said, like second-class people, like beggars. He left Somalia in 1981 and worked first in Libya and then in Saudi Arabia.

I asked if he saw a lot of Asad's parents before he left Mogadishu. Not much, he replied. Asad's father was doing well as a trader. He had been lulled into thinking that maybe he belonged in Mogadishu. Sheikh Hussein's tone seemed bitter to me.

That evening, as I left White City, I had to examine Asad's story anew. The way he had it in his mind, his was an old Mogadishu family, his parents ensconced and comfortable in the city. His mother's death and his own flight were the beginning of an unraveling. That they were refugees who had been torn from their homes, the city around them strange and unwelcome, was a notion he had not dreamed of.

Far more dramatic, though, were the implications for his time in Wardheer. Here was a lost boy, pushing barrels of water through hot sand, his family lost. Little did he know that he was home, the villages a few hours to the west teeming with his kin, many of whom had recently returned.

# Rooda

Walking his barrel through the sand in Wardheer's midday heat, Asad felt a pair of eyes on him. He looked up to see a woman standing at the entrance of a cafeteria, her hands on her hips, scrutinizing him without apology. She was young, about twenty, he guessed, and she was beautiful, her eyes wide and very large, her back straight and resolute. Her stare was curious, rather than hostile, but he nonetheless recoiled from it. He imagined himself from her perspective, a scrawny, half-grown boy pushing a barrel many times his weight through boiling sand. He stood up and returned her gaze with silent anger. She held his stare for a moment, unembarrassed, then turned away.

Later in the day, after he had delivered his barrel of water, he walked into her cafeteria and told her that he wanted to fetch water. If she could stare at me like that, he thought, she could at least do something useful for me, too. She smiled at him in a way that made it seem as if she was laughing to herself and told him to come back the following morning.

That night, Asad asked Zena about her, and Zena, who knew everything about everyone, said that her name was Nasri and that she was entirely alone: she had no brothers with her in Wardheer, no father. She ran the cafeteria Asad had gone into she was a young, independent businesswoman, her own boss. Her house was at the back of her restaurant; she shared it with another single woman.

Within a week, Nasri had become Asad's most regular client. He carried water for her at least twice a day. She said very little to him. But her waiters would reward him well, not so much with money but with a good supply of healthy food. It was, he believed, on her instructions that he was so well fed.

As his presence became routine, so Nasri began using him for other work. Once, when the cafeteria ran out of meat in the middle of dinner-time, she gave him money and instructed him to rush to the butchery. The following day, she sent him to buy camel milk. He treated these errands as urgent business, batting off all distractions and returning to her restaurant with speed. And he made a point of giving her the right change, never pocketing so much as a shilling.

Among Nasri's regular customers was a young truck driver. "His name was Abdiyare," Asad tells me. "But nobody called him that. His nickname was Rooda. It is a girl's name. I don't know why he got that name. He was in love with Nasri. He wanted to marry her. Whenever he passed through Wardheer—and it was often, sometimes as much as every week—Nasri's cafeteria was where he would chew his *mira* and eat his meals. He would stay until she closed, always the last customer to leave, every single day he was in town. He was a very warm man, a gentle, laughing man. It would be a long time before I saw him angry."

And then Asad suddenly pivots the discussion in another direction and says something I don't quite understand.

"I was suspicious of him and Nasri. Her house was at the back of the cafeteria. She did not allow anyone there, except Rooda. He was always going back there. I wondered why."

"Do you think they were having sex?" I ask.

"No. That would have been bad. They were not married. Culturally, premarital sex is not something we do."

"Maybe something short of sex, but still physical?"

"Nasri was a good girl," he replies. "If any customer tried to touch her body, she chased him away. She had a reputation for that."

"So why did she and Rooda make you suspicious?"

"Because she was always taking him back there to her house."

"But you don't think that they were doing anything untoward there?"

"No."

We were going around in circles, and so I changed the subject. But as I drove away from Blikkiesdorp that afternoon, it was still on my mind. Was Asad filtering away his subsequent, adult thoughts and simply reinhabiting his thirteen-year-old self? Was he telling me that he recognized sexual play without yet having the words or the concepts to know what it was? Or was it that his sense of decorum prevented him from talking frankly with me about sex? I am not sure about that, as he would soon share something of his own sexual experience, albeit it in the most measured way. In any event, I would imagine that he feared for Nasri: a young woman alone, running her own business; so much rested on her reputation. Perhaps he was troubled that others might see what he saw.

As Asad remembers him, Rooda spent his waking hours feeding himself a succession of stimulants. If he was not chewing *mira,* he was drinking Coke. Often he did both at the same time. That is how he and Asad got to know each other. Nasri did not sell Coke. Instead, she stocked an Arabic drink called Shani. Rooda would call Asad over and give him five hundred shillings and instruct him to come back with a few bottles of Coke. Asad would return with Rooda's drinks and his change, and Rooda would line the Coke bottles up on the table in front of him and drink them one after another in the course of the evening.

Soon, Rooda was asking Asad to do all sorts of things. Sometimes, he would remember that he had left something he needed in his truck—a pocketknife, perhaps, or an article of clothing. Asad would hoist himself into the cabin of this great beast and wriggle into the imprint Rooda's form had left in the cracked plastic cover on the driver's seat. He would finger the gear stick and press his palms down on the dashboard until the heat shot into his fingers, and he would pull his hand away.

Other times, Rooda would send Asad to the *mira* market. This was, without doubt, his most exciting task, for East African men take their *mira* extremely seriously, feeling the texture of the leaf in their fingers, burying their nose in the plant to ascertain its purity. And here was Asad, a mere street boy, expertly roaming through the plants, running leaves through his hands. He would return with his purchase and wait eagerly for Rooda to put the first of his replenished stock in his mouth and then watch his face to see whether he was pleased.

"After a while," Asad recalls, "Rooda learned everything about my life. I did not tell him, but he found out. He would ask me about being alone, about being on the street. He would ask about Islii. Once, he even asked me about my mother. But he did it in a way that did not make me want to run away. He did it in a sidewise sort of way. Sometimes, I would be sitting in the sand outside Nasri's restaurant, and I would look up and see that he was watching me. He would be laughing and talking loudly and chewing his *mira,* but while all this was going on, he would look at me out of the corner of his eye."

Expecting to hear a story about teeth, I ask Asad what Rooda looked like. But, for once, his portraiture drifts from physical description and melts into an account of Rooda's spirit.

"Rooda is a short man," Asad says. "He has white skin, soft hair, a long nose. He is a happy person. He is always smiling. And he is a great *mira* eater. You wonder when he sleeps.

"I would miss him when he was traveling. Sometimes he was away for a month, sometimes two weeks or a week. I would wait for him to come. Someone would tell me that his truck had arrived, and I would feel excited."

One afternoon in Nasri's restaurant, a couple of months after he and Asad met, Rooda tossed a proposition into Asad's lap. He was leaving the following morning, and he wanted Asad to come along. Asad had asked him several times in the preceding weeks if he could accompany him. Rooda had just laughed, as if Asad had been joking. He recalls the proposition as two great hands grabbing him by his sides and shaking him.

"How long will we be gone?" Asad asked.

Rooda shrugged. "Maybe a week."

"I have nothing," Asad said. "No food, nothing."

Rooda smiled. "*I* have food," he said, poking a finger into his own chest. He leaned back in his chair and laughed. "We will be going to Dire Dawa. I will buy you clothes there. The things you have on your shoulders are rags."

Asad picked at a hole in his shirt's sleeve.

"I do not know what a person does in a truck," he said.

"What a person does," Rooda replied, "is follow Rooda. Rooda will show a person everything he needs to know. You are not going anywhere alone. You are going with Rooda."

Asad takes my notebook and pen from me and begins yet another sketch, not of a place, but of a set of relationships: he is showing me the division of labor on an Ogadeni truck.

"You get three people in the vehicle," Asad tells me as he draws. "The first is the truck driver. The second is called the *deni.* He is the one representing the owner of the truck. He is responsible for the safety of the cargo, for negotiating with officials in and out of the Ogaden, negotiating the price of the load, negotiating with people who want to travel on the roof of the truck. And then you get the *kirishbooy,* who is in charge of the cargo, flat tires, the engine: everything to do with the truck except driving it. That is what Rooda had in mind, that he would save me from the streets by training me to be a *kirishbooy.* It was a long-term vision. I was still too small and weak. The truck jack, for instance: you let it go, the truck will crush you."

The following morning Asad found himself in the back of the truck cabin with the *kirishbooy.* Rooda was in the driver's seat, the *deni* in the passenger seat. Before the truck had even started moving, the *kirishbooy* complained to the *deni* about having to share his space. The *kirishbooy* was a very tall young man, and thin, too, which made him seem even taller. His name was Bille Dheer, *dheer* being the Somali word for "tall." He folded his arms and told the *deni* that he refused to travel with this young boy all over his space. Rooda turned around in his seat and told the *kirishbooy* to be quiet. And then the *deni* joined the dispute on the *kirishbooy*'s side, asking why a little shrimp of a boy of no use to anybody should take up valuable space in the cabin. In future, Asad would travel on the roof.

When they finally drove out of Wardheer, the vehicle that carried them seemed to Asad not so much a truck as a moving city. The back was packed to the ceiling with all sorts of cargo from livestock to furniture to an assortment of sealed boxes. And the roof was filled with people, about forty of them in all, each on his or her way to somewhere in the Ogaden.

They drove through many, many miles of desert, and it seemed as if they were going nowhere, for everything looked the same. At about midday, they stopped, and the *kirishbooy* jumped down from the cabin and began pointing out young men on the roof, commanding them to help him. Together, three of them took a two-hundred-liter barrel of gasoline off the truck. Bille Dheer uncapped it, lowered a short pipe into the petrol, sucked, and then quickly steered the pipe into the petrol tank. He filled the radiator with water and checked the tires, and by the time they were moving again, the sun was at its zenith, the temperature well over a hundred degrees.

It was late afternoon before they finally drove into a town. On the outskirts, two or three children ran alongside the truck. They were joined by more people, and still more; by the time the truck stopped in the center of town it was surrounded by an excited crowd. People pressed their hands against the windows, and some scrambled onto the truck's nose, others onto the ledge at the rear. Most were children, but Asad was shocked to see that many were not; there were elderly women thumping the windows and middle-aged men tapping the sides of the truck with sticks. The thought of climbing down terrified him. What if he lost Rooda in the mob? As the others opened their doors, Asad remained frozen in his seat.

Rooda, the *deni,* and Bille Dheer got out of the cabin, and as they moved off they resembled the corpses of large cockroaches or locusts, carried away by swarms of flies. The cafeteria where they chose to eat was in sight of the truck, and Asad watched in amazement as it filled with dozens upon dozens of people. At one point, Rooda came into clear view; he was sitting at a table eating his meal, and the people around him were quite literally reaching for his plate with their hands.

Asad sat there frozen. There was no way he was going to venture out of the truck. He feared that the crowd would rip a limb from his torso, that he would stand and watch helplessly as dozens of mouths gnawed at his severed arm. And so he waited, his hunger mounting, his hands running urgently against the plastic of the car seats.

When they had finished eating, the three men returned to the truck. Rooda started the engine and had to move at a crawl, his way blocked by the crowds. On the outskirts of the town, they had still not shaken everybody off; a few stragglers jogged alongside the truck on either side. One of them scrambled onto the side of the vehicle, and the *deni* leaned out of the window and shouted blue murder until the intruder let go and tumbled into the dust.

They were out in open desert once again. The hours passed, and Rooda chewed his *mira* and drank his Coke and laughed his laugh. Not once did he turn around and look at Asad. The garrulous man, so pleased to be on the road, had forgotten his charge.

It was very late by the time they stopped again, close to midnight, as Asad recalls. They were in a tiny village. Asad turned out his pockets and found that he had one hundred twenty shillings, enough for a glass of camel milk and no more. There was one remaining canteen open, and he went there and bought his milk and sat down. He had taken but a sip when Rooda came striding up to him.

"Before he started speaking, I knew he was furious," Asad recalls. "It was such a shock seeing Rooda's face angry. I had never seen that face before without its smile around the eyes. It was like another person had jumped inside Rooda and taken over his face. I think I stopped breathing."

"Where have you been all day?" Rooda shouted. "Did you not have lunch?"

"No."

"Why not?"

"I was afraid."

"Of what?"

"Of all the people."

"You must follow me, Asad! I have a hundred people falling over me. I cannot remember you when it is like that. You must follow me, always, always, always, you must follow me. Do you understand?"

Asad thought that Rooda might lay his hands on his throat and throttle him. But instead he turned around and stormed off.

As Asad watched Rooda recede into the night his shock gave way to a feeling of lightness. Sitting there alone with his glass of milk, he suddenly felt unfathomably merry. His mouth widened into a grin. Here was an adult who grew angry because he worried about Asad. It had been a long time since he had confronted such anger. He pictured himself grinning, as if he were watching his own face from the other side of the table, and he felt foolish.

"I traveled with Rooda for a year and a half," Asad tells me, "until I was fifteen or sixteen. I grew up. I became tall. I became strong. I could pick up a truck's wheel by the time I left."

He describes his development as physical, but it was much more than that. To live one's life on an Ogadeni truck was to be at the center of the universe. You were in the business of moving things and people, and everybody wanted to have something or somebody moved. As Asad went about his work, the world came to him. Young people, in particular, were drawn to trucks, for to be young in the Ogaden was to need urgently to get somewhere and yet to have no means to do so. The truck stops in the Ogadeni towns swarmed with the young, and there wasn't a soul among them who did not need to befriend Asad. Everybody wanted to be close to this boy who moved. Perhaps he would put in a good word with the *deni* and get one a free place on the roof of the truck.

In his memory, he was kind to everyone who came his way. He would share money freely whenever Rooda or the *deni* filled his pockets. He enjoyed being a person of consequence. It made him feel magnanimous and good-spirited. He would ride with people on the roof of the truck and talk and talk. He remembers these as the best conversations of his life.

"All we had was time," he recalls. "Those journeys would go on for hours and hours and there was nothing to do but talk. And when talk is given freedom it goes everywhere. You find out about so many lives, about so many things."

I ask him to recall one of these conversations. He thinks for a moment, and then smirks into his chin and chuckles.

"We would return to Wardheer every few weeks. When it was time to leave, I would allow Tube and Zena and Abdi onto the truck until we were out in the desert, and then they would jump off and go home. One time, Zena was in a very good mood, and he started to imitate all the adults in the town. We had to guess who he was imitating. He was so brilliant, we got it right every time. We were laughing and laughing there on top of the truck, and we lost track of time. When we realized, it was too late. To walk back to Wardheer all these miles, the boys would have died of thirst. So I banged on the roof of the cabin and told Rooda that we had to turn around, and the *deni* got so angry it looked like his eyes would explode. Zena turned his back to the *deni* and made these exploding eyes, and everyone on the roof laughed, which made the *deni* even angrier."

His lightness has filled my car, and we are smiling at each other and enjoying ourselves. He has more stories.

"At night," he continues, "Rooda and the *deni* would sleep in the town, and Bille Dheer and me with the truck. Because he was senior, Bille Dheer made his bed in the cabin. I made mine on the roof. The first time it rained at night, I lay there. I felt the drops hitting my head like someone was punching me. There was no way Bille Dheer would let me sleep with him in the cabin, even if it was raining stones. I was thinking of maybe going to sleep under the truck, in the dirt, on the ground, when, suddenly, Rooda came running.

"'I was lying in bed listening to the rain,' Rooda said, 'when I realized I had not taught Asad how to make a tent on the roof of the truck.'"

And there and then, in the pouring rain, Rooda showed Asad how to assemble a tent.

For some reason, the image of a tent on a truck roof amuses him, as if it is comically out of place; as if, for instance, a neighbor here in Blikkiesdorp had erected a kennel for his dog on the roof of his shack. He sits in my car and laughs out loud.

Rooda's truck traveled an international circuit over and again during the eighteen or so months Asad was with him. He lost count of how many times he went to Addis; of how often the truck crossed the border and went to Bosaso, the main port in Puntland; to Berbera, the deep-sea port in Somaliland; and to Djibouti, whose railway line threaded south to Dire Dawa. The *deni*'s dealings with people who wanted their goods to cross borders were none of Asad's business. He knew not to watch, not to ask, and not to look interested. I saw for myself some fifteen years later how delicate these matters are. After searching in vain for more than half a day, I discovered the truck stop in Dire Dawa where Asad slept whenever he was in town. Many trucks were parked on the side of the road, and some of them looked exactly like the one Asad had described to me. Excited by my find, I immediately put my camera to my face and began clicking. Within moments, the air was humming with muttered discontent, and I slipped my camera back into my bag and threw up my arms in apology.

Asad *was* permitted to take an interest in uncontentious cargo.

"There was often drought somewhere in the Ogaden," he recalls. "The Ethiopian government would give food aid. The trucks get notice, they go to Addis or to Dire Dawa to pick up food supplies, then they go off into the Ogaden. About forty trucks will go. You arrive at your destination, and the truck is mobbed by hungry people. The Ethiopian army is there, and they hit a couple of people with their rifle butts until everyone calms down.

"Sometimes, we transported *subag,* which is pure butter, straight from the sheep or cow. Also, we transported hides. And *masago,* which is a starch that grows in East Africa. And livestock itself: sheep and goats. When there is no order, the truck is free for anyone to hire. Sometimes it is empty. Then we just transport people, but there is not much money in that."

As ever, I am interested in how the politics of the region shaped Asad's experience on the truck; and, as always, I have to push him, asking pointed, detailed questions about the officials they met at the sides of the road.

"The best was traveling in Ethiopia," Asad says, "because the police and the army are very disciplined. The Ethiopian government is very strong. There is no space for the police to ask for a bribe. It never happened. Not even once. But when you cross the border and are in Somaliland or Puntland, there is trouble. In Somaliland, the police want bribes. It is sometimes hard to tell whether they are actually police, but you pay them anyway. But it is not so bad. You pay them, and they let you move on. Puntland, brother, is another story. There are lots and lots of road-blocks, and you pay a lot of money. And in each town, there is a group of Somalis called *qaaqlayaal.* They are not police. They are not anything. They are just very violent people, and they demand certain money. The *deni* must pay up. If he refuses, he is going to get hurt. Once, they asked for a lot of money, a lot of money, brother. And the *deni* hesitated; just for a moment, he thought about it. And one of the *qaaqlayaal* hit him hard on the front of the nose. The *deni* fell over and slowly got up again, and there was blood pouring. And the *qaaqlayaal* said, 'I have punished you for thinking. Now pay.'"

I press him about Ethiopia. "You say the armed forces didn't ask for bribes," I begin, "but surely they gave you other trouble, especially in the Ogaden, where there was armed resistance to Ethiopian rule."

He nods and, for the first time during his account of his time on the truck, begins speaking in the future tense, as if he is talking hypothetically about events that have not actually happened.

"The army will stop you and ask if you have seen rebels on the road. Sometimes they will keep you a long time. A little later, the rebels will stop you and ask whether you have seen the soldiers. They are very serious people. Both try to get real information from you. If they feel you are hiding information or lying, they get very tough with you. They unload the truck. They interrogate you individually and privately. They take two or three people off the truck, and you never see them again. Whether they end up at home in one piece one cannot know. Several times, the *deni* or Rooda was beaten. You have no recourse; there is nobody to complain to. You must be honest both with the government and with the rebels. If you take sides, you are in trouble. Tell both sides what you know. That is the best policy. Don't play games with anybody. If they are genuinely scared—if they think that the other side is nearby—the interrogations are very scary."

His account is quick and stylized, like a story written on a surface of slick, shiny steel. People get taken away, never to be seen again, and then the tale slides on, as if it cannot stop for anything, no matter how alarming or dramatic. I try to think of ways to slow it down.

"What language did the soldiers interrogate people in?" I ask. "Were they fluent in Somali?"

"The soldiers do not speak Somali," he says. "They interrogate you in the Amharic language. Some speak Oromo. A few of the soldiers know Somali, but when they are interrogating people, they speak in their own language, and they use interpreters. It makes the whole situation more uncertain. I learned a little Amharic in Ethiopia, but not much, not like English or Swahili. And so they are talking among themselves, and you do not know what they are planning for you, and everyone gets scared."

What he remembers above all from this time is being dirty. He was always covered in grass or in oil.

"In big towns like Jigjiga you can buy a shower. Some people build a business that is only showers. It is not just for travelers. In the heat of the day, the whole town comes to cool off. The showers are equipped with hair oil, a comb, a drinking glass, a mirror. You drive all day, arrive in a town, the driver and the *deni* go off immediately. They come back later with pretty faces, fresh clothes. You still stink. You are still full of grass. One of the reasons I gave up the truck was the desire to be clean."

# *Qorahay*

Asad was on the roof of the truck talking to travelers when one of them mentioned in passing that they had just entered Qorahay. Asad snapped his head up and looked about him. All around was desert. There wasn't a soul in sight.

"What is Qorahay?" he asked.

"It is a region," the traveler replied, "a region of the Ogaden. It has a town called Qabridahre and a few villages. Otherwise it is just nomads."

And then the specifics melt away.

"I looked around Qorahay," Asad tells me, "and there was nothing."

"What do you mean?" I ask. "Did you inquire about your father?"

"During my time with Rooda, we went to Qabridahre maybe three times," he says. "There was nothing there."

We do not talk about Qorahay again for a long time. And then I go to East Africa and to London, and I return with a slippery, difficult gift—some knowledge of Asad's family history.

We are in my car, as usual, but, for once, we are not outside Asad's shack. When I phoned in the morning, he said to meet him in Bellville Town Centre, for he had business there.

We met in a crowded place and strolled for some time, and then we sat in a Somali restaurant and drank coffee. But the surroundings unsettled us, and our conversation slid and drifted. Our interviews had come to require their own space, it seemed, and that space was the interior of a car. We made our way to the lot where I had parked and resumed our usual positions, I in the driver's seat taking notes, Asad in the passenger seat.

I have resolved to tell him baldly and simply what I have discovered. And so I describe my meeting with Sheikh Hussein, the London cabdriver. I tell him that Sheikh Hussein's father and Asad's grandfather grew up together in Marsin, a village in Qorahay.

He nods and says he knows of that village; he passed through it with Rooda.

I tell him that his parents were married sometime in the 1970s in Qabridahre, exactly how long before the 1977–78 war I am not sure, but they were among the nearly one million Ogadeni who fled Ethiopia in 1978. I tell him of Sheikh Hussein's escape from the Ogaden, of the time he spent in a refugee camp in southern Somalia, of the discrimination he and other Ogadeni refugees felt after they arrived in Mogadishu. Sheikh Hussein saw Asad's father occasionally in the Somali capital, I say, but he left in 1981 for Egypt and lost touch.

For a long time, Asad says nothing. He folds his fingers together in his lap and stares out of the passenger-side window.

"It would have been easy," he says eventually.

"What would have been easy?"

"Finding my family. I was told after I got to South Africa that my father had been in Qabridahre when I was living in Ethiopia. But I convinced myself that I would never have found him anyway. From what you are saying, it would have been easy. If Qabridahre is where my family is from, I could have told anyone my name, and they would have taken me to my father."

"You were a boy on your own," I say. "You were careful not to tell anyone too much about yourself. You were protecting yourself. You were surviving. That you did not find your father makes sense."

"No," he replies. "I was not alone. I had Rooda. He was always asking me: 'Who is your father? Who are you?' It would have been easy. I was *kirishbooy*. I had to stay with the truck when we spent the night in Qabridahre. But I could have sent Rooda to find my father. I could have told him to ask questions when he went into town. Given what you are saying, he would have found close family within an hour of making inquiries, maybe two hours."

"What do you think stopped you from asking him?"

He shrugs. "I was a child. I was not thinking."

He falls silent again and resumes his contemplative posture, staring out of the window, fingers folded.

"It is so strange to think about it," he says. "If the thought had come into my mind just once, only once; if I had watched Rooda walking into town and called him back and said: 'Rooda, in Dire Dawa I was staying with my father's sister and she told me maybe my father is in Qorahay. Will you ask? I will tell you my father's and grandfather's nicknames. I will tell you what you need to know to find him.' If it had crossed my mind just once to ask Rooda that, my whole life would have turned out different. I would never have come here. I would be with family."

"What happened happened," I say.

He nods. "That is how you must think. What happened happened. If you spent your time thinking that where you are now is because of mistakes you made long ago, you would not get up in the mornings. A person cannot live like that.

"But still, it is natural to wonder. I was young back then. I was like a stone in the road. Anybody could just come along and kick me, and that would decide where I ended up."

I begin to grow uncomfortable. The news is fresh and disorienting. It is best that he absorb it alone. Sheikh Hussein has asked me to give Asad his phone number in London. The two of them are to have a long talk. Perhaps we should resume this conversation after they have spoken. I offer to take him home.

"Not yet," he says. "Let's stretch our legs."

And so we stroll around the town center for a while, return to the car, and speak of other things. But as we are about to leave for Blikkiesdorp, he raises the subject again.

"This is the first I am hearing my story like this," he says, "and I am finding it very sad. As far as I am concerned, I am from Mogadishu, and the trouble started in 1991. To hear that my parents were refugees and that the place I fled to was actually home: it is a very sad story. Where is home? Do we Abdullahis not have a home? For my family to have been on the run for such a long time is a very sad thing."

"It is also ironic," I say. "The militia killed your mother because she was a Daarood of Mogadishu, but it seems that she herself was a refugee and may have felt excluded from Mogadishu."

"Yes," he says quietly. "That is a part of what is so sad."

He asks to hear more about Sheikh Hussein, whom he refers to as "my uncle in London." I tell him that Sheikh Hussein is a militant Ogadeni nationalist.

"For him," I say, "home is the Ogaden. It has been taken away, and his primary fight is to get it back. Somalia is secondary for him. He told me that only after the Ogaden has been taken back from the Ethiopians will it be necessary to think about the relationship with Somalia."

He nods. "I understand," he says. "That is what a man must do if his home is taken away from him. He must fight."

"But I am curious," I say. "In all your years in the Somali diaspora, you have brushed shoulders with Ogadeni nationalists all the time. They have websites and newspapers. They are very vocal. Hawo had told you that the Abdullahis were from Qorahay. Did it never occur to you that the Ogadeni nationalists may have been talking about your own family history?"

"I thought of them as one more political party," he replies. "The al-Shabaab people talk about Islam and purity and no *mira* and being holy. The Ogadeni people talk about fighting the Ethiopians. A lot of people make a noise about a lot of things. Until today, I did not think that what they were saying had anything to do with me."

I drop him at home and drive back into Cape Town. I am puzzled. He has said that he was merely a boy, that he was not thinking, that if he had had his wits about him he would have found his family. But Hawo had already told him that the Abdullahis were from Qorahay. Why did he not look for family when he got there?

More puzzling are the questions he did not ask in later years. He is a grown man with an adult's capacity to reflect. He has heard the voices of Ogadeni nationalists all about him. Why did he never connect the dots? The prospect that his family was among the masses who fled in 1978 must surely have crossed his mind.

Perhaps there is a simple answer. Maybe he found the story the Ogadeni nationalists tell to be foreign: foreign to him as a human being. It is, after all, a tale that is hard to own. They are like the Israelites in the desert, but the forty years came and went countless generations ago, and still they are wandering, their bitterness their sole nourishment. All they know is that they have been eternally robbed of their home.

Perhaps he decided early on that this was not his history. He needed for there to be a foundation. Once upon a time there was a prosperous Mogadishu family: that is how his story must begin. And that is how it must end. His time adrift is an anomaly, a parenthesis. It will end soon.

# *Students*

There is a truck stop in Dire Dawa. When Asad described it to me, I imagined it as a place teeming with stalls and markets and filled with noise. It is in fact just a quiet street in a tree-lined neighborhood, several trucks parked on either side of the road. A green-walled mosque is in sight, half a block away, and the loudest sound about is the dreamy, drifting call to prayer. I'd thought it so big and loud, I now realized, because of its significance in Asad's life.

The afternoon on which I visited was very hot; a lone *kirishbooy* braved the direct sunlight, crouching over the exposed intestines of his truck's engine. Everyone else sat quietly in the shade, their rest interrupted when I foolishly took out my camera.

It was at this truck stop that Asad met the students Yusuf, Abdirashid, Molid, Khadaar, and Abdiaziz.

Dire Dawa heaves with students. They come in from the Ogaden on the roofs of trucks with little more than the clothes on their backs. They rent places in the poorest parts of the city, five, sometimes ten, of them to a single room. They register at schools and at colleges and then scrounge for money to pay their fees and buy their textbooks. For the youth in the surrounding villages and towns, the only route to prosperity is the civil service, and the only way there is through a university education. And so a region's youth descends en masse on the provincial capital's schools and college, whether they can afford to or not.

"Yusuf and his friends hung around at the truck stop for two reasons," Asad tells me. "During school holidays they wanted to go home to their various places in the Ogaden to see their families, but they had no money to travel. So they thought that if they befriend the *kirishbooys* and the *denis* maybe it will be possible to get a free place on the roof of a truck. And, second, truck stops are a place of businessmen, and businessmen have money, so they come to tell businessmen about their plight."

It was on the roof of Rooda's truck, on a trip from Dire Dawa to Jigajiga, that Asad got to know the five students. Asad had told me often how much he enjoyed the conversations on the road, but it is only now, when he speaks of these particular young men, that I see the attraction. What he enjoyed was the opportunity to imagine other lives and to contemplate that these lives might be his own.

"They were clean," Asad tells me, "and I was full of grass. They had books in their bags. And I could not read properly. I asked Abdirashid to show me a book. I paged through it. Then I asked him to read some of it to me. It was about which parts of Ethiopia were high and which parts were low. Tigray, where the rulers of Ethiopia come from, was in the highlands. The Ogaden was in the lowlands. I thought about this. I kept looking up from the book at Abdirashid's face. It was so clean, the sort of clean your face gets when you wash it every day."

Asad was generous to the students. Whenever Rooda or the *deni* gave him a decent sum of money, he would hold on to it until he was next in Dire Dawa. He would either spend it with the students or simply give them half of what he had.

After a few months, it came to him that he was living for the time the truck stopped in Dire Dawa, and that whenever he was elsewhere, the students remained in his mind. This business of being in one place and imagining all the time that one is somewhere else: when it happened he realized at once that he had not felt this way in a long time.

The years he spent in Nairobi, the long trip through Ethiopia, the time in Dire Dawa: for all those uncountable hours and minutes and seconds he was, in his head, a boy on the brink of living in America. He understood now that adjusting to the disappointment that America was gone had exhausted him; that being a boy who did not imagine his future was hard work.

Without warning, he felt the presence of his mother. He thought of the two thick plaits of hair running down her back, and he realized that the image was not nearly as powerful as the feeling and that the feeling was indescribable. She was with him always; something truly terrible would have to happen to shake her out. He recalls the revelation coming to him on the back of Rooda's truck, the wind in his face, the yellow desert all around.

From the truck stop I walk down a gentle hill, past the green mosque. I turn right at the corner and come to the entrance of a large wholesaler's shop. I am retracing the steps Asad took as he went to announce to Rooda that he would be staying with the students in Dire Dawa.

"Rooda was sitting at the entrance to the shop talking to somebody," Asad recalls. "That was his standard position. He would spend hours there, talking, chewing *mira*. I stopped quite far from him, maybe ten paces.

"I said, 'I need to talk to you.'

"He said, 'Then come here and talk.'

"I didn't want to tell him I was leaving in front of the other people. 'No,' I said. 'You come here.'

"He got up from his chair, sighing, like it was a big effort, and came over to me.

"'I'm leaving,' I said.

"'Why? What's wrong?'

"'Nothing. I want to study.'

"He said nothing, nothing at all. He just stood there and looked at me and nodded his head. He is not the sort of person to shout. He just walks away. The first and last time he ever shouted at me was on that first night when he realized I hadn't eaten, and that was only because he was panicked. He was a gentle man, a very kind man.

"I sat there in the wholesaler's shop feeling quite upset, quite confused. He came back about two hours later, and I could see from his face he was still shocked that I was leaving. He put money in my hand; it was a lot of money, more than I had ever held in one pile. I think he said, 'Do not be naughty,' but I cannot remember for sure. The guys were waiting for me at the truck stop. I turned and walked away. I never saw Rooda again."

There is a long silence. We both stare at the Blikkiesdorp scene in front of us. About fifty paces away, two young men are sitting in the narrow slice of shade cast by a shack. Asad has been eyeing them carefully all morning.

"Do you regret leaving Rooda?" I ask.

"It is foolish to regret what you did when you were young," he replies. "But if I had stayed with Rooda I would have a very different life now. He wasn't pleased when I left him. He wanted to train me to change tires, to train me from bottom to top so that I could become a driver. But people disappoint you, even your children. That's not what I wanted to do.

"Looking back now, I should have stayed with him. I was a kid. I didn't know what I was doing. I could have had my own truck by now. I did not realize I was changing the rest of my life. Like I say, I was like a stone lying on the ground. Anyone could pick it up and throw it."

"What do you think would have happened if you'd gone back to Rooda a month later?" I asked.

"He would not have said a word. I just would have climbed up, and we would have driven off. But it didn't even come to my mind. I had a free life. I had no worries."

There is another long silence.

"What was Rooda's clan?" I finally ask.

"I don't know. It was not the sort of question you asked Rooda."

"Never? His clan never once came up in conversation?"

"No. Even if I were to sit here and try to imagine myself asking Rooda his clan, I can't imagine it. You spoke to Rooda only about now, about the truck, about the road, about his *mira,* about his Coca-Cola."


Including Asad, there were six students. They shared a single room in the neighborhood of Gandeqore, which was built after the fashion of the city's original French neighborhood with wide streets and stucco houses and sprawling, shady trees. Asad was the only one among them with no income, but it seemed genuinely not to matter. They lived simple lives, there was enough to go around, and, besides, Asad had been more than generous to all of them in the past.

"They were all from different places," Asad tells me, "but they were all from the Ogaden."

I find it difficult to coax to life Asad's memories of this time. His description of Gandeqore is flat and halfhearted, and it is only when I walk through the neighborhood myself that I get a sense of it. It is such a peaceful, quiet place, full of the shade cast by the trees. Groups of people lean against walls or sit on plastic chairs, talking for hours and hours and going nowhere. In little coffee shops the patrons drink espressos and cross their legs and look out into the street.

The truth, I think, is that Asad was bored. The others would leave early for school, abandoning him to this deserted neighborhood. He would pad about the room, doze and wake and stare at the ceiling. He would go to mosque and sometimes remain after prayers and talk, but the men there were mainly middle-aged, and he had little in common with them. He found himself marking time, waiting for the midafternoon, when the others would return from school. They were always ravenously hungry; they would change their clothes and go out to the canteens and restaurants to find food. Sometimes they would come home again in the early evenings and do schoolwork. Other times they would walk into the center of town and hang out all evening in the market or around the restaurants and coffee shops.

Twice, Asad tried to go to school. The first attempt was at a government-run institution in the neighborhood of Lagaharka. He sat in the principal's office growing increasingly dismayed as the man before him erected one obstacle after another. He could not admit Asad, he said, without a referral letter from his previous school. Where was his previous school? Asad panicked. Were he to blurt out that he had never been to school, but for an abortive attempt at that Muslim institution in southern Kenya, he feared the principal would laugh in his face.

"Jigjiga," Asad said.

"Well, then you must go to Jigjiga for a referral letter, so that I know what grade to put you in. I cannot assign you to a grade without knowing that you have passed the previous grade."

Asad's friends advised him to go to Jigjiga and get a referral letter, even if he had to buy one, even if he had to get somebody to forge one. But the very thought of such an expedition exhausted him, and he stayed at home in the mornings and stared at the ceiling.

He again went to see the headmaster at the school in Lagaharka, and told him that he had no referral letter.

"Then I will have to put you in the first grade," the headmaster said.

"Show me," Asad replied.

They walked through the school, and the headmaster invited Asad to peer through a window, and there, sitting at small desks made for small bodies, a group of children, no more than eight or nine years old, sat listening to a teacher. The idea that Asad might sit at one of those little desks appalled him. He was now about fifteen years old and could pick up the tire of a truck and make a tent on the roof and take care of the truck alone in a strange town crowded with strange people: that such an

Asad might sit at a little desk among little people filled him with a sense of indignity so powerful that he cannot describe it. He sits in my passenger seat and grins and shrugs his shoulders.

And so he spent a lot of his life waiting—primarily for the others to return from school. They would take out their books to study, and Asad would watch from over their shoulders, and sometimes he would ask questions, but he could tell that he was irritating them, and so soon his questions ceased. Sometimes, when a book was lying around, he would examine it, and if it was in English he would pick it up, sit himself down in a corner, and read.

"I only read two books during my time in Dire Dawa," Asad says. "One was geographical, the other biological. The geography book had a chapter called 'Civics': democratic Ethiopia, how government works, the relationship between the regions and the central government in Addis. There was another chapter on terrain, and I saw once again that the Ogaden was the lowland, the rest of Ethiopia the highland. In the biology book I learned about different trees. Two types: one with sap, one without. Also, ones that shed their leaves and ones that do not.

"I would read awhile, and then I would put down the book and join in whatever conversation the others were having."

"What did they talk about?" I ask.

"Their plans. Always their plans. They wanted to change from this school to that school because they knew that somebody from that school once got into university. But this better school costs money, so then they talk about their finances. Also, their plans for when they are finished with school. Should they live in this village or that village? There are many jobs in the civil service here, but not there.

"Sometimes, they told funny stories about girls. In fact, whenever they were not talking about their finances or their plans, they were talking about girls."

Frustratingly, he says no more.

"What did they say about girls?" I ask.

"Just gossiping, just showing off. This one is so beautiful around the hips. That one is hot for me. This one is like this, that one is like that."

"Like what?" I ask.

He shifts uncomfortably in the passenger seat.

"It was just talk," he says, "just show. They were all good Muslim boys. They prayed five times a day. And the school they went to, it was a very, very religious school. Sometimes I thought that all they do there is pray. There was no sleeping with girls for them."

"Were they ever alone with girls?" I ask.

"Never. There was no opportunity. The only girls they met were at school, and those girls all lived with their parents. They did nothing with girls, but they spoke about what they might do until their mouths were sore."

Sitting in the car next to Asad, I think of towns and cities full of pious Muslim boys, each with a sex life lived entirely in his head until the night of his wedding. That first night, then, is a canyon.

But as my imagination swells, I see that Asad's is quite dead, and that there is little point in trying to take him with me. Life on the truck was filled with adventure, with new people whose tongues spun new tales. In Dire Dawa, the days were empty, and the boys' incessant talk was boring. Their schoolbooks reminded him of what he did not have. Asad left after seven months. It happened on a whim. Yusuf had been expelled from school for not paying fees, and so the two boys found themselves alone in the house every day.

"We decided one morning to go and live in Addis," Asad tells me.

"Why?"

He shrugs. "It was the capital city. We were in a provincial place. Everyone wants to go somewhere bigger."

# Addis

Between Addis Ababa's airport and the city center runs a straight, wide boulevard called Bole Road. When I visited in 2012, more than a decade after Asad went to live there, the city's construction boom had lined it with office blocks and residential towers and shopping centers made of glass and steel. At ground level, cafés opened onto the street and well-dressed people sipped coffee and chatted. Clothes stores, restaurants, and spas filled the upper floors.

On the flanks of these buildings, sometimes beginning just meters away, were dense shacklands, stretching back for miles. Wandering off the boulevard, one saw that it was a thin spine of wealth, embedded in the flesh of Addis's poverty. Seen from above, it must make for an extraordinary scene: these shiny beacons of the new Ethiopian bourgeoisie streaked across a landscape of deprivation, as if they had been erected to show the poor the look and the smell of power.

Not far from the airport, one turns left off Bole Road down another wide boulevard, the presence of new glass buildings now much thinner. A couple of kilometers on, the boulevard narrows, then disappears entirely, and you are suddenly in a warren of very narrow streets, each lined with markets and crammed with pedestrians. The sound of Amharic now mingles with Somali. Every second stall sells clothes, the shirts and jeans and hoodies all displayed on white-skinned mannequins, dozens of them standing in a row.

This is Bole Mikhael, one of two neighborhoods in which Addis's Somali population has settled. To speak to Ethiopians in Addis about

Bole Mikhael is an education. Most have never set foot there and have no desire to. They speak Amharic and the Somalis do not. Why go to a place in your own city to be among people too arrogant to learn your language? The Somalis, they say, are loud and rude and entrepreneurial to the point of craziness; they will talk the shirt off your back. They are lazy and make their women do the work; they sleep until afternoon because their blood is full of *mira,* which they chew until late into the night.

This stream of vitriol is really a cover for ignorance, for Bole Mikhael is a truly opaque place. Who among its residents are Ethiopian citizens from the Ogaden and who refugees from Somalia is impossible to distinguish, and the residents of Bole Mikhael are certainly not going to tell you. And so the people you see in the streets may or may not be Ethiopian, and, even if they are, you can be sure that they hate you and support the rebels out in the Ogadeni desert. The Ethiopian security services are renowned for having spies in Bole Mikhael. It is the sort of place where one reveals little.

Asad arrived in this world in 2000, he thinks in March, for it was dry and cool, the rainy season still a month or two away. At first, he and Yusuf were frightened and disoriented. They had nowhere to stay, and the price of a room, they soon discovered, was three or four times that of similar accommodation in Dire Dawa. They needed to earn money and to do so fast. But they knew nobody in the big city; for the first time since his days with Zena and Tube, Asad passed a night on the streets, his bed a piece of newspaper, his bedroom a doorstep in an alleyway.

But by now Asad's capacity to surmise, to calculate, to read a terrain for its opportunities, was acute. Addis's opacity, the lack of trust among its residents, the barriers of language and culture, were to be lucrative for him.

He does not remember how long it was after he arrived in Addis, perhaps a month, maybe less. It was late morning. He stood on Bole Mikhael's main thoroughfare, watching. On the opposite side of the street, an Ethiopian taxi driver leaned against his car. The man was huge, his car quite small, and Asad smiled at the incompatibility. He pictured the big man behind the wheel, his back hunched, his head craned, his pawlike hands squeezing the steering wheel. The taxi man's eyes were red, as if somebody had just poured salt in them, and he kept rubbing them with the backs of his hands. He looked as if he ought to go back to bed.

A Somali family approached the taxi driver. From their demeanor

Asad knew that they were new to the city; it was obvious from the hesitant manner in which they crossed the street, all looking out for one another as if they were crossing a flooded river. And from the snatches he caught of their accent it seemed that they were from Mogadishu. They came up to the strong Ethiopian taxi driver and spoke to him, and he spoke back, and from the way their eyes wandered while he spoke, Asad could tell that they did not trust him.

Asad put his hands in his pockets and strolled casually into the circle the two parties had made; he listened for a moment, then put his hand on the big Ethiopian's shoulder.

"I know this man," he told the Somalis. "He is somebody to trust. He will take you to the city for a hundred birr. He will wait for you while you sort out your business, and he will take you back. One hundred birr is reasonable. Others will see that you are new, and they will ask for three hundred."

The Somalis immediately lightened, their relief palpable. They volleyed questions at Asad. Where do we go to get official papers? Where to buy food? Where to buy a mattress?

The Ethiopian stared at Asad and smiled. From the expression on his face, Asad saw that he did not understand a single word of Somali. But one did not have to comprehend words to get the meaning of what Asad had done, and in the big man's smile there was mirth and admiration. The Somali family climbed into the taxi, and the Ethiopian drove them away; Asad stood alone in the middle of the street and grinned.

Asad had just found his way into one of Addis's most enduring functions, that of the broker. When I visited twelve years later, many of the Addis residents I spoke to complained bitterly about their reliance on brokers. Never mind if you don't speak a word of Amharic and are new to the city, many of them complained; even if you have lived here all your life, there is nothing you can buy, not even a house, without an intermediary. And can you trust that he isn't conniving with the seller? Of course not, especially if your broker is Somali.

The taxi driver's name was Yared. That he and Asad barely shared a language seemed not to matter. There was not all that much to discuss. During the course of a day, Asad would bring four or five sets of customers to Yared's taxi. In the evenings, Yared would park his car on Bole Mikhael's main thoroughfare and wash it. Then he would sit and watch the world around him and count his day's takings. He would stuff most of the cash into the pocket of his jeans; the remainder, about 20 percent, he would hand to Asad.

"Yared was a wild man," Asad tells me. "Everything he felt, he felt very passionately. And he was a heavy drinker. How early he started drinking would tell me how his evening would go. If he started too early, I knew he was going to make shit with somebody. He was such a strong, powerful man. He lifted weights every day. He couldn't help fighting.

"The next morning he would come to me crying, literally crying, the tears rolling down his big face. His cheek would be swollen. Or there would be dried blood around his nose or a cut across his eyelid. 'Asad,' he'd say, 'what are these marks on my face? I don't even remember what happened. I swear I will never, ever drink again.' "

Asad's business grew swiftly. Somalis were arriving in Addis every day. None of them knew the city, none knew Amharic, and finding an honest taxi driver was just the beginning of what they needed.

"Most Somalis who come to Addis want to apply for a passport," Asad recalls. "That is not something they can do easily without a helper. First, they want an Ethiopian identity document. Mainly, the Somalis who arrive in Addis are only coming so that they can get an Ethiopian passport, which will get them to Europe, which is where they really want to go. And to get a passport, you must start with an identity document.

"To get one, they need to show that they are from the Ogaden, not from Somalia. If they can't show they are from the Ogaden, they need to pay Ogadeni Somalis a lot of money to teach them how to make the right lies. The Ethiopian officials will interrogate you about your Ogadeni origins. Show us your district on a map, they say. What are the three main roads in your district? What is the district immediately to the east? Who was elected vice president of your district in 1994?

"Then if they are successful in getting an Ethiopian passport, they want you to help them get a visa to Sudan. That is easy. The Sudanese know very well that Somalis do not want to settle there. They are just passing through, heading north, to Europe.

"Now that they have their visa, they want tickets to Sudan. There are fifteen of them. They are throwing around a lot of money by now. And they have become dependent on me. They realize now that as soon as they leave Addis, they lose me. And so they ask me to come with them and offer to pay my way to Europe, tickets, food, bribes, everything. I say, No, I am not coming with you to Sudan. They say, We are so grateful to you, thank you so much for everything. Here's one thousand five hundred birr.

"It only costs three hundred birr a month to live. So I have taken these people around for a week, maybe ten days, and I have earned a lot of money.

"And then," he says, "from those who are wanting to settle in Addis, there is a different sort of money to be made. Above all, they are looking for a place to rent, and that is a very complicated business, because it means living in the house of an Ethiopian family. And when it comes to domestic matters, Ethiopians and Somalis do not see eye to eye. It takes a lot of work on my part to make things smooth."

He pushes his head into the headrest of my passenger seat, looks up at the ceiling, and laughs.

"Some Somalis," he says, "want to rent as a family. Some want to rent single. But some Ethiopians don't want a family as tenants because there isn't enough space. Others don't want a single because he will bring friends late at night and make noise. So you have to match the right people with the right people.

"And then you have to interpret what 'family' and 'single' really mean. A young Somali woman will tell an Ethiopian family she wants a single. The Ethiopians will think it means that just she will stay. But she is actually going to bring at least six friends with her, and it is for me to explain that in advance, or there will be big trouble later.

"Then the Ethiopian will get suspicious. 'If she said single, why will it be six?'

"'You can't expect a Somali to sleep alone,' I would say. 'We need company, even when we are sleeping. So when she says "single," she assumes you know she means six, because she has never met anybody who sleeps alone, and she thinks that that goes for you, too.'

"Then there is the problem of the toilet," Asad continues. "Ethiopians stand when they pee. The Somalis are outraged by this. They think it is disgusting. They do not think it is possible to aim your penis straight. They complain that the toilets are not clean because of the Ethiopians. You cannot pray when you have even a drop of urine on you. If you use a toilet the Ethiopians use, you have to wash your whole body every time you want to pray, and that is five times a day.

"So the Somalis refuse to touch the toilet seat, which means that instead of sitting on it, they squat, with their feet on the seat rather than their legs. And they don't take off their shoes when they do this. So the

Ethiopians complain that the Somalis dirty the toilet seat by standing on it with dirty shoes.

"I must try to find a compromise between landlord and tenant. It is not easy to approach an Ethiopian man and tell him it is better if he sits when he pees. It's not easy. And to tell a Somali he must clean his shoes before he pees . . . I don't know.

"Then there is the problem of noise. The Ethiopians are very quiet people. They hate shouting. Somalis shout when they see each other. People come to visit you late at night, you shout; that is how you show that you are happy to see them. Eventually, the landlord evicts the Somali family for shouting. This always happens in the middle of the night. The last straw for the landlord is always when he is woken at one in the morning, two in the morning. The evicted ones come knocking at my door. 'Asad, help us. These people you fixed us up with are no good. It is the middle of the night, and we are sitting on the street with our possessions.' I must find them a new landlord first thing in the morning. And I must sit the tenants down and tell them that in the new place they please must try as hard as they can not to shout."

Asad giggles. "And then," he says, "there is the problem of the curfew. There was a citywide curfew in Addis when I lived there. First, it was seven thirty p.m., then nine p.m. Somalis did not obey the curfew; if you wanted to chew *mira* with your friends, you would go and chew. You did not look at your watch to see if the Ethiopian government would allow you to go and chew. It made the landlords so upset when their tenants violated the curfew. But even the prime minister of Ethiopia, Meles Zenawi, knew that you could not get Somalis to obey it. When he put the curfew back to nine p.m., he went on television to announce it. He said that this was not a slackening of rules; enforcement of the new time would be very, very strict. 'Let me warn you,' he said. 'After nine p.m., only dogs and Somalis will move.' "

When Asad started earning money, he rented a room in the house of an Ethiopian family in Bole Mikhael for himself and Yusuf. They were soon joined by two other young Somali men, Moled and Khadarmahad. Asad no longer recalls how he and Yusuf met the other two. They were all hanging out in the streets of Bole Mikhael. They spent time together. They chewed *mira* together. Before they had thought about it much, they were sharing a room.

There was a fifth person in their group, Abduraham, whom they called Hoolo, which means "animal." He was bringing up a child as a single parent and rented his own room for himself and his baby daughter. His wife was in Canada and sent him money each month. He was waiting to get Canadian immigration papers. In Addis, he had little to do. He had finished school but could not get a place at university and had thus reached a dead end.

The others—Yusuf, Moled, and Khadarmahad—were at various stages in the stop-start journey of acquiring an education. As literate boys, they refused manual labor. They wanted jobs in the civil service. But the Ethiopian bureaucracy, which a generation or so earlier had been large enough to absorb most who aspired to join its ranks, had been rapidly shrinking since the early 1990s. Government-sponsored places in the universities became scarcer with each passing year. Young people like Yusuf would travel far from home and live off the smell of an oily rag to finish high school, only to find that graduating did not help them. The more they imagined and spoke of their careers, the more mercurial these careers became. They would probably be imagining their futures deep into adulthood.

It was Asad, without an education, scarcely able to conjure the sort of adult he might become, who went to work every morning, paid the rent, and provided food.

"I was happy to support the other boys with my money," Asad tells me. "I remembered my own bad times. In Dire Dawa, it was I who had nothing.

"The others would contribute when they could. One of them would suddenly get a big sum of money, maybe three hundred dollars. And then they would also be generous. There were no cell phones in Ethiopia in 2000, so they could not tell you the news. You would get home and there would be new trousers, shoes, shoe boxes, trouser tickets. You would know that somebody got a money order."

That Asad was earning enough money to feed and clothe a whole roomful of young men meant a great deal to him.

"When I first started renting," he recalls, "I could not believe that I would be able to keep paying. We just moved in and hoped for the best. The first night, the mattresses were full of grass. After two or three days, we would buy a new one, then another, then another. It took maybe a month before it really sunk in: I was earning a living; all of this was working because of me. It was 2000, maybe 2001. I was sixteen, seventeen years old. I felt like a serious person."

"My work was always during the day," Asad tells me. "I would be home by five o'clock, often earlier. Sometimes, the others would only be waking up then. They had been chewing *mira* until four in the morning, five in the morning, and they would sleep for most of the day.

"When they were washed and dressed, we would sometimes sit and eat, and at other times we would go out. We went everywhere in the Somali parts of town. If we are not at home when we are ready to sleep, then we just sleep where we are. We wake up the next day, maybe then we go home, but maybe there is somewhere better to go. Sometimes, we were not together. Yusuf goes off; you don't know where he is for a while. Other times, we are all together for weeks.

"Except for Abduraham, we lived in one room. Sometimes there were four or five of us, sometimes eight in one room. Maybe four or five come to visit. We cut *mira*. It gets late, they say, No, we are not going home tonight. Two people would climb into your bed with you. Move over! Nudge you with their elbows. If you do that in South Africa, they think you are homosexual. With us, it is nothing.

"There are no people better in the world than young Somalis," he says. "They do not ask you questions. They do not want to know who you are or where you are from. You just move with them. You see somebody day in and day out. You share everything with him. Later in life, when you have not seen him in years, you think: What is his clan? Where did he grow up? Where was his family? You don't know these things. You would never have asked. You were together. That was all."

For the first year or so, everyone but Asad chewed *mira*. In retrospect, he is not sure why he abstained for so long. It was in part because he was the only one among them who worked, and he did not have the luxury of chewing until four in the morning and sleeping until the following afternoon. It was also the place *mira* had in the lives of his friends that made him uneasy. They would chew into the early hours, and, as they did so, they would dream and talk and plan, always about the grand things that would fill their futures. And yet the daily rhythm of *mira* chewing suggested that there was no future, only a constant present: you talk, you chew until late, the *mira* makes your mind race so that you cannot sleep, you spend the daylight hours trying to drain it from your system so that you can rest, and then night falls and you start chewing again. How can you even begin to make a future if you live like that?

"Some days," Asad said, "I worked very, very hard, taking families all over the city. I get home, I want to eat and sleep. The others are chewing *mira*. I don't want to be rude. I just quietly sleep in a corner while they chew and talk.

"When I wake the next morning to go to work, they haven't gone to bed yet. They are desperate to sleep, but the *mira* will not let them. Their eyes are glazed. Their skin is rough. They have not shaved. I say to them: 'Last night you were telling funny stories. Today you look like shit.' They ignore me. They slowly get up, wash, go to town, get more *mira,* come home, and chew."

Asad thinks that he had been living in Addis more than a year the first time he chewed.

"It was a disappointment," he recalls. "I ate nonstop for two, three hours, and I felt nothing. I thought: The whole thing is in their heads. They think that *mira* is strong, and so it becomes strong.

"Second night, also, I chew, I feel nothing. But then, late in the night, I get up to pee; fifteen minutes later, I am getting up to pee again, and then again. It is the first sign that it is working; *mira* makes you drink too much water. The other boys get excited. 'Look at Asad. Look at his face. It is working.' I say, 'Rubbish, I feel nothing.' But, actually, I am feeling nauseous, and I go outside and vomit. I come back and try to go to sleep, but my heart is beating very fast, and the blood is pounding in my head. I lie there. It is very uncomfortable. Time starts going very, very slowly. I cannot get rid of the nausea. It is stopping me from sleeping. By the time I feel myself going to sleep, it is almost light.

"It is not nice sleep. It is troubled. I'm not sure where I have been while sleeping, but it is somewhere that has upset me. I get out of bed to chase away my dreams. I go outside. The sunlight hits me deep in the eyes and makes me stumble. I cannot tolerate it. I am feeling like shit. I go back to bed and wait for evening.

"When I wake up, they are all there, eating *mira* again. 'Come, eat,' they say. 'No, I cannot.' 'Eat!' And so I eat. And now it is normal. I do not pee. I do not vomit. I just sit there, and my thoughts begin to speed up. I am thinking of all different things at the same time. I step away from myself and watch this Asad thinking all these thoughts at once. I am thinking much too much. I want to slow down, to take just one thought,

pull it out, look at it. But the thoughts keep coming in. I am thinking about the near future and about the far future. I am thinking about
tomorrow, about next year, and about ten years' time. You are thinking
who you will be when you are an old man and who you will be tomorrow,
both at the same time."

"What were some of your thoughts?" I ask.

He pauses a long time. "I don't know," he finally replies. "I don't
remember what I think when I am chewing *mira*. I just remember what
the thoughts feel like. You are planning, but you are not planning for this
world. You forget the hard things in life. You start planning for a life in
which something can happen just because you have thought it."

In early 2003, a little less than three years after moving to Addis, Asad
bought a small, wooden box. He resolved that he would put at least one
hundred dollars in it every month, a lot more, if possible. It was his exit
ticket from Addis Ababa.

His restlessness grew from his rapid success. He had landed on the
streets of a foreign city and within months had found a way of earning
a good living. Bole Mikhael was full of Somali travelers, people passing
through from here and from there, telling tales of riches and prosperity.
As he listened, he placed himself in their shoes, and his view of himself
grew increasingly romantic.

"After what I was able to do in Addis," Asad tells me, "I thought that
whatever a Somali can accomplish anywhere in the world I can also do."

The question was where to go.

Bole Mikhael was full of Somalis on the brink of leaving and of news
from Somalis who had just left. Asad had lost count of the times he had
been asked to join a group on its passage north through Sudan. He had
always declined, not because the idea of settling in Europe wasn't enticing
but because the journey there seemed unreasonably perilous.

"If you have travel documents, it is one thing," Asad tells me. "But if
you have none, trying to get to Europe can kill you. They would leave as
a big group and travel in a bus toward the Sudanese border. Just before
the checkpoints, they would break up into three or four groups. Each
must find smugglers to get them across. On the other side, they wait for
everyone in the group to arrive. Then they break again and come together
in Khartoum. Then they break again. After Khartoum, it is the Sahara
Desert for a long, long way, and that is where the people die."

"How do you know?" I ask.

"The survivors spread the news," he replies. "There are websites for just this purpose. You go online, and you see who has died: the name, the clan, the nickname. And if it was somebody from Bole Mikhael, their name will be printed off the Internet and stuck on a wall on the main street. So you were always reminded of the risk: last month you were chewing *mira* with so-and-so; now he is a name you see on the wall."

Many people in Bole Mikhael had uncles and aunts and cousins and siblings in America, in Britain, in Italy, in Scandinavia, and they all received regular wire transfers or wads of cash from *hawala* agents. So, clearly, there was a good life to be had in Europe. But who, precisely, got to live this good life was never clear, for the flesh-and-blood people one knew in Bole Mikhael who went to Europe seldom communicated much. What exactly happened to them on the other side? It was hard to form a picture.

The world to the south was even more mysterious. Asad knew South Africa only as Nelson Mandela's country, where black and white had reconciled and people were at peace. It had a constitution that made the government accountable for what it did and for what it failed to do. It was not free to lock a person in jail and throw away the key. People did not just disappear in South Africa.

And it was not just to its own citizens that the government was accountable. Somalis, who could not return home because their country was at war, could get refugee papers in South Africa. Once you had these papers, you were free to move, free to put your children in the country's schools, to go to its hospitals when you fell ill.

Sometime in 2003, a group of Somali travelers stayed over at Asad's place. They were close relatives of Yusuf's, and so the household made a fuss over them and cooked them a fine meal. They had come from South Africa and were heading for Italy.

"There were three of them," Asad recalls. "They were all young, all in their twenties, and they spoke big about South Africa. One of them said he had been down south only five years, and already he had built himself a double-story house in Somalia. 'How do you make so much money so quickly?' we asked. He told us that setting up a business was easy. First, everything was so cheap. You could buy a pickup truck for nothing. You could rent premises from a South African. And you were free to move. No soldiers asking where you were going or why. It was a free country.

" 'What if you don't have money to set up a business?' we asked. Easy, he replied. You work as a shopkeeper for a Somali. You earn two hundred or three hundred dollars a month. Money goes very far in South Africa. Even with the silver coins, you can buy a meal. You save most of your wage. You use it to buy a business.

"'If it is so good down there,' we asked, 'why are you traveling the other way?' Because South Africa was still Africa. There was no substitute for Europe."

The interrogation continued into the small hours of the morning. As the traveler grew tired, so his annoyance at his audience's skepticism increased. He wanted to sleep, but he did not want to end the evening while his hosts thought him a liar. And so he stripped his big suitcase and then his little suitcase and then his jacket, each time emerging with a small pile of one-hundred-dollar bills. By the time he was finished, they lay strewn in front of him on the floor. "Count them," he invited. Yusuf gathered up the bills into a pile and counted them, then counted them again. He announced that he was holding nearly twenty thousand U.S. dollars in his hand.

## *Foosiya*

It was about two or three in the morning. Half a dozen young men sat in Asad's room chewing *mira*. One of them, Ahmed Afgud, was talking at length about his girlfriend.

"He spoke about the shape of her hips," Asad recalls, "and what you can see of her thighs when she is sitting and her clothes are tight against her legs. He spoke about her smile. This was typical *mira* talk. Boys would talk about their girlfriends until everyone was so excited, brother, that you would not want to light a match in that room.

"Ahmed Afgud's girlfriend shared a house with five or six other women on the other side of Bole Mikhael. I thought of her sleeping while Ahmed Afgud was talking about her. If his words could travel through the night and find their way to her ears she would be having troubled sleep.

"'Girlfriend' does not mean what it means in South Africa," Asad points out, not for the first time. "It does not mean they had sex. They were never even in a room alone together. It means that Ahmed Afgud went to her house where he was received by some of the other ladies who lived there. He would ask to see his girlfriend. Ahmed would be told to wait. She would come maybe half an hour later. They would talk. Always, there was somebody else in the room. To show that she was serious, his girlfriend would maybe offer to wash his clothes for him, maybe even cook him a meal.

"Ahmed Afgud was talking and talking and talking about his girlfriend until somebody cut him off. 'Enough already! Ask her to get married!' He said, 'Okay, I am going to ask her tomorrow.' And I said, 'If you are going to ask her tomorrow, I am going to come with you.'"

And so the two young men visited Ahmed Afgud's girlfriend the following afternoon, and Ahmed Afgud proposed marriage, causing consternation in his girlfriend's house. After a tense week of waiting and interminable discussion in both houses, Ahmed Afgud's girlfriend accepted.

Asad was among the people Ahmed Afgud asked to witness the wedding ceremony. His first thought was that he did not have clothes appropriate for so solemn an occasion. And so he borrowed a jacket from his Ethiopian landlady, which he wore over a T-shirt, for he did not own a collared shirt. He stared at himself in the mirror, wondering whether the combination made him look smarter or just a little silly. He took the jacket off and gave it back to his landlady.

The ceremony was held at a mosque some ten or twelve blocks from Asad's house. Just a handful of guests was invited. The only sign of ostentation was in the transport: the entire wedding party would drive to the venue, rather than walk. They set off in a convoy of three cars, each driver sounding his horn all the way. Some of the other drivers on the road pulled up and stared. Some cheered. Others waved their fists and shouted abuse.

Asad has little memory of the wedding itself, but he remembers every moment of the car journey home. The imam who performed the ceremony was in the passenger seat. Three people were in the back: Asad in one corner, his housemate Abdirashid in the middle, and, in the other corner, Foosiya, a friend of the bride's.

The imam was boisterous and talkative. He was turned in his seat, facing the back, and remarking at length on Foosiya's beauty. He spoke also of the bridewealth he would pay for her—camels, horses, guns.

"Foosiya stayed in the same house as Ahmed's new wife," Asad tells me. "We were very interested in the comings and goings of that house. We spent hours discussing each woman who lived there. Foosiya stood out among them. First, it was because she was amazingly beautiful. She had a long, powerful face and green eyes. Her eyes were very strong. She carried herself with independence, with confidence. When I watched her I would sometimes think of Nasri in Wardheer: a young woman alone, making her way with no doubts. But Foosiya was older than Nasri had been when I was in Wardheer. Foosiya was maybe twenty-eight, twenty-nine. That made her even more powerful. We discussed her often. Who would she marry? Would she even marry anybody? Who was big enough for her? She was an Isaaq woman from Somaliland, the traditional enemy of the Ogadeni. This made her even more powerful in my eyes."

And so the imam spoke of the camels and horses and guns he would pay for the gorgeous Foosiya.

"You are too old for me," she said coolly, and turned her face and stared out of the window.

The imam smiled and pointed at Asad.

"Marry this one, then," he said.

Foosiya turned to Asad, examined him for a moment or two, as if she was taking him in for the first time, then stared out of the window again.

"He is *kurai*," she said matter-of-factly. "I cannot marry him either."

Asad leaves the word untranslated. Literally, it means "small boy." But its full import has no direct equivalent in English. "Runt" perhaps gets close. This beautiful and haughty woman had settled her gaze just once upon Asad, long enough to flick him away like dirt from under her fingernail.

Everyone in the car fell quiet. Asad stared ahead, avoiding everybody's eyes.

The imam broke the silence; he laughed and slapped his hand against the car seat. "I'm too old, and Asad is *kurai*," he said, shaking his head in mock disbelief. "Nobody in Addis Ababa is just right for Miss Foosiya. She will have to travel far to find a man."

Asad felt the heat rising from his body. His clothes sat heavily on him, irritating his skin. He found, to his surprise, that a bead of sweat was rolling down the bridge of his nose. Were he to speak, he would only draw attention to his discomfort. And yet neither would silence restore his dignity. All he could do was to sit out his shame.

When the journey finally ended, he climbed out of the car, put his head down, and walked. He wanted to storm Foosiya; he wanted to grip her by the arms and shake her hard. He imagined her composure collapsing in shouts and protests, perhaps even in tears. But that was a small boy's way of seeking attention. He kept walking.

Over the following days, he felt Foosiya's growing presence under his skin, teasing and agitating him. He believed that her image of him as *kurai* was somehow contagious, that, by now, every woman in her house saw an insignificant child whenever they laid eyes on him. The injustice of it grieved him. After all, he was the one supporting his entire household. What more did he need to do to prove himself?

His feelings confused him. Why was he so upset? He had survived a childhood of hell; he had needed to grow four or five skins to fend off the world. Yet an idle comment uttered by a woman he barely knew had felled him. An old taste settled in the back of his mouth, one he had almost forgotten. It was a taste he had slowly spat out during the two years he spent with Rooda on the truck. What was it? He had no words for it. He remembered it in his mouth as he watched Nasri and Rooda disappear into Nasri's house in Wardheer. They were inside together, and he had felt very alone. He remembered swallowing hard and feeling in his throat the endless miles of desert beyond the boundaries of Wardheer.

A week or so after the wedding, Asad announced to Abdirashid that he was going to propose marriage to Foosiya.

Abdirashid raised his eyebrows. Then he whistled through his teeth. "You'll never do it," he said.

"You're advising me not to do it?" Asad asked. "Or are you saying you do not believe that I will do it?"

"I am saying that you don't have the courage."

Asad stared hard at Abdirashid. He was a good ten years older than Asad. He was wise, self-assured. He knew what he knew.

Abdirashid smiled mischievously. "Like I say, I don't believe you'll do it. But if you do, I will back you. I will come with you. I will help you through it."

That very afternoon, the two of them called at Foosiya's house. A young woman received them and invited them to sit in the front room. Abdirashid said that they had come to see Foosiya. Asad was silent.

The young woman left and came back a few minutes later. Foosiya would see them, she said, but they must be patient. Foosiya needed to wash, then to pray. Only then would she receive her guests.

They waited almost an hour. Two or three women joined them and asked oblique questions; they were curious why these men wanted to see Foosiya, but they would not ask directly. The young men were nervous and answered the questions posed to them in riddles. The conversation grew more and more awkward.

When Foosiya finally entered the room, she nodded a polite greeting to both men and sat down without saying a word. Abdirashid took command. After a few pleasantries, he told Foosiya that he was there merely as an adviser, that the visit was Asad's, that Asad was interested in seeing her again. She nodded and looked at her fingernails, then took a long glance around the room, before finally settling her eyes on Asad. The sun was shining directly at her through the window, and her green eyes looked quite translucent. Asad returned her gaze without flinching. The imperious expression she had worn when she had looked him up and down in the car was gone. Her face was quite inscrutable. It seemed to Asad that perhaps she was curious, inquiring, but he could not be sure. In any event, she said that if Asad were to come again, alone, she would see him.

Sitting in my car outside his shack in Blikkiesdorp, Asad is bracingly candid about his intentions. He wanted to marry Foosiya, certainly, but he did not like her, and he did not want to spend his life with her. The way he saw it, the marriage would last a few weeks. He would win her and fuck her and divorce her. She had humiliated him. One of her eyes for one of his.

Asad's memories of his courtship of Foosiya are strangely ethereal. When I ask him what they spoke about, he says that he deliberately did not prepare anything to say. He looked at her across the room and said whatever was in his head.

"What was in your head?" I ask.

"Rubbish. Nothing. Whatever came, I said. Sometimes a conversation came from it. Sometimes not."

He did not know how to broach the subject on his mind. A couple of times, he was on the brink of telling her that he wanted to marry her, but the very idea that the words might spring from his head into the room seemed impossible, and he swallowed them back down his throat.

He believes it was at their third or fourth encounter that he proposed marriage. From the start, the meeting was flat and without energy. After barely fifteen minutes, conversation was running dry. It came to him that his extemporizing had lost whatever value it once had, that he had nothing to offer now, that this meeting might well be their last.

"I want to marry you," he said.

She smiled at him. "You are how old?" she asked. "Nineteen, twenty?"

"One of the two," he replied.

"You are a boy. You are not ready for the responsibility of marriage."

"How can you say I am not ready? There are five boys living in my room. I pay the rent. I buy food for dinner every night. They all chew *mira* into the early hours of the morning, and I am the one who provides money for the *mira*. To marry you would make me richer. I would be supporting one other person instead of five. You say I am too young, but what you are saying just makes no sense."

He remembers her crossing her legs and resting her chin on the ball of her hand. She was silent for a moment, and then she began asking one question after another. She wanted to know what time he went to sleep and when he got up in the morning; how often he prayed and whether he was scrupulous about washing before praying. She combed through the minutiae of his work; she wanted to know how he earned every birr. Then she wanted also to know how he spent every birr, how much he saved. When he told her that almost half of what he earned was spent on *mira,* she shook her head and mumbled under her breath. Her questions seemed like tests: "If you were to spend less on *mira* and save more," she asked, "what would you be saving for? How would you eventually spend the money?"

They met again a few days later. Foosiya sat upright and alert, her legs crossed, her back ramrod straight. Once more, she pinned Asad to his chair with a volley of questions. These were more freewheeling than her last inquiries. How did he come to live in Addis?

Asad was thrown by these questions. It was understood in Bole Mikhael that everyone's past was off-limits; people lived together in the present and kept their histories behind closed doors. Asad stared out of the window and felt that the world outside was familiar; the world here in this room with Foosiya was deeply strange.

The inequality of the exchange unnerved him. He thought of how he might formulate a few questions about her.

"Why are you in Addis?" he asked. "Alone, with no family. What made you leave your family and come here?"

In my car outside his shack, Asad shrugs in frustration and laughs.

"Some things are hard to translate," he says. "What she said was that she needed a change. We Somalis do not go on holiday like you do. We do not knock off at Christmastime and go and see relatives like South Africans. We live in the same place day in and day out. So, sometimes, someone will just decide to go and live in another place for a few months and say, 'I needed a change.' That is what Foosiya said.

"But then, later, when I knew her much better, I asked again, and she said she went to Addis because she was hoping to get to Europe or

America. And I said, 'So which was it: a change or a new life?' She busied herself with other things, like she had not heard me."

They met again the next day. Asad had barely sat down when Foosiya announced that she would marry him. It was just a question now of Asad making contact with her father in Somaliland and formally asking for permission. Asad nodded and smiled and found that he had nothing to say. He left almost immediately. Outside, the sunlight seemed much too bright. He stumbled home, barely conscious of where he was going. He was nineteen or twenty years old. If all went well, he would be sharing a bed with a woman who had humiliated him, who had angered him, whom he wanted to hurt and upset, and whom he did not begin to understand. He knew, also, that his impending marriage would prove nothing less than a scandal. Everybody wanted to marry Foosiya. Everyone had undressed her with his tongue or, at the very least, with his thoughts. And she had chosen this *kurai,* this young Ogadeni boy barely off the street. What was she doing? What were her motives?

Making contact with Foosiya's father proved difficult and laborious.

"First, I had to meet with Isaaq people living in Addis," Asad says. "They were not close family of Foosiya's but connected enough for their opinion to be important. I had to meet with them, talk to them. Then they phoned Foosiya's family to give their opinion. Then I had to phone Foosiya's father. I would arrange a time to phone the father, but he was not there. Another time, he is still not there. I was frustrated. The marriage was not at risk. I knew from the way these Isaaq cousins of hers were behaving that the family was happy. In those times, you are happy if your daughter gets married: she is away from home; she moves around; she can get a bad reputation. You worry."

Finally, after several failed attempts to contact Foosiya's father, it was arranged that he would speak to one of her elder brothers who lived in the Somaliland city of Burio. The conversation was brief and cursory. The line was not very good, and neither man could make out much of what the other was saying. The brother's voice was just audible enough for Asad to hear him give his consent.

"The wedding was in 2003," Asad tells me, "I think in July. I didn't want to spend a lot of money. I wanted just to pay an imam to do the ceremony, maybe buy some new materials for the house; that's it. I was not sure I would be married very long. So why spend a lot of money?

"But in my culture, others are in charge of the wedding, even though you are the one who pays. Yusuf was in charge. He said I must buy a suit.

I said, No, that is too expensive. Eventually, they took me off to some Somali sellers. We bought black shoes, black pants, a white collared shirt, all secondhand. I rented a black jacket. Then I was told we must buy fruit; we must buy meat. We must hire a person who is going to video the wedding. When I arrived at the ceremony there were so many people. Not just Somalis. Lots of Ethiopians. Other Ethiopians. It cost me six hundred dollars in the end. Before that day, I had never even spent sixty dollars on one thing, never even twenty dollars on one thing.

"That six hundred dollars was spent for other people, for curious people, for people who wanted to talk about this strange wedding. The beautiful older woman marrying the *kurai.*"


On the night of the wedding, the young men with whom Asad shared a room cleared out. Before they left, they washed the floor and the walls. They removed all the mattresses but one. It lay ceremoniously in the very center of the room, dressed in new linen. It was as if they had cleaned the room, not just of the signs of their own presence, but of all the lurid conversations they had ever had there; as if the place had to be expunged of its boyishness so that it might be inhabited by a man and a woman.

The only woman's body Asad had ever touched and observed was Yindy's, in the tent their neighbors had made in Dhoobley, some eleven years earlier. Asad had been a prepubescent boy then, and he had seen Yindy's body only to clean it.

Broaching the question of Asad's wedding night is awkward. It is not something I can casually toss into the confined space of my car. It is something to wait for, something that will arise in the course of another discussion. That other discussion is female circumcision. I had just interviewed a young white doctor; she was in her midtwenties, I think, and worked in the obstetrics ward of a public hospital not far from where Asad lived. What she had seen of Somali women's genitalia had filled her with indignation; during the course of our interview she had grown angry and shouted into my voice recorder.

Now, in the car, I recount the doctor's words as well as some of her fury. Asad listens carefully, the expression on his face quite neutral.

"Did the doctor explain to you carefully about Somali circumcision?" he asks. "They do not only cut the clitoris; they also do the skin around the vagina. They use strong string from a tree to stitch the vagina closed, leaving a hole so small all you can fit into it is your baby finger. If it happens when you are five years old, then for the next twenty years, until you are married, it is sore every time you pee. When you menstruate, the blood stays inside, and you get infected. But the women are ashamed, and they will not tell you.

"Foosiya had these problems after we came to live in South Africa. She was too ashamed to say. I would get home, and she was not there, and neighbors would say, 'She has gone to the clinic.' I would follow and find her there, and she would not want to talk about it. I only found out because she spoke no English, and the doctor needed a translator. I asked the doctor why this infection comes back all the time. The doctor asked when she was circumcised. She did not remember exactly. She also had kidney problems. The doctor said that to remain healthy a woman must be clear and clean, but with this circumcision the blood stays and mixes with the urine, and the kidneys get infected. Walking out of the clinic, I say to Foosiya, 'You must tell me.' She says, 'There's nothing you can do, so why must I tell you?'"

I take notes and say nothing, but he knows what my silence is asking of him. He is free either to answer or to change the subject.

"Opening that hole is a big business, brother," he says. "You can't open it with your finger. You can't take your wife to the clinic, because it is shameful if you cannot open your wife with your penis. You need to push and push, night after night. The day of your wedding, a big problem begins. It was like that with me and Foosiya. It was very painful. It took a long time. But Foosiya would not have a single discussion about it. It was weird, brother. When I tried to talk about her terrible pain, she turned her head away. We had to pretend it was not there.

"It is cruel. I will not allow my daughter to be circumcised. Not my daughter, and not anyone who gets advice from me."

It strikes me that if he married Foosiya to take revenge, the task of opening her vagina offered ample opportunity.

"You married Foosiya to hurt her," I say. "Is this—?"

"No, brother," he interrupts. "No, no. You are there naked together, exposed to each other, and one of you has this terrible pain. It is not right. It is an injustice. I think maybe it was when we were alone on the first night that my feelings for her began to change."

# *North or South*

The day after the wedding, the boys moved back into Asad's room, and the newlyweds moved out. Asad's landlady had a grandmother who lived in a room in the house. The old lady gallantly agreed to give it up and share a bedroom with her great-grandchildren so that the newlyweds could have their own space. As a wedding present, she waived the first month's rent. With the money he saved, Asad bought a bed, a bedside table, a cupboard, and new curtains. He kept paying for his old room, now occupied solely by his friends. He had become the breadwinner in an eccentric household, his dependents consisting of a wife and a group of unemployed, *mira*-chewing young men all older than he was.

On the third morning after the wedding, Foosiya rose early and walked unannounced into Asad's old room. Five young men lay there, fast asleep. She took a spoon and hit it against the door to wake them. Once she was sure she had an audience, she began to speak. While her husband was paying for the roof over their heads, she said, and for the food on their table, they were to follow her rules.

She would cook three meals a day, she announced, and attendance at meals was compulsory. A person who persistently missed meals would be evicted. Second, she would wash all their clothes, but on two conditions. First, they were to stop sharing clothes. They had reached the point where they did not know whose clothes belonged to whom. Adult men didn't behave that way. They knew what was theirs and what wasn't. Second, she said, it was time to end this business of one's girlfriend washing one's clothes. In fact, the girlfriend business must end entirely. Either you were married to a girl, or you went about courting her in the proper way. This in-between business was unhealthy. It led to disrespect of young women. The Somali women in this city, Foosiya said, were far from home. Many were here without their families. To be a woman alone in a foreign city was not easy. Such a woman should command special respect.

Finally, Foosiya said, her husband would no longer spend the money he earned on *mira* for them. He was going to be saving as much money as he could so that they could plan their future. And even if they managed to find somebody else to buy their *mira,* they could not bring it there. If they wanted to chew *mira* at home, they had to find somewhere else to live.

Foosiya went back to her own bedroom and asked Asad a long series of questions about how he earned his income. He was asked to estimate how much came from helping people acquire documents, how much from helping people settle into Addis, and so forth. When she was finished asking questions, she made a pronouncement: Asad was to cut ties with Yared. He was not the main source of his income, he did not need him, and he was not the sort of person a good Muslim man spends his time with.

"There are no gangsters in Addis," Asad explains to me, "not like here in South Africa where you have people who kill you, then never think about you again. The closest you get to a gangster in Addis is a taxi driver. They are undercover people. They are involved in all sorts of business, aboveboard, below board. Foosiya did not like Yared. She would look at his filthy vest and the way he walked with his arms showing their muscles. She just stared with her strong green eyes, and she was not thinking good thoughts."

Each member of the household responded to Foosiya's presence in his own way. Some were angry and challenged Asad to manage his life by his own lights. Others, like Yusuf, took to Foosiya immediately and reformed themselves, cutting *mira* out of their lives and falling gratefully into the rhythm of her days. Most kept chewing *mira* but not at home; they would wander off after dinner to feed their habit out of sight. If they were unable to rise for breakfast the following morning, they would find their dirty clothes returned to them unwashed.

Asad refused to cut ties with Yared. He liked the big man, and he especially liked the money he earned by working for him.

"It was an unreasonable demand," Asad tells me. "It would have made us poor, which would not have been good for Foosiya either."

But aside from this one moment of dissent, Asad was simply dazed. His life had been snatched from him and was now being refashioned in her hands, and he watched in amazement.

"Something was going on that took me a while to understand," Asad says. "She was the wise one. She was the one deciding how things should be. But it didn't seem like that. She was so respectful toward me, so polite to me. Even when she was angry, she never failed to be respectful. So maybe she was molding me, but she was molding me into the sort of man a woman respects. You understand, brother? I didn't feel she was taking over my life. I felt that I was for the first time becoming the sort of man who takes over his own life."

Their marriage was built over the ensuing weeks by two cycles of labor, one performed at night, the other during the day. After dark, they would persist in the bloody business of consummating their marriage. Asad would turn off the lights, close the curtains, and come to Foosiya in pitch darkness. She would not permit him to see her face in pain. He experienced it only in the shuddering of her body and in her dulled moans.

They set about the task with grim purpose, both now of the same mind about what they were doing. They were not tearing open a cavity in which Asad might pleasure himself or take his revenge. They were parting the entrance to the womb in which Asad was to deposit his seed. For as time passed, it became clear to Asad that he wanted to settle with Foosiya and father her children. His idea of marrying her in order to hurt her, perhaps even to ruin her, seemed, already, embarrassingly boyish and wantonly cruel. She was offering him something infinitely richer than the quick satisfaction of revenge.

But what was she offering him? Today, Asad struggles to put words to the unsettling ideas he began to entertain in the weeks after his wedding. They were at once about the past and about the future.

"Something happened when I knew that I was going to have children with Foosiya," he says. "The best way I can explain it: I started having regrets. Why did I not go to school? Why did I leave driving trucks? Why did I not stay in Kenya where I maybe would have found my family? For the first time, I saw that my life was a series of decisions. I saw that each decision decided who I was going to be from now on. That is a big realization, brother. I felt dizzy and had to sit down. It is the sort of realization that can make you fall over."


Asad had kept some vital information to himself. He did not let Foosiya know, for instance, about the small wooden box he had begun to keep, about the money he added to it every month, and about his plans to go to South Africa. As he began to commit to her, so his South African plans receded. He had always imagined going alone.

He kept filling his wooden box with money. And he kept its existence a secret from Foosiya. Quite how or when he would put it to use, he no longer knew. He and Foosiya would stay in Addis for a while. They would have children here. And then they would see.

But no sooner had he put his South African plans on hold than they beckoned again, this time for quite different reasons.

Asad and Foosiya were married in August or September 2003. Around this time, the political currents that streamed through Addis began to grow rough and nasty. The Ethiopian government had for a long time had an uneasy relationship with the student body at the Addis Ababa University, and with the city's youth more generally. And it was also in perpetual conflict with several insurgencies in its borderlands, some Oromo, others Somali, all supported by the Ethiopian government's bitterest foe, Eritrea. In late 2003, the currents of these various conflicts kicked at the foundations of Asad's life. He thought that he could read them in ways that other Somalis could not. And what he read scared him.

"There was a student march on the campus one day," Asad tells me. "I'm not sure exactly when, but very soon after Foosiya and I were married. A student was killed by the soldiers. There was a rumor among the students that the soldiers were coming to their residence to kill more of them, so they fled all over the city. Many ran to Bole Mikhael; there were a lot of students living in the neighborhood. And government people came after them. All of a sudden, government men were walking around Bole Mikhael. They were knocking down doors and breaking into houses. They had lists of names. They were looking for particular people.

"And then things became hard to understand. There was this old Amhara man who lived in Bole Mikhael. He owned some flats. He was a harmless old man. He used to just sit all day in the sun on a plastic chair, greeting people. One day, he was gone. I was told that intelligence people came to his house in the middle of the night and took him away. He never came back, not while I was still living in Addis.

"Then about a week after the old man disappeared, soldiers came for someone I knew well. His name was Faizel. He used to chew *mira* with us. We would call him Fooljeex, which means 'cracked front tooth.' He was taken away. This was maybe three months before I left Addis. I did not see him again. I'm not sure if he ever came back.

"My fear was a very lonely fear, brother. Other Somalis did not understand what was happening the way I did. To most of the Somalis in Bole Mikhael, all Ethiopians were the same; they were all Amhara. I was different. I got to know Ethiopians better than that, so I could see things other people could not see, and what I saw was frightening me.

"There are layers among any group, brother. Even Somalis. Most Ethiopians thought we were all the same. But no. There are those from Ethiopia and those from Somalia. And then even within those two groups there are Daarood, Hawiye, Isaaq. You have a group in general, and then you look deeper. I went deeper into the Ethiopians. I knew more than most Somalis about what was going on. I knew because some taxi drivers were talking to intelligence: they were spies. And I knew the taxi drivers, I knew Yared and his friends. Yared had many lives, brother.

"And so I knew that the sort of people they were after were specific. They were after student activists, Oromo nationalists, Ogadeni nationalists, and some Amhara people who were against the government. But I also knew that their information systems were rubbish, brother. They just listened to talk. And then a person disappeared. That old Amhara man: somebody whispered about him; he had nothing to do with anything.

"And I was an Ogadeni, brother. And I was out and about, talking to this one and that one. It was my work to be out and about. I thought: It's a matter of time before somebody finger-points me. I will be taken away one night, and Foosiya will never see me again.

"So that is why I thought again about South Africa. Of all the many things we'd heard about that country, one of them was this: if the police come and throw you in jail, you have a right to a lawyer. You do not just disappear into the prisons and never return. There is justice."


When I visited Bole Mikhael in April 2012, I searched for people who had lived there in the second half of 2003, the time that Asad decided to go to South Africa. I wanted other people's recollections of that time; I wanted to know, in particular, how other people experienced the Ethiopian military.

Bole Mikhael is a transient place, Somalis coming and going all the time, and it took a while to find the sort of people I was looking for. Even then, it was not easy. For one, only a fool would talk openly with a stranger who comes asking questions about the secret activities of the Ethiopian security forces. And, besides, something happened after Asad's departure that tampered with the memories of those who remained.

In July 2005, nineteen months after Asad left, the Ethiopian government went to war with Addis Ababa's youth in the wake of a disputed national election. More than a hundred students were killed on the streets. Tens of thousands of people were rounded up and thrown in jail. Such dramatic events scupper even the most meticulous memories. My interviewees couldn't really distinguish between the second half of 2003 and the second half of 2002, or 2004, for that matter. The past was divided into a before and an after. July 2005 was the only moment they could pinpoint with precision.

I spoke, too, with scholars of the Ethiopian youth movement and also with scholars of Somali resistance to Ethiopian rule in the Ogaden. Neither marks the second half of 2003 as a time of unusual fragility or of heightened repression. All I spoke to were puzzled that this was the moment that Asad took fright.

I am guessing freely, and I may well be wrong, but I do not think that Asad was fleeing danger. On the contrary, he was courting risk; he was plunging from the shore of a life he knew into the depths of one he did not.

There were two ways to get to South Africa. One was to head for the Kenyan coast and buy a place on a boat heading south. It would dock in secret on a quiet beach in Mozambique. Its passengers would make their way to the South African border on foot. The idea filled Asad with dread.

"You do not want to mess with the sea, brother," he tells me. "You want land under your feet. On the boat, it is just you and the ocean, and you have no control over the ocean."

The other option was to stuff his pockets with his savings and head south by bus. There were many borders to cross: first into Kenya, then Tanzania, then Zambia, then Zimbabwe, then, finally, South Africa. At each border, a smuggler of human beings would have to be hired; officials would have to be bribed. As Asad describes it, the journey seems to me so obviously uncertain, the chances of safe arrival much too scant. How does one begin to read so treacherous an environment as a lone stranger? One must serially place one's life and liberty in the hands of the most dubious strangers.

"I didn't even think of the journey," Asad tells me. "I thought only of life on the other side."

"But you were so frightened by other journeys," I protest. "You thought that the Sahara would kill you, that the ocean would kill you, but this . . ."

"Ah, brother," he says. "It makes so much sense when you say it here in this car. It was different back then in Addis. I really wanted to go to South Africa more than anything I'd ever wanted before. I couldn't afford to think about the dangerous journey. If I'd done that, I would have been stuck in Addis."

At the beginning of December 2003, just three or four months after their wedding, Asad proposed to Foosiya that he would leave for South Africa in early January. He took out his wooden box and showed her the contents. It contained twelve hundred dollars to take with him, plus enough to pay for Foosiya's rent and food in Addis for three months.

At first, Foosiya was unsure. She asked Asad many questions about his plans for the journey to South Africa. He had no plans; he had not even imagined the journey. She asked what he'd do to make money when he got to South Africa. He had barely pictured South Africa beyond the fantastical land the tongues of travelers had spun.

She looked at him skeptically. "I will not live in this city alone," she said. "If I do not hear from you, I am going back to Somaliland."

"I will send for you within three months," Asad recalls replying. "If you do not hear from me by then, it means I have been arrested and cannot contact you, and you must wait."

"I will not wait," she replied. "If you contact me within three months, I am yours. If you do not, I am not yours anymore."

There was no question in Asad's mind: he would send for Foosiya. He was only making this move in order to share with her the sort of life he had just begun to imagine. He was hardly fleeing her.

And what of Foosiya? What was she thinking? By now, Asad was referring to her as a "great woman." He was somewhat in awe of her. But in truth he still knew little of her history and did not yet have the wisdom to divine her motives. Foosiya was from Somaliland. Much of her family lived there. By 2003, Somaliland had been stable and at peace for some time. Foosiya was thus not in any sense a refugee. Why was she living alone in Addis? Why was she marrying an Ogadeni man, with whom her clan, the Isaaq, were on bitter terms? And an orphan Ogadeni barely out of his teens, to boot. And why was she about to follow him all the way to South Africa, a journey that would take her even farther from home?

That she had chosen a clever, hardworking man as a husband, one who seemed to make money easily, made sense. But perhaps she had picked such a young man because she might be able to fashion him into the sort of husband she wanted. And perhaps she chose an Ogadeni precisely because it would be awkward to take him home.

Maybe, for her, South Africa represented fresh ground, far from old constraints, on which a woman might be free to build the sort of life she coveted.

# PART III

# To South Africa

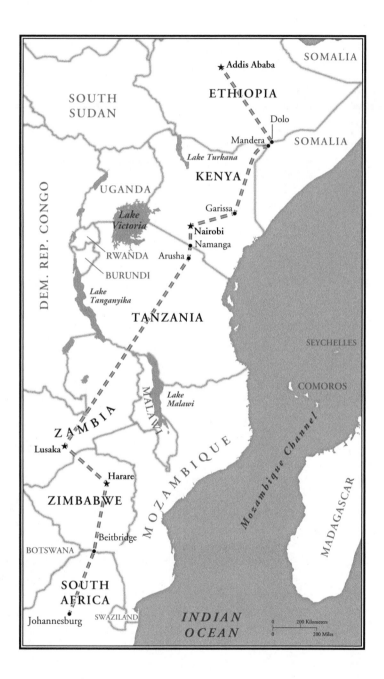

*Journey*

Eight years after he left Nairobi for Addis Ababa, Asad did the journey in reverse. He had walked into Ethiopia carrying a Koran, a thin pile of photographs, and a couple of changes of clothes. Now, he left with the possessions he had gathered in the intervening years.

He divided them into two groups: the expendable and the precious. The first were his daily clothes—T-shirts, jeans, sweaters, a down jacket—which he stuffed into a large duffel bag. The second bundle he carried in a small Samsonite briefcase, not a counterfeit but the real McCoy, which he had bought from a trader in Bole Mikhael. He had selected it with care: it had to be big enough to carry its cargo but sufficiently portable to be always in hand.

Among its contents were Asad's smart clothes: a white ankle-length cotton *thobe;* a tailored suit that he had had made just a week before he traveled; a brand-new pair of jeans. Also, an album filled with photographs of his wedding, of Foosiya, of Yared leaning against his car, of the boys with whom he had shared a room for four years, of his Ethiopian landlady and her grandmother. And, finally, a thick red-covered journal that Asad called his Red Book. Rooda had given it to him in Wardheer—to keep a record of all his travels, he had said—and Asad had been carrying it ever since.

"What did you write in it?" I ask.

He throws a hand up to his ear and scratches it urgently, a sign of annoyance, I think, as if my question is fingering open the book itself.

"Whatever happened that was worth remembering," he replies cautiously. "And, also, things that were funny."

"Like?"

He shifts his weight in the passenger seat and glances out of the window. "Like when Zena imitated the *deni* getting so angry and everyone on the back of the truck laughed until their stomachs hurt."

"What else was worth remembering?" I ask.

"I'm not sure. When I started planning to come to South Africa," he replies, "I used it to practice my English. I was okay to speak English. But I thought maybe my work would require me to write it."

I ask him again months later what was in his Red Book and get a different answer.

"It was a record," he says, "of the very best and the very worst. Like the day Foosiya agreed to marry me. I wrote down the date, the time. And on days when I had nothing and saw no future, I would write down the date on which I had that thought."


Seated next to him on the bus out of Addis Ababa was Khadar, one of the boys who had shared his room in Bole Mikhael. They would journey together as far as Nairobi, where each would make separate plans. Khadar had no interest in South Africa; he was determined to get to America.

Half an hour out of Addis, the flicker of headlights from a passing vehicle warned of an army checkpoint ahead. The bus stopped, the undocumented passengers got out—there were seven or eight of them, as Asad recalls—and walked through the bush, giving the checkpoint a wide berth. They returned to the road several hundred meters beyond the soldiers, where the bus was waiting for them. An hour later, the same thing happened again, and then again, and again once more.

The bus journey ended in the town of Dolo in the far south of the Ogaden, right up against the Kenyan border. They found a cafeteria in which to eat. That they were illegal travelers was obvious, and by the time their food arrived they had paid a man to give them information.

The stranger advised them to go the following morning to a town called Suufka, where they would find the border post to Kenya. The smugglers on the Ethiopian side of the border worked with the smugglers on the other side, he said. "You leave your bags with the Ethiopians, you walk across the border empty-handed so that the officials believe that you are going only for the day, and then you collect your bags from the Kenyans on the other side."

Asad kept his thoughts to himself, but his incredulity must have been written across his face, for the stranger smiled.

"You need to learn whom to trust," he said.

And then the man reeled off a list of smugglers, and each time a new name crossed his lips, Asad and Khadar wanted to know more. What is his tribe? How old is he? How long has he been in the business? Do you know people he has helped cross the border?

The seventh or eighth name was that of a woman, and both Asad and Khadar pricked up their ears. Who was she, they asked. An Ogadeni, he replied. Very strong. Very reliable.

"We chose her," Asad says. "We feared other smugglers. They might have us arrested and then want more money to get us out of jail. We thought that a woman would not do that. A female would not have such plans."

They got a lift to Suufka the following morning to find that the woman smuggler was waiting for them. "She was very black and very thin. She did not look at all like an Ogadeni to me. We greeted her. We listened closely to her accent. She took us to a Somali cafeteria where we drank tea.

"She asked us our names, how we got to hear of her, our tribe. She asked what money we had, but we would not tell her that. She said she would arrange to have our bags put on a donkey cart that would cross the river. She also said we must separate and cross the checkpoint alone and say that we are going to Mandera only for the day.

"She wanted us to give her all our money to keep. We were an easy target, she said: anyone could look at us and know we were traveling far and had lots of money. I said no. We each gave her fifty dollars to exchange for Kenyan money.

"We slept in a lodge and woke while it was still dark, washed, prayed in the mosque, and drank tea in the cafeteria. The smuggler did not come for a long time. It crossed both of our minds that she had run away with our things, but we said nothing to each other. Then suddenly she appeared. She sat with us. She was relaxed, cheerful. She said she was hungry. It was like we were just meeting to be social. Not to cross a border. We ate *anchera*—flour pancakes. We were sitting and sitting and sitting, and the sun was getting high, and I was wondering whether maybe I was going mad and that we would maybe have to remind this woman that we had just paid her a lot of money.

"Then suddenly she said, 'Now is the time; your stuff is crossing the river as we speak.' How did she know? Did she have a third ear that we did not have? We had no choice. We had to do what she said."

The two men parted and crossed the border separately.

"The rule at the border post—if you are going to sleep on the other side, you need an ID. If you are coming back the same day, they just search you. The smuggler had told me to say I am going to Mandera to visit people. I stood there, and the soldiers were asking me questions in Amharic, and at the last second, I changed my mind. I didn't want to say what the smuggler told me to say.

"'I am just going to Mandera to look,' I said. 'I have never been.'

"That was good enough. I walked. Next came the Kenyan soldiers. They asked me nothing. They did not even search me.

"When I was sure that they wouldn't stop me, I slowed down so that Khadar could reach me. We looked back, Ethiopia was gone, we felt no fear; it had been easy."

The Ogadeni smuggler had said that a middle-aged woman would be waiting to meet them just beyond the border post. All sorts of people were standing and watching the travelers stream in from Ethiopia. Some were men, some women, some middle-aged, others young.

A woman in the crowd raised her hand briefly and looked Asad in the eye. She turned and walked away, and Asad and Khadar followed.

"She greeted us and said that we must walk with her to Mandera. It was a long, long way. It took a couple of hours. And it was very hot, and she was very quiet. Once or twice, we asked her a question, but she said nothing, as if she hadn't heard us. All the time, we were wondering: Where are our bags? Is she taking us to our bags?"

In Mandera, the woman walked the two travelers to the back of the market and settled them under a *balbalo*. Having barely said a word the entire journey, she now burst into life.

"'Kenya is different,' she said. 'Soldiers ask to see IDs. Everyone is hunting illegal people. If they catch you, you are stuck here. They put you in a cell and take your money. Or they take you elsewhere and torture you and take your money. Or they ask for a lot of money and send you to a refugee camp.'

"She said she would arrange tickets and all we needed, and that our bags were safe and would be with us soon.

"She said, 'If you want *mira* or anything else, ask now, because later I will be busy.'

"We gave her money; she went to a *mira* kiosk and came back with a lady who showed us an assortment of *mira* from which we chose. We could not calculate the prices. We did not know the money. But while we were choosing, our bags arrived, and we were so relieved that we did not care how much the *mira* cost. I think that we spent a lot of money."

They left for Nairobi that same night. The woman who had led them to Mandera and to their bags told them that the bus ticket would cost them seven hundred shillings, that they must pay another seven hundred to soldiers at checkpoints, and another seven hundred for the conductor's fee. They never found out precisely what that amounted to in dollars, but it was a lot. The fifty dollars they had changed in Suufka weren't nearly enough, and they each changed two hundred dollars more.

The passengers were separated into those who had and did not have a *kibanda,* the Kenyan national identity document. There were fifty-nine of the former, Asad tells me, and twenty-eight of the latter; why he recalls this detail I do not know. He remembers that the conductor gave each of the undocumented ones a false *kibanda.* The one handed to Asad sported a photograph of a woman. He examined it skeptically and put it in his shirt pocket.

The charade began at the first checkpoint. Soldiers boarded the bus, and everyone showed their *kibanda,* and the soldiers could tell immediately which were fake. They got off the bus and negotiated for a long time with the conductor, and then they reboarded and the bus drove off. The same happened at the next checkpoint and the next and the next.

They spent a night in a lodge in the town of Garissa, and the following morning, everything started anew. Another bus, another fee for the ticket, another for the soldiers, for the conductor. Only forty-eight hours had passed since they had left Addis Ababa, and Asad's wad of dollars was shrinking at a pace that made him uneasy.

This time, there were just eight passengers without documents, but they were not given a fake *kibanda,* and Asad remembers wondering whether there could possibly be any difference between traveling with an obviously fake *kibanda* and none at all.

There clearly was, for at the first checkpoint of the day the eight were thrown off the bus by a group of flamboyantly irate soldiers and herded into a cafeteria. From where they were sitting, they had a clear view of the bus, and they watched as the soldiers searched it from top to bottom, unloading every bag, unzipping every zipper, pulling out shirts and underwear and then tossing them onto the ground in disgust. Every now and again, one of them would scream vehemently at the conductor.

Asad thinks that about six hours had passed when the soldiers suddenly walked from the bus, and it drove off. The undocumented ones downed their coffee and began to chase after the bus, but the soldiers began remonstrating all over again and pointed their guns and shepherded the travelers back into the cafeteria. Ten minutes later, the soldiers returned and shooed the travelers onto the road in the direction in which the bus had driven off.

As they began walking, Asad felt light-headed. The road was long and straight, and the sky was clear; one could see a far way. There were houses on the horizon that appeared to be hovering some distance above the ground.

They caught up with the bus after about an hour of walking. Asad settled into his seat and stared out of the window; the landscape appeared to tilt and then slowly to spin. He closed his eyes, hoping that if he could not see the world, it might stand still. As the bus began to move, a thought so odd crossed his mind that he heard himself laughing. He was no different from his duffel bag, for he was as powerless as it was, as uncomprehending about the rules of this journey. He would sleep, he thought. For what was the point of sharpening one's wits when one was powerless? He would let the conductors and the soldiers work it out among themselves. What would be would be.

He made a pillow for himself against the window and shut his eyes once more. The motion of the bus sent gentle messages up and down his shins, and he felt his mental armor sliding away. The sheer leisure of not being on the defensive felt utterly glorious. He willed himself into the deepest sleep.

He has no memory of the remainder of the journey. Although he knows it is impossible, what he recalls is that he slept the rest of the way. He remembers being nudged and pushed and coming back to consciousness and realizing, in that split second before waking, that he had been very far away, somewhere beyond dreams. Then he heard Khadar's voice telling him that they were approaching Nairobi.

# Kenya

The bus dropped them in the center of the city, and they immediately went to Eastleigh.

"Brother," Asad says, "you cannot believe the changes. All the places we played in were gone. The lane where we rode bicycles and roller-skated was gone. There were buildings there now, *smart* buildings. There were Internet cafés everywhere with glass fronts and umbrellas. There was a beautiful, big restaurant. Upstairs, there were beautiful cafeterias.

"And there were so many Somalis everywhere. Before, Islii had been just Daaroods. Now Daaroods were a minority. The Hawiye had fled from starvation and war. There were lots of Oromos from Ethiopia. *Everyone* was in Islii. There had been a few dozen school students when I was there; now there were thousands."

Despite all the strangers, Asad had been in Eastleigh less than an hour when he came across two AliYusuf girls with whom he had lived in the Hotel Taleh. He stared at them, and they stared back at him, the moment of recognition slow in coming. They were eleven or twelve years old when he had last laid eyes on them. Now they were grown women.

"We looked at each other with big eyes, and then we all laughed and couldn't stop laughing," Asad remembers. "It was like being asleep for eight years and then waking up. They couldn't believe how tall I was. And them: they were both married. Married! Their husbands were Somalis who lived in America. They were men who had walked across the Mexican border into America, had made a lot of money but then could not find wives. Maybe because there were no virgins there. So they came to Addis or Dire Dawa or Nairobi. Before they came they had spies out to spot the beautiful girls. So they would arrive, meet the young woman immediately, and go straight to her family to talk."

Both of these girls were waiting for green cards. Their new lives were in America. But they had never been to America. They were frustrated with all the waiting. One of the girls took Asad and Khadar to a restaurant for lunch. That evening, Asad slept at her house. They spoke of all the people they had known in Eastleigh in the early 1990s.

"There were very few AliYusuf people left in Islii, brother," Asad tells me. "Everybody was gone, gone, gone. This one is in America. That one is in Europe. That one is in the refugee camp."

Asad absorbed properly for the first time the catastrophe his move to Ethiopia had been.

"I had gone from civilization to deep bush, brother. If I had stayed in Islii, I would have gotten to Europe or America. Or even if I had not, the UNHCR was in Nairobi. Many NGOs were in Nairobi. One of them would have done something for me, sent me to a good school, maybe. And even if they had not picked me up, look at all the money that was washing through Islii: the buildings, the lovely shops, all the goods from the East. I would have made a good living. Ethiopia was a prison, brother. There was nothing there. Nothing."

He did not sleep well. The idea of paths not taken was manageable during the waking hours. He could brush it to the side of his mind, from where it would quietly watch him, out of the way. But as he lay in bed, when thoughts materialize from nowhere, the notion that who he was had turned on the careless decisions of others upended him. His time on the streets of Wardheer, the soccer table in Dire Dawa: that the Asad who had lived these experiences might never have existed—the implications ran too deep. He was watching himself from the ceiling, this inanimate lump of Asad, a puppet waiting for his strings to haul him upright. He felt his anger rise. And almost immediately, he felt it nourishing him, restoring him, making him, once again, into a person. He willed sleep. He needed to be fresh during the day. There was much to accomplish.

Early on his second morning in Nairobi, Asad set out to chart a course to South Africa.

"I met Khadar in the market," he recalls. "It was still very early, just a few people. Khadar had found family. He had spent the whole night on the phone to America. He thought he had a good plan to get there. It would take a while, though. He would have to settle into Islii to do this work. We ate breakfast, then Khadar went home to get some sleep until night was over in America, and he could phone again.

"I started looking for people going south. By lunchtime, I had spoken to many smugglers. There were Ogadeni smugglers, Hawiye smugglers, any sort of smuggler you could think of. They give you different prices. They offer you different things. Some are making passports with *kibanda*. Others are offering to take you by boat. Others are just offering papers.

"One of the first people I spoke with was offering the whole thing in one package. Everything for seventy thousand shillings: a fake Kenyan passport, a bus journey to Lusaka, to Harare, to Johannesburg. That's a lot of money, brother; it is nearly one thousand dollars. I said no."

The idea of being swindled was intolerable. The banks of anger that had formed inside him during the night had puffed him up; he felt about him an aura of the possible.

"People spoke of a border town called Namanga," he tells me. "I had been there. It was the town where I went to that Muslim school and kept running away. I decided to go there. I needed to deal directly with the smugglers rather than go through an expensive middleman."

"Why?" I asked. "You had a thousand dollars. You hand it over, you sit back on a bus, and next thing you are in Johannesburg. Why go for the most dangerous route?"

"There were so many other people also not paying that one thousand dollars," he replies. "That morning when I started looking for smugglers, within two hours, I found twenty-seven people going to South Africa. Some had come from Mogadishu, others from various parts of Ethiopia. They were all hanging around where the smugglers were, talking, talking, talking. Some wanted to go by sea. Others said no, they have already traveled by sea to Yemen, and it is not nice. We shared ideas. Sea was risky. The boat can overload—fifty-fifty chance. Others said, 'What Allah wants, nobody can stop. If you go to the border, you may be arrested.'

"Seven of us decided to go to Namanga. I don't like the sea, brother. I have this fear for it."

The seven who had chosen Namanga hired a private car together. They were all Ogadeni. The car they hired was owned by an Ogadeni. As they left Nairobi, Asad thought that he smelled Wardheer on their clothes and their skins; he smelled Jigjiga. The idea that these were familiar people taking familiar smells into foreign lands stayed with him a moment. He was not sure what to make of it.

In Namanga, the seven travelers went their separate ways. Asad does not recall why. In any event, he did not think that he needed help. He was feeling stronger than he had in a long time. His duffel bag on his back, his Samsonite case in his right hand, he walked alone through the streets of Namanga, looking for a place to spend the night.

The front room of the inn he found was a public space for guests, it seemed: several people were sitting lazily on chairs, drinking, smoking, talking. Behind the reception desk stood a pudgy, middle-aged man wearing a shirt unbuttoned to the top of his stomach. Asad approached him, put down his duffel bag, and asked for a room.

The man opened a ledger and picked up a pen.

*"Kibanda?"* he asked.

Asad shook his head.

"Passport?"

Asad shrugged.

The man put down his pen and looked at Asad with great interest. He leaned over the counter and peered at the duffel bag on the floor.

"Where are you from?" he asked quietly.

Asad looked over his shoulder, as if something had suddenly captured his attention.

"Where are you traveling to?" the innkeeper asked.

"Nowhere. Here. Just to Namanga."

The man nodded. He named the price of a room, and Asad gave him money, and the innkeeper handed Asad a key.

It was enormously hot and the car journey had been sapping. Asad put both bags in his room, locked the door, went to the communal ablution facilities, and stood under a cold shower. He was there a long time, the water washing over his back, then his chest, then the top of his head. He turned off the tap only when he began to worry that other guests may begin to complain. Back in his room, he changed into fresh clothes, put his bags under the bed, locked the door again, then returned to the front room and took a chair.

"It was so hot," he tells me. "The car journey had given me the sort of thirst it takes a lot of drinking to recover from. I sat there drinking soda, drinking soda, and trying to talk to the people in the room. Nobody would answer me. It was like I was invisible. I drank another soda. I watched. I tried to speak again. Whoever I spoke to would turn his head."

If Asad was beginning dimly to work out what was happening, he suppressed the revelation. He went outside into the stark sunlight, leaned against the wall, and squinted into the street. Standing there, watching, he felt the innkeeper's presence alongside him. The fat man put an arm around Asad's shoulder. Asad felt the intense heat coming from his body and wanted instinctively to wriggle free.

"Brother," the innkeeper said, "*everybody* is in that room."

Asad looked at him blankly.

"Do you follow what I am saying? *Ev-e-ry-bo-dy.* The one in front of you, wearing the safari suit, is CID. Do you know what's CID? He works for Kenyan intelligence. Look at the bulge on his hip. That is his gun. The small one with the pointy beard: he works for customs. The very dark one and the tall one: they are smugglers."

In my car, outside his shack in Blikkiesdorp, the scene now safely in the past, Asad begins to giggle.

"You know a fishing net, brother?" he asks. "They all go fishing there in that lodge. They go and cast their net. I'm carrying luggage. I have no documents. Everyone immediately knows what I am doing. It's obvious."

The first thing that came into Asad's head was his money. It was in his room. One of these men was going to cart him away, and when he returned, his money would be long gone. He went back into the inn, tucked his head deep into his chest, and lurched toward the passageway.

For a heavyset man, the one in the safari suit was impressively swift. He was out of his chair in a flash, his hand pressed firmly against Asad's chest.

"Where are you from?" he asked. His voice was surprisingly high-pitched for a big man. His Swahili was delivered with an accent Asad couldn't place.

Asad shrugged, and in broken Swahili said that he didn't understand.

"We will get a translator," the CID man replied. "What language?"

"English."

The CID man looked at Asad skeptically. "We do not have an English translator here," he said in English. "Let's go."

He bunched his fingers around Asad's bicep and pulled.

Asad tried to grab on to the reception desk. "I need to speak to the innkeeper before we go," he said.

"This is not the innkeeper's business," the CID man snapped.

At that very moment, the innkeeper appeared with Asad's duffel bag over his shoulder and his Samsonite case in his hand. Asad smiled at him with the deepest gratitude. The bags were loaded into the CID man's trunk, Asad was ordered into the passenger seat, and they drove off.

"You will never guess, brother, but the moment we left, the two smugglers, the very dark one and the tall one, jumped into their own car and followed ours. I was a fish, brother, and all the sharks were circling, circling, circling.

"The CID man sees the two smugglers in his rearview mirror.

"'You know them?' he asks.

"Brother, I did not know *anybody*. I had never felt so alone in my life. And this CID man is driving me to I don't know where. To prison? To a police station? To his office somewhere in the city?

"He drives me to his *house*. He personally takes my bags out of his car and he leaves them on the ground, and I carry them into the man's *house*. His wife is in the kitchen cooking dinner. He shows me to a room and closes the door when he leaves. Brother, I had been kidnapped."

He lay down on a single bed and listened to himself breathing. Soon, the sounds of the world outside came to him. He heard roosters in the yard and, somewhere down the road, the shouts of children playing. Husband and wife talked quietly to each other, in Kikuyu, Asad thinks, somewhere in the house. He lay and listened, and the domesticity soothed him. The feeling that he had been captured slowly seeped away. Perhaps, he now felt, he was somewhere sane.

An hour or two later, the CID man let Asad out of his room and invited him to sit and talk.

"I started to relax," Asad says. "Observing this man in his own home made him . . . How can I say? I thought, I can deal with this man.

"So I decide it's best to get straight to business. I tell him I want to walk over the border tonight.

"'How much?' he says.

"'Fifty dollars.'

"Brother, he looked at me like he was about to spit in my face.

"'Then we'd better take you to prison right now,' he says.

"We bargain. It takes maybe half an hour. We settle on one hundred dollars.

"He tells me how it is going to work. He is calling this Masai tracker guy, this nomad, to come in a taxi. The Masai is a genius at walking at night, he says. The Masai can see in the dark. I am going to walk with the Masai for a long, long time, far around the border post. He stops talking, gets up, and brings my bags through. He looks at them carefully. 'You can keep the small one with you,' he says. 'The big one I will get across the border. The Masai will take you to a taxi. Your bag will be in the taxi.'

"I look at this man, and I am thinking to myself, Why should he take the trouble to get my bag over the border? I will have paid him. He will never see me again. But what else could I do? I put myself in his hands.

"The Masai came in a taxi. He was a little guy, wearing clothes of the bush. He and the CID man spoke together in Masai. I couldn't understand a word they were saying. It made me nervous. I looked closely into the Masai's face to see if I could understand what the CID man was saying he must do with me. The Masai's face was completely blank, brother, completely blank."

Asad followed the Masai into the night. The man's footfalls made hardly any noise, while Asad's shoes banged and creaked whenever they hit the ground, and he wondered whether the nomad was barefoot. The Masai was perhaps ten paces ahead, his head to the ground.

Asad wanted to know for how long they were going to be walking. He called out in Swahili. The Masai stopped, half turned, put his finger in his ear, and then shrugged—he didn't understand. Asad spoke in English. This time, the Masai didn't even bother to signal that he had heard.

It was very dark, and Asad soon lost track of where they were going. It occurred to him that perhaps they were tracing wide circles around the CID man's house. He stared at the back of the Masai's head, as if doing so for long enough might allow him to peer inside. He still had more than seven hundred dollars on him. The Masai might turn around and stab him and share his money with the CID man. Perhaps the two of them had killed a dozen Somalis over time. Perhaps it was with the money of dead Somalis that the CID man had built his house.

Asad cast his eyes to the ground and strained to see what was there. He was looking for a weapon. But it was very dark, and to find anything he would have to slow down, which would arouse the Masai's suspicions. Eventually, he kicked something accidentally and reached down and picked it up. He was holding a stick, about four feet long. He examined it briefly, tapped it, then stopped and broke it in half over his knee. He kept walking and felt the break with his fingers. It was as he wanted: he had created two sharp ends. He clutched his two makeshift knives, one in each hand, and walked.

He thinks that it took the better part of three hours, but eventually they crossed the border. It was easy. There was a large hole in the fence. He wriggled into Tanzania, flat on his stomach, his two sticks abandoned in Kenya.

On the Tanzanian side, they walked only a short way before Asad saw passing headlights in the distance and heard the sound of an engine, perhaps fifty or so meters away. The Masai directed Asad to a clump of tall trees and motioned for him to wait there. Then he headed for the road. Asad watched. He thought he could make out the man's silhouette crouching a short distance from the highway. Then he blinked and could no longer see him and wondered whether he was trying too hard.

While he waited, he tried to work out the route on which the Masai had taken him. On the Kenyan side, they had given the border post a wide berth. The Kenya-Tanzania highway had in the meantime twisted to the right and followed them. Clever, Asad thought to himself. The Masai and the CID man must have worked this out long ago. They had probably been doing this for years.

He did not hear the Masai return; the little man was suddenly a few paces from him, gesturing for him to come. He turned and walked toward the road, and Asad followed. A taxi was parked on the shoulder, its headlights on, its engine running. The sliding door on the side was open, and the Masai gestured for Asad to get aboard. Asad hesitated. For the first time, the Masai showed irritation, a sharp click, his tongue hitting his palate.

Asad climbed into the taxi. Lying next to him on the seat was his duffel bag.

## To South Africa

The lodge in Arusha to which the taxi driver took Asad was run by an Ogadeni, but if he felt any kinship with Asad, the feeling was faint. Once his eyes had taken in the duffel bag and the briefcase, once he had learned that his visitor had no papers, he scanned Asad's body without shame, searching for the telltale bulges of U.S. dollars.

"He told me that the neighborhood was swarming with police, that if I took even two steps I would get arrested. He said I must buy safe passage from him. For two hundred and fifty dollars, he could arrange to get me from his front door right to the other side of the border with Zambia. I told him I'd think about it, paid him only for the room, and went to bed."

Asad decided to leave very early the next morning, hoping that the innkeeper would still be asleep. But the moment he stepped out into the passageway with his duffel bag, the man was upon him.

"You won't last two minutes," he shouted. "The police will arrest you and interrogate you and you will tell them you slept here and they will come and make trouble for me."

For the first time since leaving Addis, Asad considered the prospect of using his fists. He strode past the innkeeper, and his duffel bag, which was slung over his right shoulder, nudged the man against the wall. He heard the scuffing of the innkeeper's shoes as he struggled to keep his footing. Asad kept going, his body tensed, waiting for the man to come after him. And then he was out on the streets, walking, the innkeeper now a problem of the past, the danger of police filling up the present.

As he made his way through a strange city, unsure where he was going, a feeling of great unhappiness descended upon him. His bags and his long Somali face and its expression of uncertainty were like a town crier announcing that he was primed for fleecing. He stared at his feet taking one step after another, and he imagined himself walking through Bole Mikhael, through Islii, through the town circle at Wardheer, through all the places in which he had once felt sure of himself. He allowed the reverie to continue for just one more moment, knowing that he must snap it shut. It was too much like dreaming, like the moments before sleep when the mind drifts. Were he to slip into such a state, the vultures would tear the flesh off him.

He found his way to an intercity bus terminal and began negotiating. The touters picked up at once that he had no papers, and each wanted hundreds and hundreds of dollars. He said no to them all, then wandered around the vicinity of the terminal until he found a taxi driver who would drive him to the Zambian border for no more than forty dollars. As he climbed into the taxi, he knew as well as he had ever known anything that the journey would not go as planned.

At this point, the stability of the story Asad is telling me begins to give way. From Arusha, things went badly, and his memories of the next few days come in the form of flashes and scenes and spectacles, the connections between them not entirely clear.

He was not in the taxi for long. He soon ran into a group of traveling Somalis who persuaded him that undocumented travelers who used taxis were always arrested and that he should join them. They were on a bus, and it was cheap.

He did just that. No more than an hour or so into the journey, the bus was stopped at a roadblock, its occupants ordered onto the street, and he and his new Somali friends arrested. The hold at the rear of the bus was opened, and Asad was allowed to take his duffel bag, but when he protested that he had another bag in the cabin he was clipped on the back of the head and told to keep moving. And so Asad was driven to a police station while his Samsonite briefcase disappeared forever into the inhospitality of Tanzania.

There were times in the following weeks when he wondered who might be wearing his *thobe,* how many times it had changed hands, in how many street markets it may have been displayed. He wondered, too, about his photographs and his Red Book. But the moment he contemplated the fate of the Red Book, he felt from deep inside him a determined voice shooing its memory away; such indulgences were not healthy for a man on the move, and he focused on the present instead.

Asad was among a group of seven Somalis taken off the bus. After a night in police holding cells they were driven to a court, their stomachs empty, their throats dry, and locked in a room, waiting for their hearing to begin. A hat was passed around, and they offered their guard a bribe. In return, each of the seven Somalis was given a thick official-looking piece of paper stamped with a coat of arms. They were summarily released. Not surreptitiously. Not through a back entrance. Right out of the front of the court building.

As they walked into the sunlight, Asad scrutinized his paper.

"I was the only one among us seven who could read English," he recalls. "The others, they just take the paper, put it somewhere safe, give it to the soldiers at the Zambian border post. Brother, the paper was bullshit. It said we were in Tanzania illegally and that we had forty-eight hours to cross the border back into Kenya. We hand that paper to the soldiers at the Zambian border, they laugh in our faces and put handcuffs on our wrists."

Asad's memory dissolves, or, at any rate, his will to recall fades, and now he is talking about being in the border town of Tunduma. The seven Somalis had thrown away their worthless papers and negotiated their way onto a bus.

Tunduma lies right on the border. Zambia was quite literally in sight. But how to get there with dwindling money and no documents?

They scouted Tunduma and asked questions and were soon guided to a border control office. The officials there already knew that they would be coming and were kind enough to offer them seats. Then the negotiations began. The talks twisted and became opaque and confusing, and then they became nasty. There was a lot of shouting and many threats of immediate arrest. Sitting in my car, Asad is struck, not so much by the negotiations themselves as by the document each of the travelers purchased from the border officials once the shouting was through.

"It was very beautiful. It was like money because it had a stamp or a picture that was inside the paper. Not on the one side or on the other, but somewhere inside. It also had a place for my picture. I had a photograph taken and bought glue and stuck it in its place. It was some sort of regional travel document, I'm not sure for what. Southern African Development Community, maybe, I don't know. It said I was Tanzanian; it gave me a Tanzanian name. The border officials explained that it could get us from any country in SADC to another."

"Did you believe them?" I ask.

"I don't remember. I liked the document very much. It looked like it was going to work."

The impressive new document was not tested just yet, for, in the end, they were smuggled across the Zambian border to a waiting bus that drove them through the night to Lusaka. Asad was utterly exhausted. His last decent sleep, he believes, was on the bus somewhere between Garissa and Nairobi. In Lusaka, another bus, another handing over of dollars.

Asad's narrative is racing, desperate to leave this time of transit behind. Next, the seven Somalis were on the Zimbabwean border, and Asad was now very nervous. A long, narrow pedestrian pathway led to the border post; it was fenced on both sides. He felt the fence close around him, as if he had suddenly been tunneled, all choices slammed shut. He stared at the beautiful document he had bought in Tunduma, and its beauty was now beguiling and ominous. The watermark seemed to be mocking him, taunting him, telling him that it was too late to run.

"What was the watermark?" I ask. "What was the picture of?"

He thinks awhile. "I don't remember," he says. "I remember only that it was beautiful."

On the bridge, the Zambian and Zimbabwean soldiers mingled, doing their work side by side. This frightened Asad all the more; at no previous border post had the two sides been so friendly, so at ease with each other.

His paper was taken from him. He was questioned in English. What is your name? What is your occupation? Why are you traveling? Where are you going?

"Namibia," he replied.

To this day, he is not sure why the word came from his mouth. Perhaps because all Somalis were going to South Africa; perhaps because to say that one was going to South Africa was to surrender one's entire story. But Namibia? He had never heard of anybody wanting to go to Namibia.

The seven travelers were told to wait at the side of the border post. Hushed word was soon sent to them that they must attempt to enter

Zimbabwe again. This time, they were to clip thirty dollars in notes to their watermarked documents. They pooled money, made sure that everyone had thirty dollars, and approached the border post again. Their documents were stamped, the dollar notes removed. Within minutes, they were through the border post and back on their Harare-bound bus.

Sitting there, waiting for the bus to start moving, Asad examined the new stamp on his watermarked travel document. He glared at it resentfully and restrained himself from tearing it to shreds. It occurred to him that the document itself had probably been invented for the purpose of fleecing people without documents. It was something for which you paid one set of officials dearly; and when you presented it to another set, many hundreds of miles away, it announced that you were up for more fleecing. Not for the first time in the last few days he felt a fool, a person whose purpose on this planet was to be duped.

Strange things began happening on the bus. First, bread and sodas were distributed to all passengers free of charge, as if they were children on some outing. When Asad asked why, he was told that the journey to Harare would take thirty hours and that the bus would at no point stop for long enough for passengers to buy a meal. The idea of so long a journey dispirited him. He prayed that he would be able to rest. He did in fact drift off and was soon sleeping the sleep of the very tired, only to be awoken by an unpleasant, synthetic smell in his nostrils and a strange, hissing sound. When he opened his eyes, they began to burn. He rubbed them and looked around. A uniformed official was walking up and down the aisle spraying a can.

Asad's fury came to him like a sharp blow. He was literally dizzy with anger. Of everything that had happened to him since leaving Addis, this, unfathomably, was the greatest indignity. Why were they not asked permission before a chemical was sprayed in their faces? Were they cattle being shipped to market or, worse, to slaughter?

Dimly, it occurred to him that he was caught in the spell of a kind of madness, that he was utterly exhausted and frightened, that were he to close his eyes and breathe evenly his emotions would soon settle once more into a pattern he could recognize. He sat there, eyes closed, seething. He imagined a person walking down the aisle and glancing briefly at him. What would this person see? Just a sleeping face, a face blank because of the fact that its eyes were closed. Little would such a person guess at the tumult inside. He tried to banish the thought, for it seemed to draw him closer to madness.

.  .  .

The moment the bus stopped in Harare the travelers were swarmed, once more, by all sorts of people offering all sorts of services. It seemed that there were a hundred ways of getting into South Africa. Asad was by now the group of seven's spokesperson and its primary decision maker. He chose the border post of Beitbridge, for no particular reason, he says, other than that the alliteration of the two b's was pleasant on the tongue.

The man who had offered to get them to Beitbridge wanted to be paid, and this turned Asad's attention to the question of Zimbabwean currency.

"Somebody walked past with a huge pile of money, brother. Just like that. In his hands." He holds his hands in front of him and feigns to slump forward in the passenger seat, as if the weight of his load is folding him double. "I asked the smuggler man: 'How much money is that man carrying?' Smuggler man says maybe five dollars."

Of all he had seen since leaving Addis, this, oddly, was the starkest reminder that he was in a strange land. For a moment he imagined a country full of people weighed down by sacks of money, people hiring horses and donkeys to carry their savings to a safe place, people buying a mule merely to take home their change from the market.

He asked the smuggler how much it would cost to cross the border at Beitbridge, and the smuggler named a price in South African rand, not for the crossing, but just for information on how to proceed. Asad knew nothing about the rand. He gave the smuggler a ten-dollar note and asked for change as authoritatively as he could, well aware that he was about to be robbed.

Now the seven were on a truck bound for Beitbridge, another fifty of their thinning pile of dollars in the truck driver's pocket. There was nowhere for the passengers but the cabin, and all seven were crammed into it, a space with room for three at most. One of Asad legs began to prickle and then to numb. The sharp end of an elbow stabbed painfully at the back of his upper arm.

An hour or so into the journey, one of the two women in the party lost her composure. With a measure of panic that startled Asad she demanded to get out of the truck. When it was clear that the driver would not stop, she began choking and gasping and lashed out with her fists and feet. There was nowhere to take cover; Asad dug his arms out from the heap of bodies and sheltered his face. It was as if a creature of the wild had been let loose in the cabin. He believed for a moment that if the woman were to suffocate and die, the driver would still not stop. Her corpse flashed momentarily before his eyes, its graying, cooling skin pressed up against him.

To his relief, she began gradually to still, but at that very moment, the other woman in the party announced that her bladder was full and that she was about urinate all over the cabin. All the while, the Somalis pleaded with the driver to stop; each time he shrugged and smiled benignly and drove on. Asad imagined that if all seven of them were to die he would keep shrugging and smiling.

As is his custom, Asad takes my notebook and sketches the Beitbridge border post. But this time it does not help me to understand. I listen closely to his account of the border crossing and check it against the map and ask him to repeat several things, but the journey remains clouded. Back in my office, I play back our interview; the sequence of events he recounts makes little sense.

I wonder if, by now, sleeplessness and anxiety had not robbed him of much of his sentience. Perhaps, too, something else was at play. Beitbridge is the busiest crossing into South Africa, the most coveted destination on the continent. Tens upon tens of thousands of people cross there each year. The border economy has shaped itself around these transients. Almost everyone there who is not an undocumented traveler earns a living by servicing the needs, both real and fictitious, of people on the move.

At Beitbridge, Asad was swept into a pattern of movement designed to bamboozle him. Together with a man in his party of seven, he walked onto the bridge where a taxi driver immediately offered his services. The man directed them to a place, just out of sight of the border post, where the seven were to traverse the river.

"It was easy to cross," Asad recalls, "and nobody tried to stop us. We were wondering if it was really going to be this simple. A taxi met us on the other side. We drove and drove for a very long time, two hours, maybe. It was hard to tell in what direction we were going, but it seemed somewhere very remote.

"Suddenly, the taxi stopped, in the middle of the bush where these nomadic people were living: just three or four homes in the middle of nowhere. The driver shooed us out of the taxi and said this was it, he was handing us over to the nomads."

"Why do you say they were nomadic?" I interrupt.

"Because of their homes. You could kick them down with your foot. It would take maybe a day to build new ones.

"One of the nomads spoke to me. He took me inside his house in the bush. He offered us homemade bread and tea. We sat there several hours. Then, at eight p.m., an old man arrived and said, 'Let's go.' We walked a long, long way, back to the river. It was waist-high. It is midnight. We crossed again.

"Back into Zimbabwe?" I ask.

He shrugs. "It gets even more confusing, brother. A few minutes later, we met the next taxi driver, a very young boy, maybe sixteen at most. He wanted another twenty-five dollars. We grumbled. He argued. We disagreed among ourselves. Eventually we paid him, but not twenty-five dollars, more like fifteen. He said, speaking partly in English, partly in Swahili, that if we see police, the last thing we must do is run. Just lie still.

"I said, in Somali, 'The Bantu is just trying to scare us.' The taxi driver stopped and turned around, very aggressive, 'What did you say?' 'Nothing.' After that, he did not like me. He targeted me. I thought maybe I'd have to fight him.

"He led us to a big fence which had signs on it saying it was electrified. There was a hole in the fence and many, many footprints around it. The taxi man lifted the fence and we started to crawl through. Half of us had made it to the other side, the other half not yet, when two cars drove by—one a police car, the other an immigration police car. We lay very, very still. I thought to myself that this boy who I called a Bantu had given us good advice after all and I felt like a fool. The police kept driving. The boy gathered us around. He said, 'We are going to walk to the pickup now. Don't sneeze. Don't cough. Don't even blink.'

"Three of us spoke English. The other four did not. We translated for them. 'Don't sneeze. Don't cough. Don't blink.' Then we walked to the pickup, and we all piled into the back. The young boy drove us to a town. On the way, we Somalis in the back had a debate among ourselves. 'Does it really make a noise when you blink?' Someone agreed. Some disagreed.

"Brother, I burst out laughing on the back of that pickup. Stupid Somalis."

# Home

Asad is not sure to which town the young man drove them. It may have been Musina, just a few kilometers from the Beitbridge border post. The youngster took them to his own home, a two-room brick-and-mortar house, and promptly went to bed. The seven Somalis slept on the floor of the other room, huddled under their own jackets, until just before daybreak. When they tried to wake the young man, he would not budge. They left him another hour and tried again, but he remained dead to the world.

"He was not interested to get up, brother. His work was done, and now he was going to sleep. So we just took our bags and walked."

Dawn had not long broken. The Somalis asked whomever they encountered how to get to Johannesburg. Each person offered a different answer. Some said a bus, others a taxi. Still others said that it was not possible to get to Johannesburg from this town and that they would have first to make their way to somewhere bigger. Eventually, somebody told them that the only way to get to Johannesburg was to hitch.

"What does it mean 'to hitch'?" Asad asked.

"It means to stand in the street and wave," one of his companions explained.

The party of Somalis found a piece of a tomato box and borrowed a thick pen from the proprietor of a trading store. On the scrap of box they wrote: JOXANAZDEG. They made their way to the main road leading south and flashed their sign whenever a car drove by.

"Nobody stopped, brother. Hour after hour after hour, and nobody stopped. At the time, I thought we were unlucky. Now, when I think of what we wrote on that box, it is a miracle we were not thrown into jail—seven foreign-looking people with big bags, just near the border, with this ridiculous sign. It was a joke."

The sun was directly above them and the party about to abandon the roadside when a minibus finally pulled onto the side of the highway. Asad strode up to the driver's window to find two white men peering out at him.

"They said they were going to Johannesburg," Asad recalls. "They had space for us all. Then one of them says, 'But . . . ,' and he rubs his thumb and finger together. I'd never seen that sign before, but I knew it meant money.

"Out of the one thousand two hundred dollars I took with me I had one hundred and sixty-five left and I was worried because the journey was not over. I gave sixty-five. I hid the rest from the other Somalis. Nobody else knew what I had. Some of the others put in more money, but it still wasn't enough. We agreed that we would give them more when we got to our destination."

The Somalis sat in the back of the minibus, the two white men in the front. Asad chose the seat directly behind the driver and watched the white men as closely as he could.

He was struck, above all, by their size. They were beefy men, very strong, their forearms thick and red and covered in a layer of soft, light hair. He calculated that they were in their thirties, but the more he thought about it, the less sure he became.

He strained to listen to their conversation. They were switching languages, it seemed, for one moment he could understand their talk perfectly, and the next their tongues were emitting the thick, grinding consonants he would later recognize as Afrikaans.

"As I started hearing what they were saying, I felt fear, brother. The one is saying, These people are illegal. We must take them to the police. The other says: Look at the state they are in; take pity. The first one: Pity is fine, but we are aiding and abetting; we are committing a crime.

"I was getting very suspicious now, brother, so I leaned forward so that I could see more of them. That is when I noticed that one of them had a gun in a holster on his hip.

"Brother, in East Africa, the only people who carry guns are soldiers. So I turned and spoke to the others: 'These people are military. We are being arrested.'

"The others were very upset. One of the ladies started crying. But two of the others said, Don't worry, it's fine, if they arrest us, they will take us to the border.

"I didn't like that, brother. I had almost no money, no contacts. To be stuck on the border like that: that is how you end up dying. I wanted to get out of the minibus. And as soon as I say that, as soon as I say I want to go my own way, something else starts happening: the other Somalis say, No, if you try to leave, we will fight you. Because, brother, I had money. They couldn't know how much, but they knew that whatever I had they would need. So now I have enemies in the front seat and enemies in the back."

He had been with the other six ever since the day he lost his Samsonite briefcase in Tanzania. And yet, until this moment, they had barely been shadows in his story. Only now, right at the end, does this shapeless group of six take definite form, and it does so as a foe.

For the first time, the extent of his loneliness strikes me. Every alliance he formed on the road, every friendship, was always thin, always circumstantial. Each could turn on a dime. It is no wonder that he was so very tired; he needed a cocoon, a place where he could relieve his internal sentinels of their duty and truly rest.


He mulled over his options. They were on a highway, moving very fast. But at some point, the white men would have to slow down. He could fling the door open, roll onto the ground, and run. The Somalis were not so brave as to chase him through the streets of this foreign land.

But he was soon distracted from his getaway plans by the scenes outside the window. The highway had widened and was double-laned on both sides and was full of traffic. The surface of the road itself was as smooth as a varnished table, as if it had been laid yesterday. And the cars on the road were also new, like they had just come off the factory floor. Beyond the roadside were straight rows of houses with deep terra-cotta tiles on their roofs, thick beige paint on their walls, and manicured gardens. They, too, looked as if they had just been built, and Asad imagined a city in a constant state of renewal, each car, each house, each road eternally replenished, a place where nothing is permitted to grow old.

"Johannesburg?" he asked.

"Pretoria," one of the white men replied. "Johannesburg is still nearly an hour away."

Pretoria? He had never heard of a place called Pretoria. He stared out of the window. A cluster of tall buildings was silhouetted in the distance. Between here and there were uninterrupted concrete and houses and buildings, all of them new. He did not believe that this much wealth had ever before been laid out before him. And they were in a city so inconsequential that Somalis who had been to South Africa had not even mentioned it. He wondered how many such cities this country contained. The stories the northbound travelers had spun about South Africa's riches had been an understatement. He looked again at the cluster of tall buildings and at everything in between and wondered at the scale of human endeavor, and at the reserves of wealth, that had put all of these things on the landscape.

The men in the front consulted among themselves in their indecipherable language, and then the one in the passenger seat turned around and announced that they would stop for a while in Pretoria.

"You can't come to your people in Johannesburg dirty and hungry," he said. "We'll stop at a garage where you can have a shower and a good meal."

Asad knew immediately that his earlier calculations had been wrong. These were not soldiers. It was not so much what the man had said as the feeling that filled the car when he said it. The feeling was not entirely good—it was a mixture of curiosity and idle kindness; these men, Asad surmised, had found themselves on an adventure to somewhere exotic, and they wanted to see it through.

They stopped in Pretoria and showered and put on clean clothes and ate hot takeaway chicken, and were soon back on the road. The white men wanted to know where in Johannesburg the travelers were going.

"Where the Somalis live," one of Asad's companions offered.

The two men shook their heads and murmured between themselves. Then the man in the passenger seat turned around and spoke, his voice now clipped with anger. They would drive around the city in a big circle, he said, until the Somalis could tell them where to go. They would not let anyone leave until they had their money.

One of the two women had a cell-phone number for a relative in Johannesburg. He was duly phoned, and word made its way to the white men in the front that the place where Somalis lived was called Mayfair and that there would be money waiting for them there. They were given a street address. The one in the passenger seat consulted a thick road map, and the two men spoke to each other again and seemed happy.

"Brother, we are driving through this very big city and you can see

from the way things change that it is a city with many sorts of people. And, then, suddenly, everybody on the street is Somali. The noses
and mouths are Somali. The way the teeth are arranged in the mouth is
Somali. The clothes people are wearing are Somali. You put your head
out of the window and you hear Somalis shout at each other. Not like
in Islii, brother, where there are all sorts of people, many of them not
Somali. Not like Bole Mikhael, where there are also Ethiopians. Everything and everybody was Somali.

"I do not have the words in English to tell you what happened inside
me. I don't think I have the words in Somali. I would have to sit down
alone for a long time and write a poem, and, even then, maybe it won't
come out right. I felt like I was in Mogadishu. You know when something has been so deep inside you that you did not know it was there?
And even once you know it is there, you still are not sure exactly what it
is? I remembered something. Walking through a crowded street. Something. I realized that there were parts of Mogadishu that I had forgotten
but that were still inside me. I wanted to jump out of the car and run.
I knew I would be safe. I knew these people on the streets. And I did
not want to have to pay these white men extra money. They had already
taken more than enough."

But the white men were very keen for their payment. They found the
woman's relative's house, steered their car off the road and onto the pave-
ment, and parked right in front of the gate, so close that a person would
struggle to get in or out.

The woman's relative, a middle-aged man, came outside and spoke
to the white men briefly and gave them some money. And then the white
men went around shaking the hands of all seven travelers and wished
them luck. Then they climbed back into their minibus and were gone.


"The man invites us in," Asad tells me. "He tells us his name is Sheikh
Mohammed. We all wait our turn to have another shower, even though
we just had one in Pretoria. When we come out of the bathroom, there is
something waiting for us to eat. We are asked to give dirty clothes to be
washed. It is all very nice, very comfortable.

"Once we are all sitting together, Sheikh Mohammed takes out a
notebook where he has long lists written down. And he goes around
the room asking each of us our tribe. He listens and nods and then says,
'Good.' No matter what your tribe, he says, 'Good.' Then he looks at

his lists and finds the right page and then he asks more questions. Your grandfather's name and nickname, your uncle's name and nickname. He writes these down. He is Ogadeni, brother. And we are also Ogadeni. He has a whole map of the Ogadeni in South Africa, and next to each name on the map he has a cell-phone number."

Three of the travelers were of the same subclan. Sheikh Mohammed decided it was best to deal with them all together. He made one call on their behalf, then another, then another. For every new person he found at the other end of the line, he consulted his notebook and read out the names of the travelers' fathers and grandfathers. He listened carefully and took more notes in his book.

"You three will not be a problem," he pronounced after the third phone call. "We will come back to you later."

Then it came to Asad.

"I am Mohammed Zubeyr," Asad said. "And AliYusuf."

"I did not even bother with Abdullahi, brother. What are the chances there would be Abdullahi?"

"And your lineage?" Sheikh Mohammed asked.

"Abdullahi."

Sheikh Mohammed made a call.

"There is an AliYusuf man just around the corner," he said, as he waited for the phone to be answered. "I am trying him now."

A long phone discussion ensued. Sheikh Mohammed asked Asad his father's name, his grandfather's name, then spoke on the phone. Then he asked Asad the names of his father's brothers. He spoke on the phone some more.

He hung up, put his cell phone down carefully on the table in front of him, and, raising an eyebrow, looked at Asad closely.

"Do you know Abdicuur Abdullahi?" he asked.

"I have never met him," Asad replied. "But I know who he is. He is my father's oldest brother's oldest son."

Sheikh Mohammed nodded and, again, examined Asad carefully.

"When did you last hear news of him?"

"Brother," Asad replied. "I have not heard news about *anybody*."

"Abdicuur is a wealthy man, an important man," Sheikh Mohammed said. "He lives in a place in South Africa very far from here called Uitenhage. It is near a big city called Port Elizabeth."

Sheikh Mohammed read a phone number out of his notebook and

punched it into his phone. Now he was talking to Abdicuur. And now he was handing the phone to Asad.

Asad put the phone to his ear and spoke.

"My name is Asad Abdullahi," he said. "My father is Hirsi."

"Immediately, brother, the man on the phone asks me: 'Have you seen your father?' I tell him, 'Uncle, I have come a long, long way. I am tired.' I hand the phone back to Sheikh Mohammed."

Sheikh Mohammed spoke into his phone briefly, nodded, then put the phone down.

"He says you are his son. He says I must keep you safe."

Asad smiled briefly, then looked at his hands. He felt his tiredness as a weight bearing down on his head. His chin dropped, and his neck creaked. But inside the tiredness, Abdicuur's voice echoed. With great mental effort, Asad captured the voice and sealed it into his interior, then listened to it rebound inside his head. It was the first Abdullahi voice he had heard since the whistling mortar had wrenched him from his uncle in the town of Qoryooley. How much time had passed since then? It was now February 2004. It had been thirteen years.

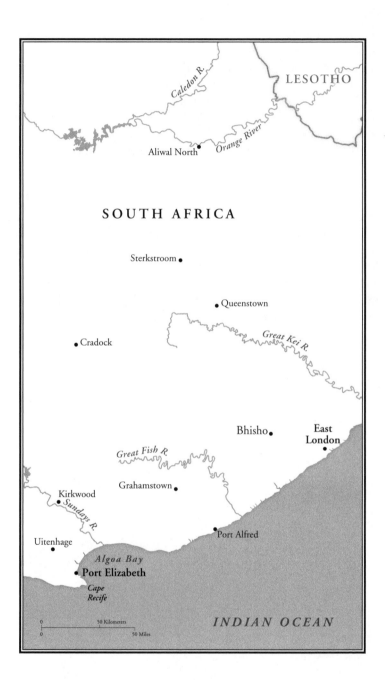

## Uncle Abdicuur

By nightfall, five of the seven travelers had been scooped up and taken to the homes of family. Just Asad and a man named AbdiKeni remained. Sheikh Mohammed walked them to a lodge a few blocks from his house, informed the proprietor that he would pay the bill however long they stayed, and left them to rest.

Asad slumped onto his bed. He lay splayed on his back, his arms outstretched, and stared at the ceiling. He listened to the sounds coming from outside: several conversations were going on at once, each one shouted in voluble Somali, the voices full of passion and fire, as if these were their last conversations on earth. In the background he heard the blaring of an international news channel.

He closed his eyes and listened. He could be in Eastleigh or in Bole Mikhael—he could be anywhere Somali travelers gathered in lodges.

An image came to him: dense gatherings of Somalis, represented as clusters of flickering lights, scattered across a map of Africa. The east of the continent was aglow, but down here, too, in the south, the Somali lights blinked. He got up, had yet another bath, then tried to watch television. He was too tired to focus; he fell asleep almost at once.

"The next day was very strange," he recalls. "When I went down to the restaurant for breakfast it seemed to be facing the opposite way from the way it faced the day before. I went onto the street to try to trace the direction from which we had come. I had no idea. I realized I would not be able to find my way back to Sheikh Mohammed's house. There was nothing to do but sit in the lodge. I spoke to people about changing my hundred dollars. But it seemed too much effort."

Over the next three days, he occasionally joined AbdiKeni's attempts to find family. But the task could not hold his attention for long. He chewed *mira*. He watched television. He ate. He slept. Dimly, he observed the systems and circuits inside him shutting down. The spectacle was of momentary interest. The feeling of thinking of nothing at all was far preferable.

Ten days after his arrival in South Africa, he found himself sitting on a Greyhound bus in Park Station, Johannesburg. It was two o'clock on a mid-February afternoon in 2004. At six the following morning, the bus journey would terminate in Port Elizabeth, where Uncle Abdicuur would collect him.

He did not sleep a wink. Whenever he looked about him, he saw people slumped in their seats or buried under mounds of blankets. He heard snoring and sleep murmuring. He seemed to be the only person awake.

He remembers being very cold throughout the journey, which is odd, since it was February, an unfailingly warm month throughout the country. He remembers staring out of the window, into the night, trying to gather from the little he could see the character of the country in which he now lived.

Every town the bus passed, he noticed, was divided into two distinct sections. There was always a settlement on the outskirts: it consisted of straight, narrow rows of identical houses, each as modest as the next. And it was always in darkness, save for the occasional blinding light mounted on a towering pylon. The effect was eerie, the homes around the light brilliantly lit up, everything beyond it dissolving slowly into darkness. He wondered why anyone would choose to cast such sharp, naked light from on high.

While the settlements at the outskirts seemed to have been slapped down in a day, the towns proper appeared to have grown organically and with grace. The steeples of fine churches stared at him, like ones he had seen in Addis and Dire Dawa, but much sharper, much more severe. And there were many, many trees, some of them heavy and ample and clearly very old. Lights burned behind drawn curtains. He tried to imagine the families inside, but he could not; he was not sufficiently familiar with this place.

He knew, from what he had been told, that the outer settlements were black townships, the inner towns white neighborhoods, that what he was seeing had been built under the infamous system of apartheid. It occurred to him that the home to which the young taxi driver at the Zimbabwean border had taken him and his companions was in a township. That is why everyone on the streets had said that there was no transport to Johannesburg from that place. What they meant, he now realized, was that intercity transport departed only from the white town.

From what he had seen thus far, South Africa was as prosperous as promised. Every Somali he had met lived in a good house and drove a good car. It appeared also that South Africa harbored far more prosperous places still, places Somalis seemed not to venture to. About the country was a general sense of plenty, a sense he couldn't quite pin down. There seemed to be an abundance of food and drink. Everything was cheap. You could use small coins—two rand, five rand—and buy a lot with them. What they said about South Africa was true.

He knew, from the talk around him, that many Somalis made their money selling food and drink to black people in townships. You cannot arrive and simply settle in Mayfair, he was told, as if jobs in Mayfair grow on trees. You have to go out into the townships and open a business; that is the way to make money. But he had still not set foot in one, aside from that first night on South African soil. As the bus passed one township after another, he tried to imagine himself walking down one of its streets or sleeping in one of its houses.

He thought, also, of his uncle Abdicuur, and this made him a little anxious. His uncle would want to confirm that Asad was indeed who he claimed to be. The first hours, perhaps even the first day, would consist of an unannounced test.

"How does the test work?" I ask Asad. "If you were to receive a call now saying that your brother's son was in Johannesburg, what would you do?"

"I would tell my nephew to come. I would pay for his journey to Cape Town. I would meet him and hug him and welcome him into my home. But I would be examining him: the nose, the cheeks, the way he talks."

"The teeth?" I ask.

He looks at me with laughing eyes. "Especially the teeth," he says.

Nobody was waiting for him at the bus terminal in Port Elizabeth. Two young Somali men who had been on the journey from Johannesburg invited him to come with them. He took in their worn bags, their casual clothes, and their slight, young men's frames; it seemed he was looking at the last decade of his life. These rootless Somalis who hook up with one another on a whim, spend the next year or two together, night and day, without respite, without asking a question, sharing everything. And then, at a moment's notice, one of them drifts off, never to be heard of again.

He was filled with warmth, with pleasure, with gratitude. But he felt, too, a rising nausea, a sense of panic. He declined politely and waited for his uncle, who appeared just as the young men were leaving, an unmistakably Somali face beaming at him from the driver's seat of a smart new pickup.

Abdicuur got out of the car, revealing a prosperous belly, and embraced Asad and addressed him as "my son" and insisted on picking up the duffel bag and putting it very carefully in the back of the cabin, as if it contained recently blown glass.

On the journey home, he asked Asad where he had been. For a brief moment, the question seemed ridiculous. How could he possibly answer in one sentence?

"Everywhere," he replied. "Islii, Addis, Dire Dawa, Wardheer, then all over the Ogaden on a truck—"

"All over the Ogaden?" his uncle interrupted. "Did you not hear on the BBC that your father was looking for you?"

"No. When was that?"

"In 1998 and 1999. He sent out messages twice. He was in Qabridahre in Qorahay. The message said you must make your way to Qabridahre."

"Where is my father now?" Asad asked.

"We heard news that you were in Islii," Abdicuur replied. "Then we heard that you had left and we did not know where to find you."

Asad does not remember what they spoke of next. He thinks that his uncle told him a very long story and that he struggled to follow, in part because he was very tired, and in part because the news that his father had been looking for him was upsetting.

Abdicuur's house was in a suburb in the white town of Uitenhage. It was full of things. Asad is at a loss when I ask him to recall precisely what, but they were the sorts of things, he says, that gradually fill a house inhabited by people who have money.

He wanted desperately to sleep, but his uncle was hovering anxiously; it seemed that he had taken the day off work, probably at great trouble, to be with his lost nephew. The two men danced awkwardly around each other for some time, each wanting to please the other but unsure what he might want. Eventually, Abdicuur went off to work, and Asad slept. When he woke, his aunt had prepared lunch.

Abdicuur returned in the early evening and took Asad out. A big soccer game was about to start, he said. His team, Real Madrid, was playing. Long-lost son or not, there was never an excuse for missing Real Madrid.

They drove to a Somali canteen nearby. It was packed with Somalis, perhaps fifty or sixty people sardined into a small room. Half of the clientele appeared to support Real Madrid and the other the opposition, and each side took turns shouting and exclaiming and sometimes both shouted and exclaimed at the same time.

When the game ended, Abdicuur chatted merrily.

"Where is my father?" Asad asked.

An invisible hand washed the merriness off his uncle's face.

"He died two months ago. In Qabridahre."

"How long had he been there?" Asad asked.

"Since 1991. He went straight there at the beginning of the war. He remarried there. You have a new brother. He is maybe seven or eight years old. He is growing up in Qabridahre."

"How did my father die?"

"His time was finished. He got sick and died."

Asad was silent a long time. He desperately wanted to ask a question. But he did not know how to formulate it. He was not even sure what it was that he wanted to know.

"How is it I never heard about him all the years I was in Ethiopia?" Asad finally asked.

"Well, where were you?"

"In Qabridahre!" Asad shouted. "I was in Qabridahre three times!"

He heard the incredulity in his voice and tried to calm himself. Then he told his uncle everything: about the decision of the AliYusuf in the Hotel Taleh to send him to Dire Dawa; about Yindy's cold and loveless family and the months it took them to shake him off; about his abandonment in Wardheer; about the time on the truck with Rooda.

His uncle listened carefully but said nothing. Whether Asad's story shamed him or just saddened him, he did not know. Perhaps he had heard a dozen versions of the same story before. Maybe the tale of Asad's life was old and familiar and filled his uncle with nothing but weariness.

Abdicuur began telling him what had become of his siblings. A sister and a brother had settled in the North East Province of Kenya, near

Garissa. A brother was in Somalia, in Kismayo. A sister was in a refugee camp in Yemen. As for the uncles Asad knew in Mogadishu, the one whom he lost in Qoryooley and who he later heard had lost an eye: he had been captured the very same day Asad lost him. He had been severely tortured but had eventually gotten away and was now safe and in good health. Another uncle, who had been a senior police officer in Siad Barre's old regime, had been captured when Mogadishu fell; his torturers had broken one of his legs. He, too, was fine now and was living in Kenya.

"There's something I'm struggling to understand," I tell Asad. "In all the conversations you had with your uncle, you never discovered that your parents came from the Ogaden."

He shrugs. "He said that my father was in Qorahay, but my brothers and sisters were in Kenya, in Yemen. There didn't seem to me to be anything special about Ethiopia."

"You didn't ask your uncle why your father chose to go to Qorahay, of all places?"

"There are so many things I regret not asking my uncle," Asad replies.

# *Shopkeeper*

He stayed with Abdicuur for two weeks. On some days he would accompany his uncle to work. On others he would sleep late and then walk down the road to a place where young Somali men played pool. These days reminded him a little of his time in Dire Dawa. But there, the soccer table stood in a public space and a cross-section of the city came to play—young and old, Somali, Oromo, Amharic. Here, only Somalis set foot in the little canteen where he played pool. He slept under a Somali family's roof, walked down the street, and played pool with Somali men, then went back to his Somali home for dinner. He felt that he was both in, and yet not in, South Africa. He could be anywhere.

His uncle earned a living running a general trading store in a black township. In South Africa these stores are called *spaza* shops. But he had still barely set foot in one of these townships. Thus far, they came to him only in the form of news reported around the pool table.

"One day, we were playing," Asad recalls, "I think it was maybe five or six days after I had arrived in Uitenhage, when someone walked in looking upset and said, 'In Motherwell, they have killed one of us.' Everyone went silent. Everyone was upset. For the rest of the day, the mood was very heavy.

"The following afternoon, we all went to the funeral. There was fear, brother. People huddled in groups saying there is too much robbery in this country; it is not safe having a cash business. There was talk about buying illegal firearms, about hiring Xhosa people to be security guards.

"I had not heard about this at all before I came to South Africa. The people passing through Addis, who showed us all the dollars they had earned down south, they said nothing about Somalis dying in townships. But right from the start, it was something that was there, always, something in the background."

It entered, too, into Abdicuur's plans for Asad.

"He was looking for a job for me," Asad says. "He'd come to South Africa in 1998. He was an old hand. He knew every Somali who ran a *spaza* shop in the whole region. His own *spaza* shop in Motherwell township was very successful. But he said I could not work with him because of the risks in Motherwell. He started listing all the townships: here is safe, there is not; here is okay; there is not so okay. He said he would choose where I was going to work."

"He showed me how to write stock," Asad recalls, "how many items must be left before you restock—four or five items. When he writes the order, he makes signs next to each item. This one is very low, this one less of a priority. This one is on special this week; buy more of it because there will be more profit."

They would climb into Abdicuur's impressive pickup and drive out of Motherwell to an enormous wholesaler on the outskirts of Uitenhage. The inside of the store was square and cavernous and very tall. The shelves were stacked impossibly high, brown boxes towering many meters above their heads, and men and women in blue overalls drove forklifts down the aisles.

Abdicuur gave Asad a trolley and a list of items to purchase and then watched quizzically as his nephew stumbled around the giant cave of a store, entirely lost.

"When I started," Asad said, "I would look for the Omo washing powder next to the rice. 'No, no,' Abdicuur would say. 'This part of the shop is dry goods, this part is fresh food, that part clothes, that part cigarettes and cell-phone airtime.'"

Back at the shop in Motherwell, watching his uncle selling the goods he had just bought, Asad was struck by the artistry of Abdicuur's trade.

"In the wholesaler I noticed that he had bought sixty-five cans of Fanta grape, but only a dozen of Fanta orange. In the *spaza* shop, I saw why. For every six cans of grape his customers bought, only one would buy orange. The trick was to watch very, very closely. Do they like salt-and-vinegar chips or tomato chips? How many salt and vinegar sold for how many tomato? Brother, he knew his customers better than they knew themselves. He had a rule: never run out of stock; never turn a customer away because you do not have what she wants."

Abdicuur's store was in the heart of Motherwell township. But even here, deep inside a South African settlement, Asad did not feel that he was inhabiting this new country. Abdicuur's shop was a shack. The yard was surrounded by a wooden wall so high that those inside the property could not see out, and those outside could not see in. The storefront itself was covered in wire meshing and bars. The only gap was a little half-moon at the level of the countertop, through which coins and notes and merchandise were exchanged.

The glimpses he got of Motherwell's street life shocked him.

"My first feeling about blacks was that they have too much sex," he recalls. "I have now adjusted a little. But back then, what I saw on the streets, to me it was illegal, uncultural, a shame to one's reputation. A man holding a woman who is not his wife, squeezing her bum, putting his hand up her skirt. I could not even look at them. I would look to the side."

He pauses and sighs. Hearing himself speak of these things has unearthed emotions. When he continues there is an uncharacteristic note of bitterness in his voice.

"Even if you consider many different beliefs about the world," he says, "nobody allows that. Christianity, whatever: it is in nobody's culture. It is a democracy here. You say nothing. It is how they are. But I tell you, they do not get this from their religion. It is not in their culture either. But they do it. They have lost what their ancestors once knew. Christian, Jewish, doesn't allow it. Nobody allows it."

His uncle drove him to the Department of Home Affairs office in Port Elizabeth to apply for asylum-seeker status. It would be a formality, Abdicuur said. You get a piece of paper saying that you have applied for asylum, and you are now in the country legally, pending the outcome of your case.

"And what if they decide I'm not a refugee?" Asad asked.

"It all takes a long time," his uncle assured him. "And if it is not going right, there are things that can be done."

They drove into Port Elizabeth on a pristine highway, the asphalt as smooth as wet cement. The suburban houses on either side were like the ones he had first seen in Pretoria, built yesterday, only much bigger and smarter. And then, suddenly, the suburbs were gone, and they were outside a tall brick building, surrounded by line upon line of people. Asad and his uncle joined the queue and waited. They stood there a long time, and it did not seem to move. A little sheepishly, Asad asked his uncle how long they would wait. Abdicuur smiled and put a hand on his shoulder.

"The office only opens in two hours," he said.

Waiting in the line, Asad thought he heard a snippet of what sounded like Swahili. As he strained to listen, another conversation drifted toward him, and it was unmistakably Amharic. Amid these familiar tones, he heard a fragment of his native Somali. He stood stock-still and opened his ears. It was as if fragments of his own biography had taken audible form and were now being thrown at him, as if a random selection of memories had left his head and found their way to the tongues of others.

As the day wore on, he heard more languages. He thought that one must be French. Of the rest, he could not make head or tail.

The country he had chosen as his destination now seemed vast beyond his comprehension. He pictured the highways and the suburbs through which they had just passed, then looked at the people of Africa gathered about him, then at the locked building in front of them. He wondered at the power of South Africa: without expending any effort, it could gather people from every country on the continent outside one building and force them to wait all day.

Aside from a pool table, the canteen in which he spent his days also had computers and an Internet connection. On his second day there he sent Foosiya an e-mail. It was a selective distillation of his experiences: barely mentioning the dramatic journey to South Africa, it announced triumphantly that he had found close family, that they were prosperous, that they were providing him with food and with shelter and that they were soon to find him work.

For a long time he received no reply. Concerned that the message may never have reached her, he sent it again.

On the very afternoon he resent the e-mail, his phone rang. He remembers it as a momentous occasion; it was the first time during his years on this earth that he had received a telephone call. The phone was a Nokia 3310. The moment it rang, he knew it must be his uncle, for Abdicuur had bought it for him the previous day and was the only person who knew the number.

His uncle's voice was urgent, agitated.

"Asad," he said, "can you drive?"

"Yes," Asad replied. "A taxi driver taught me in Addis."

"This is no joke, Asad," Abdicuur said. "Tell me the truth."

"Honestly, I can drive."

"Are you a perfect driver?"

"Yes."

"Do you know cars that are different from the one in which you learned?"

"I can drive any car."

"You can drive a right-hand drive?"

"Yes."

"You know the road signs?"

"Yes. Why do you not trust me to drive?"

A long, skeptical silence followed. Then his uncle hung up.

That night, Abdicuur phoned Asad from outside the house and told him to come outside. Asad walked up to the truck, and his uncle got out of the driver's seat and offered it to his nephew.

"We drove to a Somali restaurant down the road," Asad says. "All the parking around the restaurant was taken. When Somalis close their shops for the day, they all go to this restaurant—to store money, to watch television, to talk. So I found a very, very narrow parking space, tiny, and I parked the pickup perfectly, one inch between me and the car in front, one inch between me and the car behind."

He turned off the ignition and looked up to find that his uncle was smiling broadly.

"I have found you a job," he announced. "It involves a lot of driving."

The job was in a *spaza* shop in a small township on a hill overlooking the rural hamlet of Kirkwood. It was about a half-hour drive from Uitenhage. The salary his uncle had negotiated on his behalf was extremely attractive. He would earn one thousand four hundred rand per month—about two hundred dollars at the time—plus one hundred rand extra for Saturdays and twenty-nine rand in cell-phone airtime per week. He would also get free food and lodging. It was very good by South African standards: the average wage for a Somali shop assistant was between nine hundred and twelve hundred rand. It was considerably more than he had ever earned in one month during his four years in Addis. In one fell swoop, his journey down the African continent seemed justified. He resolved to save every cent. Quite for what purpose he was not yet sure, but with money came choices.

One person's good wage, of course, is another's slavery. In March 2004, when Asad began working in Kirkwood, one thousand four hundred rand per month was well below the minimum wage in every sector of the South African economy. The lowest grade of workers among South Africa's gold and platinum miners—generally considered to be among the most exploited of the country's formal labor force—was around four thousand rand per month. Asad found himself at the floor level of South Africa's vast, unregulated service industries. That he celebrated it as an opportunity to become rich would have come as a shock to most South Africans. That most South Africans regarded his wage as below their dignity would have left Asad dumbfounded.

Asad was in fact given two jobs, which is probably why he was paid well above the average wage of a Somali shopkeeper. He was responsible for the stock, a task that required him to drive to a wholesaler, either in Uitenhage or in Port Elizabeth, every third day. And he was also the assistant shopkeeper; whenever the regular shopkeeper took a break, Asad would stand at the counter and sell.

His life in Kirkwood sounds unremittingly bleak. He and the shopkeeper, a young man named Osman, shared a room at the back of the store. As with Abdicuur's shop in Motherwell, a tall wooden fence surrounded the yard, and the storefront was screened with bars and wire mesh. His trips to the wholesaler aside, Asad left the store only to use the outside toilet the two Somali men shared with their South African neighbors. And even these adventures were restricted; it was considered unwise to unlock the bolt on the front gate after dark; this was a cash business, after all, and a predator could simply wait in the darkness outside the gate. If Asad had to urinate after the sun went down, he did so in a bottle and emptied it the following morning.

And so the two men were confined to a small cage, sometimes for as long as seventy-two hours at a time. They cooked for each other, ate together, sat in the shop together, and slept on mattresses at opposite ends of the same room.

"Did you like Osman?" I ask cautiously.

"He was a good guy," Asad replies. "When you live like that, you both behave very well because there is no choice."

He came to know the people of the township primarily as pairs of eyes on the other side of the wire mesh and as dark hands that slid money through the opening above the counter. As slight as these encounters may seem, they were both invasive and profound.

"Brother, the customers were very rude," he tells me. "I first saw it even before I started working, when I went with my uncle to his shop in Motherwell. Abdicuur is a very proud man. People much younger than him would come up to the counter and ask for salt-and-vinegar chips. He'd bring a packet, and they'd say: 'Hey! Are you fucking deaf? I asked for airtime.' He'd put the chips aside and look at them calmly and say, 'How much airtime would you like?'

"I was shocked. I wanted to unlock the gate and go around to the other side and challenge this man.

"My uncle watched me. He saw exactly what was happening inside me. He smiled. 'You've just learned the most important three lessons about running a shop,' he said. 'One, you must be clean twenty-four hours; two, never be rude; three, when the customer is wrong, he is right.'

"It was an unnatural thing to me, brother. To be nice to a person who is behaving like a piece of shit—I had to ask myself many times why a man like my uncle would allow for something like that."

By the time I meet him, he has developed an elaborate theory about the value of his uncle's rules.

"Most of our customers are unemployed or on welfare," he says. "They are the laughingstock of South Africa. But when they come to our shops, they are king. They can come with two rand. There are only a few things you can buy with that: single cigarettes, one or two chewing-gum sticks, sweets. The customer can come with his coins and say, 'Give me a cigarette.' I get one. He says, 'No, I've changed my mind; I want chewing gum.' I say, 'Yes, *bra*,' and get it. By the time I am back at the counter, he has changed his mind again. 'No, *kwerekwere*, I want sweets.'

"A South African shopkeeper will not tolerate that. He will say, 'You are wasting my time. Fuck off.' A Somali cannot afford to say that. He can only say, 'Yes, *sisi*. Yes, *bra*.' The laughingstock of South Africa come to us because our shops are the one place in their own country where they can say, 'I want this!' and someone will respond."

And so Asad suspended his honor, or, at any rate, kept it in reserve for the other parts of his life, and kept a serene face.

The exchanges over the counter were not Asad's only encounters with the people of the township. Whenever he returned from the wholesaler in his goods-laden pickup, young men would emerge from nowhere.

"It is a tricky time, brother," Asad tells me. "You have to open your gate, open the back door to your shop; you have to walk in and out carrying goods. You and your property are exposed. The young men gather around you the way ants go for an ice cream a child has dropped on the ground. They are wanting to help.

"First time, I said, 'Okay brothers, thanks.' There were so many of them, the packing was over in a few minutes. Then they stood around and wanted money. Whatever I was going to give them, brother, whatever, no matter how much, was not going to be enough. The situation was becoming difficult. Some of them were clicking their tongues and shaking their heads. They were talking to each other in Xhosa, and I did not understand. I backed away and bolted the gate and felt my heart beating very fast."

The township was inhabited in part by Xhosa-speaking people and in part by mixed-race colored people. Asad was astounded at the differences between them.

"Chalk and cheese, brother," he tells me. "The colored people are like children. They are ruled by whatever they are feeling at a particular moment. You make one little mistake behind the counter with a colored person and he will say something terrible to you, like, '*Jou ma se poes!* [Your mother's cunt!].' The next day, you run outside to fight with him for insulting your mother. He looks at you like you are crazy. '*Naai, broer* [No, brother],' he says, 'that was yesterday.' He's happy now. He's forgotten.

"The Xhosas are something else. They never show what is in their heart. And if they are going to insult you, they do it softly. A customer will stare at me through the wire mesh and say, so soft I can hardly hear, '*Uthanda imali* [You like money].' If I challenge him, he will throw up his hands and say, 'You are right, my friend. *Ixolo* [I am sorry].' Brother, they do not show you what is in their heart. When I think of them, I feel cold."

Aside from the two men who had driven him and his companions from the Zimbabwean border to Johannesburg, Asad had barely come across white people.

"I only knew stories about whites," he tells me. "I was told about apartheid, how whites did not like blacks. But from what I could see, whites were educated and had power, so I was very keen to make white friends. But I did not know how to meet white people."

Among his first customers in Kirkwood was an elderly Xhosa man.

He appeared unfailingly each morning to buy bread and milk and two cigarettes. He would greet Asad with a smile that appeared to carry genuine warmth. Asad took pleasure in addressing him each day as Tata, the Xhosa word for "father."

Every now and again, Asad and the old man talked. In the little language they shared, Tata told Asad something of the history of the settlement in which he now lived. At some point, he nodded his head in the direction of the Kirkwood town center, where white people lived.

"I want to go there, Tata," Asad said with a light smile. "I want to be where the money is."

The old man laughed at Asad's foolishness. "Black people cannot live there," he replied. "You cannot be a part of what is there."

Asad stared back at the old man in astonishment.

"Brother," he tells me, "I never thought I would see the day I am described as black."

He returned the old man's stare. "I am not black," he said sternly. "I have my own culture."

The old man laughed: not his usual quiet chuckle, but an open-throated, mirthful guffaw. "When you are here in South Africa," he said, turning away, his milk tucked under one arm, his loaf of bread under the other, "you are black."

At the end of his first month in Kirkwood, Asad received his salary in one-hundred-rand notes. He phoned his uncle immediately.

Abdicuur was confused by the call.

"That's nice," he said. "But what do you want me to do?"

"I thought I was meant to give it to you to manage for me," Asad replied.

"No. It is your money."

Asad was now a little confused in turn. This is not how he had imagined things. He asked his uncle to keep his savings anyhow.

When he next drove into Uitenhage to buy stock, he handed his uncle one thousand eight hundred rand—his fourteen-hundred-rand salary, plus overtime he had received for working on four Saturdays.

Abdicuur counted the money and looked at his nephew in astonishment.

"You haven't spent a cent," he said.

"There is no need to spend," Asad replied. "I eat in the shop. I sleep in the shop. I do not smoke cigarettes. I do not chew *mira.*"

Actually, Asad and Osman did chew *mira,* but he kept this concealed from his uncle.

"If he knew," Asad tells me, "it would have been a big problem. He was a pious man. He did not chew. If he knew, I would lose my reputation."

I ponder Asad's relationship with his uncle. He was about twenty years old now. For much of his childhood, he had had nobody to tell him how much to save and how much to spend. In Addis, he had used his own wits to conjure a living. He had supported a large household, paid for a wedding, saved to go south. Now he had adopted the position of a minor, surrendering his will and his judgment to a man he had just met. He did so hungrily, it seems, like a small child climbing under the sheets and blankets of an inviting bed.

His job in Kirkwood did not last. About six weeks in, he received a call from his employer's wife summoning him to her home in Uitenhage. Upon arriving, he discovered that all she wanted was to have him drive her to friends less than a kilometer away. He had to wait in the car all afternoon while she drank tea.

A few days later, she called again. This time, Asad was to take her grocery shopping.

On the third occasion, Asad phoned his employer.

"I have a problem," he said. "I am being paid to take care of stock in your shop, not to be your wife's driver. I cannot do both jobs at once."

The two men exchanged words. Abdicuur was brought in to mediate. Asad went back to work, but under what terms he was not sure.

A week later, his new mistress phoned again. Another trip to the grocery.

This time, Asad phoned his uncle and told him he was quitting his job. He was in a stronger position now. Via the network of Somalis he encountered whenever he went to the wholesaler, he knew of an opening as a shopkeeper in a town quite close to Kirkwood. The pay was not as good—just twelve hundred rand a month, no overtime, and no free airtime—but he was prepared to cut his losses.

"Was your uncle sympathetic?" I ask.

"Very. He said, 'This is bullshit. Abdullahis do not work like that.' I was very proud when he said that. I took strength from that."

. . .

Just days after Asad changed jobs, Foosiya replied to his e-mail.

During her extended silence, he had begun to wonder. On some days, when it was just he and Osman and their shop, and he had too much time to think, he imagined that Foosiya had drifted into another life, one replete with a husband and children. He would shake the thought from his head and chastise himself for his mental wandering.

His trips to the wholesaler were often too rushed to permit him to stop at an Internet café. He was only able to check his e-mail every ten days or so. He had come to numb his excitement each time he logged in. He had trained himself to expect nothing.

Now she was back, and as he read her news, he grew angry. She had left Addis before Asad even arrived in South Africa. For the past two months or more, she had been living in the port town of Berbera in Somaliland. She had broken the first line of their agreement—to stay put for three months.

She explained what had happened. A week after Asad had left, she had been attacked one night in Bole Mikhael by a group of Ethiopian youths. They had ripped her necklace from her throat and had even tried to tear an earring from her ear. She had realized, on that very night, that she could not be in Addis without a man; it had been a mistake to allow Asad to go. She had wasted no time; within a week, she was in Berbera, with family.

She stressed that she had not reneged. She was his wife. She was waiting for him to send for her.

At the bottom of the e-mail was a cell-phone number. When he tried to call it he found that his phone did not reach beyond South African borders.

Lying in bed that night, two Asads danced before his eyes. The first was a young man saving a lot of money, a man waiting for his wife to come. There would be children soon and a thriving business and a good home. The second Asad was a boy locked in a bolted room. He was trapped there, day in and day out, a lone Somali in a very strange land, the people outside toyingly hostile, his employer an exploitative man who would squeeze him for all he was worth.

Where in this life was there a place for Foosiya? He had much to do before he could send for her. And she was clearly not a patient woman. When he woke the next morning he felt very alone, as if he had known Foosiya in another lifetime.

# Uncle

On the evening of April 9, 2004, an hour or so after he had gone to bed, Asad was woken by a phone call.

"Abdicuur is dead," the voice at the other end announced.

"Who is this?" Asad asked.

"Asad, listen. Abdicuur was shot in his *spaza* shop. He is dead."

Asad sprang out of bed and looked at his watch. It was a little before ten o'clock. He had no car. Taxis to Uitenhage would only begin running in six hours' time. He looked around his bedroom and took in its contents. Everything suddenly seemed unfamiliar—the bedclothes, the chair, the duffel bag—as if he had just walked into a stranger's private quarters. His uncle was dead, and he was stranded here in a room and in a town that seemed, now, the most inhospitable place he'd ever been.

He began pacing like an animal, drawing an invisible square over and again along the perimeter of the room. Then he lay down very carefully on his bed, as if the news had turned his body into something brittle, something that might snap.

"Brother," he says, "what happened when I lay down on that bed: I lost control of my body. My legs started to shake. The muscles in my stomach started to jump up and down. It was like that all night. Until four o'clock, I lay there trying to keep my body under control. Then I ran outside and looked for a taxi."

He arrived at Abdicuur's house shortly after dawn to find it locked up and empty. For a moment, he wondered whether it wasn't all a joke, whether his uncle had simply taken his family on a trip to Johannesburg.

He put his head down and walked quickly to the Somali restaurant down the road.

From a block away, he saw the crowd. He believes that there were as many as three hundred people standing there in the dawn. He did not know that so many Somalis lived in the Port Elizabeth area. They were mainly men and largely silent, and in their white *thobes* and prayer caps they looked ethereal against the morning's gray light, as if they might vanish at any moment.

Asad walked into the crowd. He did not tell anybody that he was the dead man's nephew. He stood shoulder to shoulder with people he did not know.

A man was beginning to address the gathering. He spoke in a quiet voice that Asad strained to hear. He was saying that he had been the first on the scene, that he had watched Abdicuur Abdullahi die. It happened shortly after dusk, he said. Five men had walked into the store and demanded money. Whether Abdicuur had tried to resist, he could not say, but the men had opened fire, and Abdicuur had been shot nine times. Still, he was not dead, the man continued. He lived another ten or fifteen minutes. He was conscious for some of that time. The two men had exchanged parting words.

A murmur rose from the gathering, as if it had just this moment become a single being and was taking its first labored breath. Then people began to speak softly to one another, and the illusion subsided.

Asad no longer recalls how long the crowds lingered outside the restaurant, only that they gathered again at the mosque later in the day. Still, he remained anonymous. He walked slowly through the gathering, head bowed, eavesdropping on myriad conversations. In each one, he heard a note of panic.

"My uncle was a big man in that area," he says. "It was like a pillar had fallen, and now the house was going to fall down with it. It was only then that I realized what a very big man my uncle was."

Sometime in the midafternoon the body arrived. Asad followed it through the crowds until two men blocked his way.

"I asked to see it," he recalls, "and they shook their heads and said no."

When he explained that he was the dead man's nephew, he was examined with skepticism. Strangers had taken over the scene, people he could have sworn he had never seen before in his life. It dawned on him how little he knew of South Africa's Somali community. A crisis arises, and people come from nowhere to take command. He did not know how and by what rights they had come to control access to the body.

"We negotiated for some time," Asad says. "Eventually, they allowed me through."

I have asked him twice what he saw and felt when he stood over his uncle's corpse. His two answers are not at odds with each other, but they are very different.

A white sheet covered Abdicuur's body, up to the top of his neck, and his face seemed exposed and disembodied.

"It is for a son to wash the body," he says. "I felt sorry that I had not been there to do it."

He took the sheet in both hands and slowly pulled it down to Abdicuur's waist. There were two wounds in his chest and two on his left side. They were small and neat, almost as if a craftsman had made them, laboring away delicately and with much care.

"Then I saw the stitches from where they had cut him open after he died," Asad recalls. "It is against Islam to remove the organs from the body. I do not believe that what they were doing was ascertaining the cause of death. I believe that because we are Somali and defenseless they were taking the organs for other people to use. We do not accept this. They did not ask us."

In the months and years following Abdicuur's death, it became an obsession. Asad has written to the newspapers. He has tried to speak on the radio. Of all the terrors inflicted upon Somalis in South Africa, it is this, the surgical work performed upon the corpse, that he feels most deeply.

"They did it without our permission," he says. "They need to ask a relative for permission. They see it as a chance: 'These people do not have anybody to stand up for them. They do not know their rights.'"

The second time I ask him about that day, his response is very brief.

"It was the first relative I've seen dead," he says. "There was a switch in me. A change. It has happened. Now it will continue."

On the tip of my tongue is an observation: this was not the first time he had seen a relative's corpse. There was his mother. I hesitate a moment and then say it.

He nods very quickly, his face inscrutable, and changes the subject. It is an image, I think, that he has long cast from his head. He remembers holding on to her leg as the door to their home was being bashed down. He remembers the two thick plaits that ran down her back. And he has the sense, always, that he carries her in his being, for she was the first to love him. Her corpse does not figure among these images and feelings. She represents a foundation, not its shattering. It is Abdicuur's dead body that must stand in for the feeling that the bottom of the world has fallen away.

He remembers sitting with other members of the family as one person after another filed past and said sorry. Of the burial itself, he says only, "We carried the body very slowly. It was not a hurried affair. The feelings must come out."

Afterward, about thirty people gathered at Abdicuur's house, all of them AliYusuf.

"We talked and talked and talked," Asad recalls. "All the shop owners agreed: we must sell and leave. We must take Abdicuur's wife and children with us and go to Johannesburg.

"Fourteen of us left immediately, within a week of my uncle's burial. We took his wife and children with us. The AliYusufs all chipped in to pay their first six months' rent in Johannesburg. The remaining AliYusuf remained in the Eastern Cape long enough to sell their property. Then they also packed up.

"My uncle was killed in April 2004. By July, to my knowledge, there were no more AliYusuf people in the Port Elizabeth area."

## Sterkstroom

He was back in Mayfair. When he had last been there, South Africa was new and unknown, and this little piece of Somalia had seemed a launching pad to an adventure. Now, it was more a lung, a corner of this vast country where one could breathe the air.

He wanted desperately to stay. He wanted to live his life within the four corners of this Somali island, never to have to face South Africa again. He wanted to wake up and hear Somalis shouting and to go to sleep listening to the sounds of the international news channels they watched into the night. He wanted to be able to walk the streets without fear.

Since his uncle's death, the two rooms he had inhabited in Kirkwood—the first with Osman, the second alone—seemed like dungeons. When he thought of himself inside them, he saw the scene from a great height, a shivering wreck of a Somali man in a sea of hostile people. He felt bitter. Walking to the mosque one morning for five o'clock prayers, he found himself, much to his own astonishment, in angry dialogue with his God.

"If you designed my life," he heard himself asking, "why make it this way? Why deliver me into the arms of family when I am least expecting it, only to take them away? Wouldn't it have been better if you'd never led me to my uncle? At least then I would not have known. I would not have had to stand over his corpse."

He could not find work in Mayfair. Work, he discovered, came through close family connections and through very old friendships. There were several AliYusuf families in Mayfair, but they were only distantly related. They were the sorts of people who might keep him safe for a while but would soon tire of the burden.

Among the AliYusuf people who had abandoned the Port Elizabeth area was another Abdullahi, a cousin named Kaafi, and his wife and small daughter. Asad had met him several times during his time in the Port Elizabeth area. Now that their uncle Abdicuur was dead, they were the only Abdullahis in South Africa. They resolved to stay together.

Kaafi mentioned a hamlet in Eastern Cape called Sterkstroom. He had passed through it several months ago. He and his companions had stopped in the black township next to the town center in search of something to eat and drink. They had found nothing; there wasn't a single trading store, just a boarded-up old place that seemed to have closed its doors many years before. Kaafi wanted to go there and open a shop.

"Where is it?" Asad asked skeptically.

It was in Eastern Cape but very far from Port Elizabeth, much farther north. The nearest town was a place called Queenstown. It was unlikely to be dangerous, Kaafi said. It was so small.

Asad was not sure. The words "Eastern Cape" did not sit well with him now. And the idea of hurling himself back into the thick of South Africa seemed rash. But he and Kaafi were both living on savings now, and every cent they used was a cent less to invest in their lives.

Kaafi had about ten thousand rand in savings. Asad had saved almost every penny he had earned since coming to South Africa, about four thousand rand. It would surely be enough.


Abdicuur died on April 9. Before the end of May, Asad, Kaafi, and Kaafi's wife and child were in Sterkstroom.

The black township alongside the white village was very small. Just a dozen or so dirt streets lined with little old houses with corrugated-iron roofs. In the distance, on a hill, was a new settlement of what South Africans called RDP houses (referring to the Reconstruction and Development Programme), provided by the democratic government. These were all identical, laid out in rows, as if they were marks on a map somebody had drawn on a piece of paper.

Kaafi was right. There wasn't a single trading store in the township. To buy anything—a liter of milk, a box of matches, a chocolate—the residents of the township would have to walk into the white town or board a taxi to Queenstown, about a half hour's drive south.

On their first day in Sterkstroom, their bags at their sides, Asad and Kaafi stood outside the township's boarded-up shop. Above the entrance was a sign saying MANGALISO STORE. Much time had clearly passed since it was last open for business. Most of the windowpanes were long gone, and the plaster around the windowsills was cracked and broken. From the ground, it was hard to see whether the roof was intact. The wood of the door at the entrance was warped and swollen.

In their broken Xhosa, the Somalis asked passersby who owned the place. They were directed to a home just a block away where an old woman came out to greet them leaning heavily on a hand-whittled cane. Asad surmised that she was eighty at least, her cheeks sunken by the absence of teeth and marked with deep dry crevices.

"She invited us into her house and gave us tea and treated us like people," Asad recalls. "When we told her we were interested in her shop, she laughed and shook her head and told us a long story about the shop and why it was closed, but we did not understand. She was happy for us to use it. The rent she asked was cheap: I think seven hundred rand."

The space was hardly ideal. The shop itself was tiny: just a narrow counter and a short, shallow shelf behind it. There was no space for a fridge, which was essential if they were going to stock fresh produce; it would have to stand outside, exposed to the elements, connected to a plug by a long extension cord.

Behind the shop was the house proper. It had four or five tiny bedrooms, and each was in disrepair. The Somalis touched the walls gingerly and treaded lightly on the floors, for the place seemed very fragile.

"We told the old lady on day one that we needed to do work to the place," Asad tells me. "She said we could do what we like, as long as we pay for it. So we hired builders. They were three brothers. They lived just a few blocks away. First, we got them to build an extension so that we could stock the shop properly. Then we changed the roof—it was very old and leaked in so many places it was not worth trying to fix. Then we knocked down some of the walls to make bigger rooms. We made a nice place."

They were the first foreigners to live in Sterkstroom. Every third or so day, when they went to restock in Queenstown, they would meet other Somalis. They soon ascertained that several AliYusuf families lived in a large radius around Queenstown. They punched the phone numbers of their kinspeople into their cell phones; they made contact; they met. They discussed family. They discussed business. Then they would retreat to the isolation of Sterkstroom, where the people spoke a language they were only slowly learning, and where the expressions on faces were hard to read.

"Twenty-four hours we were suspicious, brother," Asad tells me. "We remembered Abdi's death. When we were sleeping, the zinc in the roof made a noise, and we lay awake wondering."

The more they came to know Sterkstroom, the more comfortable they felt. In Uitenhage and Kirkwood, there had been blacks and coloreds, and many people had seemed strangers to one another. Here, the Somalis soon realized, everyone knew one another, and everyone's parents and grandparents and great-grandparents had known one another.

"The people in Sterkstroom were not only Xhosa," Asad says, "they were from the same clan, the ones who cut off half of a finger of the girl children. Kaafi was the first to notice it. He pointed it out to me and his wife. We thought he was mad. Whenever a woman came to buy, we would watch her hands closely. It was true. Each had half a finger missing.

"At first, we were scared to ask why. We thought that maybe it is some secret, something they don't talk about. Maybe if we ask, they will become angry and throw us out of town. But the people were so nice to us, especially the old mothers and the old fathers, that in the end we could ask quite easily. They laughed. 'It is something we do.' And they would show how it was done, when the girl was still very small and her bones had not yet formed."

It took a few months, but they eventually realized that the whole township was connected by family ties.

"It's something you realize as you get to know people," Asad says. "This one's that one's auntie. But she is also the other one's auntie and another one's sister-in-law. You see how the families are connected. You discover this big family, that big family."

"They were lovely people," he recalls. "The old ones were especially kind to us. They would come and sit and drink tea with us, and we would talk and laugh. They would ask us about home, and did we not miss home, why did we travel so far? They had lived in this one village for seventy years, eighty years. They said that if they traveled as far as we did they would die."

It helped, no doubt, that the money the Somalis made was spread around. There was the old lady's seven-hundred-rand-a-month rent. And the renovations they had done to her house were contracted to neighbors. Also, Asad and Kaafi did not have their own car; they would hire a pickup from a local, together with a driver, every time they went to Queenstown to restock. They distributed this business between three neighbors and would use each in turn.

And, of course, residents could shop for food in their own township for the first time in more than a decade. Soon it seemed that everybody was coming to the Somalis to buy their daily bread and milk, their crisps and chocolates and cell-phone airtime, their frozen chickens. Business was brisk. Asad and Kaafi eyed the RDP settlement on the hill; it was surely large enough for its own *spaza* shop. Perhaps, they surmised, they could open one there, too.

Asad called Foosiya promptly at the end of each week. And via the Western Union office in Queenstown, he sent fifty dollars to her in Berbera at the end of each month; the Somalis' famous informal money exchange, the *hawala,* had not yet reached this remote part of Eastern Cape.

I ask him to describe their conversations. Were they tender? Did they laugh together? How much of his life did he describe? He shrugs and changes the subject. I suspect that what passed between them was brief and formulaic; each was just checking that the other was still there. He barely described Sterkstroom to her, it seems. And while he told her briefly of his uncle's death, he evaded the troubled questions she asked in the wake of this news.

Then in September 2004, during one of their weekly conversations, her tone suddenly changed.

"You don't love me anymore," he recalls her announcing.

"What do you mean, I don't love you?"

"It's been eight months. You no longer talk about me joining you."

"You're ready to join me?" he asked.

"Yes, right now."

"Now?"

"Tomorrow, then."

"Foosiya, it takes time—"

"How long?"

"I will send you money at the end of the month."

"At the end of *this* month?"

"Yes, this month."

"Do I have your word?"

As he recalls it, this conversation took place on September 20. Eight days later, he was standing behind the counter in his and Kaafi's shop, when his phone rang. The number on the screen was Kenyan.

"It's me," said the voice on the other end of the line. "I could not wait until the end of the month. I'm in Nairobi."

Asad stood there with the phone to his ear and squinted into the Eastern Cape sunshine. Foosiya answered the question he could not get out of his mouth. "I used the money you've been sending me," she said. "Every fifty dollars you sent, I saved it all. But it's not enough."

"Of course it's not enough!" Asad finally spat out. "It's nothing!"

She told Asad that she had found a smuggler who would get her to South Africa for four hundred dollars. She also wanted another two hundred for food and drink.

"I only had four hundred dollars," Asad recalls. "I went to Kaafi and told him what was happening and asked if he had another two hundred. 'Of course!' he said. 'Of course!'"

Asad went immediately to Queenstown to arrange to send the money to Nairobi. Only once he was on the road, in the passenger seat of a neighbor's car, did he gather his thoughts. Two different versions of his wife formed in his head. The first was the Foosiya he thought he knew: wise, thoughtful, deliberate. In Addis, he had the sense that she had spent years and years thinking about every word that came out of her mouth. Now, here was a second Foosiya, impulsive to the point of madness. He strained to remember this side of her in Addis and for a moment entertained the thought that the woman who would soon be coming to live with him was a stranger.

Once the money had arrived safely in Nairobi, Foosiya made two admissions. First, she had another woman with her, a member of her clan without a cent to her name. The six hundred dollars would cover both their journeys.

"She kept it from me," Asad says, "because she was afraid that I would refuse to pay for this woman. Foosiya is a very sly person. She *does* think about everything first."

Second, the smuggler had not offered to take her to South Africa for four hundred dollars. He had offered to take her and her friend for six hundred. She had handed over every dollar Asad had sent her. Aside from the few dollars she had left of his monthly payments, she had nothing; she was making her way down half the length of the African continent with empty pockets.

Asad begged her to stay in Nairobi while he found more money, but she refused. The smuggler's troupe of migrants was leaving that day, and she had handed over the money already; there was no going back.

A day went by and Asad did not hear from Foosiya. Then another day. Then another. At first, he imagined the terrible things that might have happened to her. He cursed himself for allowing her to concoct such a harebrained journey. On day four, he thought of Allah and his intentions: the life he had mapped for Asad was thus far signposted by tragedy; it would be in keeping with those intentions if he lost his new wife in this way.

He kicked himself for not even getting the name, never mind the phone number, of the smuggler. He made several calls to Nairobi, but these proved fruitless. He obtained the phone numbers of two Somali smugglers in Tanzania. He called them. They had not seen Foosiya. How on earth was he going to get to Kenya? The thin slip of paper he had received at Home Affairs in Port Elizabeth, affirming that he was applying for asylum, did not give him the right to leave South Africa. Yet a husband does not abandon his wife to whatever fate will befall her.

On the seventh day, he was standing behind the counter, giving a customer change, when it came to him in a flash that he had just risen above the scene, watched himself from on high, and had seen a widower. He passed the change through the cage and sat down. Such thoughts had been going through his head for days, he now realized. In increments so small that he had not noticed, he was growing numb. Deep inside, beyond conscious thoughts, he was preparing to leave Sterkstroom for long enough to look for a wife. Perhaps he would find one somewhere as close as Queenstown, maybe in Johannesburg, perhaps even in some other country.

On the fourteenth day he answered his phone to hear a man's voice ask whether this was Asad Hirsi Abdullahi, whether he had a wife called Foosiya, whether he was expecting her.

"What has happened?" Asad pleaded.

Then Foosiya was on the line. Her voice sounded both close and startled, and Asad imagined that she had seen terrible things.

Then the strange man's voice was back and he announced who he was and what had happened.

"The smuggler had left Nairobi with sixty people," Asad tells me. "But he realized on the journey that he had miscalculated, that there were too many of them to cross the border into Tanzania. They must divide into two groups. Foosiya was in the first group. The smuggler left them on the Kenya-Tanzania border in the care of a woman. He paid the woman one week's board and lodging for all of them and went back into Kenya to fetch the second group. But he did not come back. The landlady in the bush was not getting paid. She started robbing the people who the smuggler left with her.

"In these conditions, people began to divide into clans. There were no other Isaaq people. Foosiya was scared. She said she was Ogadeni. The Ogadeni interrogated her. She said she was AliYusuf and Abdullahi. Somebody there knew Abdullahi. They accepted her. They took her and her friend under their wing. That is the one who phoned me. He was an AliYusuf. He said they were stuck, they had all been robbed, none of them had money. They had nowhere to stay."

Asad asked for the cell-phone number of the smuggler. The man answered at once, and in a cold, even voice Asad threatened to come to Kenya and kill him.

"He was very apologetic. He said it was not his fault. Fourteen of his people had been arrested. He could not leave them in prison. He was trying to get them out. I said I didn't care what his problem was. If he valued his life, he would get my wife to South Africa."

Four days later, Foosiya was in Maputo, just four hundred kilometers or so from Mayfair. She phoned Asad and told him she needed another four hundred dollars to get her and her companion to Johannesburg. Asad borrowed the money from an AliYusuf family near Queenstown and wired it straight to Maputo. The following day, Foosiya was in Johannesburg.

"I phoned an AliYusuf person in Mayfair. I asked him, 'Please fetch these ladies. Please keep them safe.'

"She stayed in Johannesburg a week. She said she did not want to rest anymore. She wanted to come to me."

## *Foosiya in Sterkstroom*

Asad woke a neighbor before dawn to take him to Queenstown to meet Foosiya's bus. Of the journey, he recalls that the grass plains were gray in the predawn light and that he felt anxious. But he has no memory of Queenstown that morning. He does not recall waiting for the bus or seeing Foosiya get off it. He no longer knows what they said when they laid eyes on each other, whether they touched, or how. Nor does he remember the journey home. He no longer knows, for instance, whether he sat in the passenger seat and Foosiya behind the driver, or whether they sat together in the back, as if in a taxi.

I am guessing freely, for all I have is my imagination. I see him in the front and her in the back, and throughout the half-hour journey they exchange barely a word. To swivel in his seat far enough to face her is a gesture that imparts import, weight. He is not sure that he has anything weighty to say. It is safer to stare straight ahead. He is about to introduce his wife to her future; there will be plenty to talk about soon enough.

What Asad does recall, as vividly as if he has just seen it, is Foosiya's face when she saw Sterkstroom. Her lips began to form a perfect O, but before they could get halfway there, they slammed shut, as if she feared that by seeing into her mouth Asad might see into her soul. And he remembers, too, what he thought: such self-possession, to be able to catch so powerful an emotion so early.

"Brother," he says, "that look on her face was pure shock. On the phone I had told her that I work, not where I work. She didn't have a picture. She thought I was working in a big city. She had an image of the township in her head, an image of a very tough place."

"What did she think?" I ask.

"That is a question I did not want to put to her."

"But what do you think she thought?"

"I don't know. Maybe that she had jumped from Addis into the bush. If she thought that, she did not tell me. On her second day in Sterkstroom, she was already behind the counter working. What choice did she have?"

Of all the moments in his past Asad has described to me, it is this October day in 2004 I wish to have witnessed with my own eyes. A woman waits nine months to join her husband in a new land. They have behind them a briefly shared life. While it is true that each has felt strongly for the other, their coming together was calculated, the nature of the transaction opaque, for both had kept secrets. Now the woman makes a hair-raising journey to join this husband whom she does not quite know. She gets through it by the skin of her teeth. And she arrives to find a place more remote than any she has seen. She is in a house of four Somalis, two of them strangers; beyond it is a tribe of inscrutable people; beyond them, empty blond fields roll into oblivion.

There is no turning back now. This is her life.

"Was it easy to live with her again?" I ask Asad.

"Yes," he replies. "I still loved her. The excitement I felt in Addis when I realized that she was a great woman: it came back straightaway."

"Immediately?"

"I woke up the morning after she arrived. She was still sleeping. I rested my head on my elbow and looked at her for a long time. I was excited. It did not take away my uncle's death. But it brought something new."

Foosiya seems to have fallen pregnant during her first week in Sterkstroom, for by early December, Asad was noting strange behavior in his wife.

"First, she started oversleeping," Asad reports. "When she finally got up, she would be angry. I would say something and she would fight. So I was just quiet. Then she would complain that I was not saying anything.

"One day, she started moving produce out of the shop. Kaafi stood and stared at her. He said, 'What are you doing with our stock?'

" 'It stinks,' she said. 'Either the stock goes or I will vomit.'

"Then I realized. I said, 'Foosiya, why didn't you tell me? We are going to have a child!'

"She gave me a terrible look, brother."

His memories of Foosiya's olfactory disturbances bring a spirit of mirth to the inside of my car. The space between us is now alive with something rare: nostalgia.

"I did not know what to expect in the mornings," he says. "Some days I woke up and she would tell me I stink so bad she was going to vomit. Other days, I would be about to go out for a few hours, and she would ask for my shirt so she could hold it to her nose and smell me while I was gone."

Now he is laughing out loud. He says he has a story about watermelons.

"We sold them in the shop. They were very popular. One day, she was sitting behind me, dealing with the change; she said she didn't want us to sell watermelon anymore. I asked why not. She said they were making her unhappy. Unhappy? How can a watermelon make you unhappy?

" 'You'll never understand,' she said. 'Just get rid of the watermelons.' "

He is on a roll now. The memories are pouring out and will not cease.

"She stopped eating food, brother. Stopped altogether. She would only drink milk. I was worried for our baby. I was trying to think of how to get her back to food. So I told her a story about South African milk. In Somaliland, she drank milk fresh from a camel or a goat or a cow. In Sterkstroom, she was drinking long-life milk. I told her it isn't actually milk. It doesn't come from an animal. They make it from plants. She was shocked. She stopped drinking it. But she did not go back to food. She just had nothing at all now. Brother, she was driving me crazy!"

Word reached the Somalis' landlady that Asad's beautiful wife was refusing food. She came around one morning leaning on her stick, flanked by three others. The women pronounced that they had seen this problem more often than they could count. They were going to take Foosiya on an outing. But first, they said, they were going to do her hair.

A chair was brought out, Foosiya was invited to sit, and half a dozen Sterkstroom women hovered around her head for the rest of the morning.

"They liked Foosiya's hair," Asad says. "They liked its softness. They would insist on doing her hair every so often, and it would take hours.

"Sometimes, though, they asked what was the point of doing her hair so nice when she would only cover it in the Muslim way. She said it was for her husband. They would like that. They would wink at me and tell me that they were making my wife beautiful for me."

Once her hair was done, the old ladies swept Foosiya into a taxi and she was gone—where to, Asad did not know.

They all returned in the early evening. When Asad asked Foosiya where they had taken her and whether she had eaten, she ignored him. He walked down to his landlady's house and asked her.

"They had taken her to eat potato crisps," he tells me. "The old woman was looking very satisfied with herself. She said she had never known a pregnant woman who does not eat potato crisps."

For the duration of Foosiya's pregnancy, Sterkstroom was pretty much the sum of Asad's world. He only ever went to two other places: to Queenstown every third day to buy stock, and to Home Affairs in Port Elizabeth every third month to renew his, and now Foosiya's, asylum-seeker status.

The trips to Home Affairs were dispiriting. He would get a taxi to Port Elizabeth, a tiring six-hour drive, and take his place in that grim, endless queue. When he eventually got to the front, the official he confronted would tell him that his attempt to acquire refugee status had made no progress and that he would have to renew his asylum-seeker papers. He would ask questions, try to ascertain whether there was something he might do to speed up his case. But the officials were rude and harried and disinterested.

These trips cost him a great deal. Each time, he was away from work for two days. He would have to pay for a hotel to spend the night in Port Elizabeth. And, when he finally returned home, he was so tired and frustrated that he took a day to recuperate.

Besides, there was something about the experience that haunted him. All these people from the four corners of the continent waiting lamely in that long line, then filing into the great building like sausages into a butcher's machine, the officials inside so callous, so utterly indifferent. It struck him again, as it had when he first stood in that queue with Abdicuur, that South Africa was immensely powerful in ways he did not understand.

He knew little about refugee law. Snippets of information circulated in South Africa's Somali community, but they were entangled in rumor and opinion, and he could not say for certain what was right or wrong. But it seemed clear that without refugee status, he was not free to travel outside South Africa. To cross a border one needed a refugee identity-document book. To get a refugee document, one needed refugee papers.

"Eventually," he tells me, "I went to a Somali smuggler. His name was AbdiNoor. He lived in Port Elizabeth. He specialized in smuggling between Somalis and Home Affairs. He asked for fifteen hundred rand. I said it was too much. I could give him one thousand. He took out his notebook. He wrote down my name and age. I gave him one thousand and my asylum seeker's permit number."

Asad waited all day at AbdiNoor's place, and the smuggler returned in the evening with refugee papers for Asad. It was as simple as that; Home Affairs worked very well if you greased the right palms.

The very next day, he took his new papers to the Home Affairs office and applied for a refugee identity document. He was given a receipt and told to return in three months. He did: he stood once again in that queue, and when he got to the front the official told him that his receipt meant nothing and that there was no record of him ever having applied for a refugee document. He applied again and put the second receipt in his wallet.

He returned home troubled. It is true that Sterkstroom was treating him and Kaafi well. Business was good; shortly after Foosiya arrived, the Somalis opened a second shop, this one in the RDP settlement on the hill, and it was making almost as much money as the first. And the people of Sterkstroom had accepted them and were kind.

But the idea that he was stuck in this country, that he could not show his identity document at the border and walk out, made him immensely uncomfortable.

"You didn't plan to stay for long?" I ask.

"No. I wanted to work hard and to save and then to move on."

"Move on to where?"

He sighs deeply. "How do I answer that question? I didn't have an exact plan. I was always on the lookout for peace. Not necessarily Europe or America. I wanted to travel, I just wasn't sure where to."

Foosiya went into labor in the afternoon of July 28, 2005. Asad was at the shop in the RDP settlement when he heard the news. He worked until shortly after seven o'clock that evening, closed the shop, and went to the hospital in the town of Molteno, a twenty-minute drive from Sterkstroom.

He arrived to find the nursing staff in the maternity section ruffled and indignant.

"You need to speak to your wife," one of them said to him sharply.

When she had been admitted, a nurse had invited Foosiya to lie down. She had refused.

"In Somalia," he explains, "when a woman is giving birth she stands and holds on to something. Here they say: Lie down and stay there. But she couldn't do that; nobody has given birth like that in Somalia. You couldn't."

"We cannot deliver the baby if the mother is standing on her feet," a nurse had reportedly told Foosiya. "How do you expect us to get down there? Stop being silly now."

She had smiled benignly at Foosiya and laid her hand gently on her shoulder. Foosiya had ducked from it as if a snake had just dropped onto her. The nurse stared at her openmouthed. Then she stormed Foosiya, gripping her shoulders with her hands. Foosiya had fought back.

"I saw the nurse who had fought with Foosiya," Asad says. "She was little. Foosiya is a fierce woman. She is very strong."

Asad went to talk to his wife. "'Listen,' I said. 'We are in a foreign country. They have their own training. They do not know how to help you unless you are lying down.'"

"Fuck that," Foosiya said in English.

Asad stared at her in amazement. To his knowledge, these were the first two English words to pass her lips. Where did she learn them?

Asad was then told to leave. He does not know whether Foosiya gave birth standing or lying down. When he asked her some months later, she stared at him a long time and, by way of reply, invited him to give birth to their next child.

In any event, Foosiya was in labor all night. Their son, Khalid, was born the next morning. That afternoon, they went home.


When I ask Asad about his first experiences of fatherhood, he says that he has no words to explain.

"My excitement was too deep, brother. It was beyond words. It was beyond me. It was something very big."

Here and now, during the time of our daily interviews, I am watching him father a subsequent infant, this one a girl. And so I take what I am seeing and transport it to Sterkstroom in August 2005.

Asad and his daughter are in love. When I follow him into his shack, after we have spent hours sitting in my car, he takes the little one from whoever has been holding her, cradles her head in the crook of his arm, and finds her eyes with his own. They stare at each other without blinking, as if each is daring the other to look away first. Asad is usually the one to blink. As he does so, he bursts into laughter. His attention is locked on her face, his absorption uncompromising. As I look upon this, I think of the way he is in my car, a piece of him always detached and watching the street for signs of trouble.

I tell him all of this. I tell him that I am watching how he is with his daughter now because it is helping me to imagine how he was with Khalid then. He looks at me and grins. My words have triggered a memory.

It was a cold August, and he had wrapped Khalid in two thick blankets. He was carrying his son down the street when he ran into his landlady and two of her friends. The old Xhosa ladies were delighted. They huddled around Asad and poked fingers at the little one and gave Asad all sorts of advice. He thanked them and walked on. He does not believe that he has ever been happier than at that moment.

# *Pickup*

In January 2005, while Foosiya was still pregnant, Kaafi went to Port Elizabeth in a taxi and returned two days later in a single-cab Nissan Courier pickup truck. He stumbled out of the driver's seat in a state of high anxiety. He had just driven across Eastern Cape without a driver's license, he said. He never wanted to do that again.

Asad laughed at his cousin. He knew many Somalis who drove cars, but few who had a license. If the police stopped you, you paid up.

"Some police are even friendly about it," Asad tells me. "They say, 'You people pay fuck-all taxes on your businesses. Now is your time. Do it with a smile.'"

That is not how Kaafi saw it, Asad recalls. He was terrified of South African law enforcement, terrified that he would end up in jail where South Africa's famous prison gangsters would tear his limbs from his body. He had bought the pickup because it was good for business; they were spending far too much for the use of other people's vehicles. But he did not want to drive it again until he had a license.

It strikes me that this is the most substantial portrait of Kaafi that Asad has painted. They lived under the same roof day in and day out. They ran a business together, shared every meal, watched their respective children grow. It is like this with all the men with whom Asad lodged—with Yusuf in Dire Dawa and Nairobi, with Osman in Kirkwood. Only rarely does a man come to life in his recollections, and it is usually an older man, a father figure, a person who scoops Asad from the floor and cares for him: like Rooda and Uncle Abdicuur.

It would take some time until Kaafi would be able either to buy a license or to test for one. And while Asad could drive well, and had in fact for several months driven all around the Port Elizabeth area without a license, Kaafi refused to countenance the idea of him behind the wheel of the pickup. And so they looked around Sterkstroom for a driver.

It did not take long. Few young men in the township had gainful employment, and many could drive. In the end, the person they found was a neighbor. His name was Madoda, which means "old man," his nickname Elvis. He was a son of one of Sterkstroom's old families, which encouraged the Somalis. That they had now stopped paying for the use of three of their neighbors' cars made them a little apprehensive, and they were pleased to be putting money in the pockets of another old family.

Asad liked Madoda. He describes him as "an open person."

"He was very serious," Asad recalls. "He was not a light person. He was not the sort of person to make you laugh. But he felt things strongly. If he thought you were angry with him, he would really feel it. It would upset him deep inside. He would try to make you happy."

Madoda had an old car that stood forever outside his house. He seemed always to be just short of enough money to have it repaired. Sometimes it stood on blocks, covered in a tarpaulin. And then, out of the blue, the cover would come off, and Madoda would spend an afternoon working under its hood, and by evening the engine would be running. But never for long.

That Madoda had a car but not the means to run it seemed to the Somalis an emblem of the village itself: cars that used to work but now stood idle; a shop that was once open for business but was left rotting; roofs once solid and weatherproof now leaking like fishnets.

In the privacy of their foreign language, the Somalis would talk to one another about their neighbors. They were Bantu. Bantu had once been slaves. They had lost their pride many generations ago and had yet to recover it. A man stands forlornly staring at his old car, and instead of starting a business to earn money to fix it, he laments over it.

They had to remind themselves that Madoda was forty years old, that he had a wife and children. From the way he lived his life he seemed a mere youth.

"They were waiting for someone to come and help them," Asad tells me. "That was their attitude toward their new democracy. Now that they have voted, somebody must come and save them. Nobody has ever saved a Somali. From hundreds of years ago, when we were nomads, life was very tough, and either we fought or we died."

The Somalis' relation to the people around them was Janus-faced. They appreciated the kindness of the old people and took delight in discovering another layer of old family ties. But they had genuine contempt for their neighbors; watching them sit helplessly in their poverty brought to mind a child crawling on the floor.

"We think of black people as teenagers," Asad tells me bluntly. "Their democracy is so new and precious to them, but it confuses them. When it does not bring them what they want, they start to get violent."

A month or two into his employment as a driver, Madoda asked Kaafi for a loan in order to repair his car. The Somali said no; he did not believe that Madoda was in a position to service debt. Madoda was furious. He stormed out of the shop and was more than an hour late the next day for an urgent trip to Queenstown. For the following week, he sulked, his usual openness gone, his face down. He would not meet Kaafi's eyes.

The Somali took pity on him. Now that he had a car of his own, he wanted to learn how to service it. Why not practice on Madoda's car? He called upon a local mechanic, and the two men stood over the hood while Madoda watched from a distance. The mechanic explained what was needed and why, and Kaafi stood next to him, utterly absorbed, imbibing, for the first time, the logic of what made a car move. The two men went together to Queenstown and bought parts and spent a day restoring the car. Madoda seemed embarrassed. He mumbled a word of thanks and disappeared into his house.

A month or two later, Kaafi acquired a driver's license, and Madoda's services were no longer needed. He was not happy to be dismissed; once again, he bowed his head and went silent and refused to meet Kaafi's eyes. But he had known from the start that the work was temporary. And besides, he had gained more than a meager wage; he now had a working car.

The ban on Asad driving Kaafi's pickup began to slacken. The need for an urgent trip would arise when Kaafi was busy. Asad could drive, after all, and there was a business to run.

Asad remembers well his first trip alone to Queenstown. It was spring. He rolled down the window and felt the breeze on his face. He was simply going to buy airtime and a few other items of stock—clients were incensed when the Somalis ran out of airtime—and he would be back among his people in a couple of hours. But the time alone was quite lovely.

Somalis from all over the region converged on one Queenstown wholesaler. They did not go to Metro Cash & Carry, the most well known in the country. Nor did they patronize another famous chain called Browns. Instead, to the last Somali shop owner in a fifty-kilometer radius, they all patronized a business called Big Daddy's.

"Why there?" I ask Asad.

"Because the manager respected us. Metro Cash & Carry was not rude to us, but they were not on our side. If you fight with a local trader—say, for example, there is a long queue and people get upset with each other—the security at Big Daddy's will help the Somali. They know it is the Somali who is vulnerable. You feel safer there.

"I do not remember the real name of the manager at Big Daddy's. We called him Gamagab, which means 'short arm.' He was stocky with very thick, short forearms. We really liked him. And we found out later that he was Jewish. We liked that, too. Isaac and Ishmael were both sons of Abraham. Jews and Muslims are brothers."

"Was Big Daddy's cheaper than the others?" I ask.

"Sometimes, sometimes not. But once Gamagab knew that Somalis would always come back to him, he was kind to us. If we were short, he would loan us money on low credit. If we bought a lot of something, he would lower the price a little."

I smile at this story. Across the country's townships, South Africans tell tales of Somalis conspiring to buy in bulk. They may look like lone entrepreneurs, it is said, but they are in fact organized into quiet networks that secretly bargain with the big wholesalers. A Somali can thus walk into a wholesaler and get the same cheap price as a large supermarket chain. South African businessmen don't stand a chance.

I smile because, in Asad's account, Somalis converge on one wholesaler primarily from a sense of fear. They go to the one who will protect them from South Africans.


When Khalid's first birthday came around on July 29, 2006, Foosiya was five months pregnant with a second child. Her asylum-seeker papers were also on the brink of expiration. Asad phoned around the district and discovered that an AliYusuf man who lived not far from Queenstown and had a pickup of his own was also planning to take his wife to the Home Affairs office in Port Elizabeth. He offered Asad and Foosiya a lift.

The four set out for Port Elizabeth in the early afternoon. They spent the night at a lodge in the city and woke at three o'clock the following morning to stand in the queue outside Home Affairs.

By midday, their business was done. They were eating lunch at a Somali restaurant when Asad took a call from an AliYusuf man named Mohamed who lived in the Queenstown area. He asked Asad about Kaafi's condition.

"Kaafi's condition?" Asad asked.

"Are you not in Sterkstroom?" Mohamed asked.

"I am in Port Elizabeth."

"Kaafi was stabbed this morning in his shop. They took him to the clinic in Sterkstroom, but his injuries were much too serious for the clinic. He is in the hospital in Queenstown."

Ten minutes later, Asad and the man who had driven him to Port Elizabeth were back on the road. They had left their respective wives at the lodge where they had just eaten.

Over the next three hours, Asad made thirty, perhaps forty, phone calls. Each was to relatives sitting in the waiting room at the hospital in Queenstown.

Kaafi had been stabbed many times, they said. His injuries were very severe. It was not certain that the hospital in Queenstown was equipped to treat him. There was talk of emergency surgery that could only be done in East London. But the hospital staff was also saying that it was dangerous for him to travel as far as East London. It would be better if he stabilized first. They were deciding where the greater risk lay: in moving him or in not moving him.

Asad put his phone in his lap and stared at the road ahead. It was impossible that another Abdullahi might die. Impossible because unthinkable. The murder of another Abdullahi would be catastrophic beyond description. Remaining in this country would be intolerable. And yet leaving now was intolerable, too. He narrowed his focus. He thought only of whether Kaafi was to stay in Queenstown or move to East London. He calculated the quickest way to East London should they get news that Kaafi was being moved. He did not allow his mind to wander any further.

He kept phoning. He kept looking at the route ahead of them. It was still possible to veer off the road to Queenstown and head for East London. The news at the other end of the phone was to shape their journey. He hung up and stared at his phone and could not stand its silence. He phoned again. And then again. And then again.

They were less than an hour from Queenstown when he received the news that Kaafi had left by ambulance for East London. His condition had improved enough for him to travel, the family was told. They were expecting him at the hospital in East London. They were preparing to receive him.

Asad and his driving companion turned around and headed in the opposite direction. They had missed a turnoff to East London some time back. It would take them the better part of an hour to get there.

Asad's phone rang. It was the first time since he left Port Elizabeth that they were phoning him, rather than he them. The person at the other end was in a car driving behind the ambulance that had taken Kaafi from the hospital. Not far out of Queenstown, the ambulance had stopped. It had remained stationary on the side of the road for five or ten minutes. Then it had turned around and headed back to Queenstown. Kaafi had died on the road. Kaafi was dead.

# Kaafi

By the time Asad returned home that evening, the whole of Sterkstroom knew what had happened.

When Asad and Kaafi came to town and rented the old Mangaliso Store, they saw at once that the site of their new shop was far too small. Their first and most urgent renovation was to increase their floor space by four or five times. What had been the original shop was now a cage of mesh and bars in which the cashier locked himself. That is how it was with all Somali shops in South Africa. Asad had never known any different.

After Kaafi was rushed to the clinic, his Koran was found lying on the floor outside the cage between the ten-kilogram bags of maize meal and the fridge. It appears to have been a quiet morning. The shop empty, Kaafi had left the cage and had sat on a chair to read his Koran.

Madoda had walked in accompanied by two other men. One was Aubrey; he was a regular customer; the Somalis knew him well. Like Madoda, he was a member of one of Sterkstroom's old, large families. The other was a man called Mike. The three had probably come to buy cigarettes or airtime. They were regular customers. Kaafi had no reason to think that he was in danger. He was probably going to finish the passage he was reading before wandering back to the cage to serve them.

As for the three men, they walked in and saw the cage door standing wide open. One of them must have nudged the others and pointed. Kaafi read while his customers plotted.

The door to the shop usually stood open. Now, Mike closed it behind him and stood outside. Two women came to shop.

"The man is praying," Mike had told them. "Come back later."

.    .    .

A few minutes after the three men left the shop, a customer found Kaafi lying in a pool of blood. She ran to his house and shouted for Kaafi's wife. What happened next is legendary among Asad's branch of the AliYusuf clan. Aside from Asad himself, I heard the story from a relative of his I met in London, a man who had never met Kaafi and had lost track of Asad. But he knew about the fate of his unknown relative's corpse.

Kaafi's wife was nursing a young child when she heard the shouts. Still carrying her child, she ran to the shop. When she saw her husband lying on the floor, she put the child down and cradled Kaafi's head in her hands. She looked up to find her baby daughter crawling through a pool of her father's blood, her clothes and her hands stained red.


Kaafi was taken to the clinic at Sterkstroom on the backseat of a car, his head still cradled in his wife's lap. When the party of Somalis got to the clinic, they found Madoda slumped on a chair. As Kaafi's unconscious body was carried through the front door, Madoda sat up and stared at it, then slumped in his chair again. Kaafi's wife asked him what he was doing there. He mumbled something in Xhosa she did not understand. Then he put his head in his hands and wept.


Aubrey and Madoda were arrested that afternoon. Aubrey had not bothered to change the shirt he had worn when he killed Kaafi. It was speckled with blood. Mike was gone; Asad never saw him again.


I twice ask Asad about the aftermath of Kaafi's murder. He goes very quiet. He takes a long time to reply to a question. His answers are brief.

And so, what I know of Asad's experiences of this time takes the form of a series of short reports. The first is Foosiya's immediate response to the murder. When she returned from Port Elizabeth the following day, she told Asad that they must leave South Africa at once. They must take their Khalid and the unborn child in her womb and go to live with her family in Somaliland. They could no longer live here.

She will calm down in the next few days, Asad thought. She is in no condition to make decisions. Once she has taken a step back, she will change her mind.

Asad sold one of the two shops he and Kaafi had opened. With the proceeds, he bought Kaafi's wife and children plane tickets to Nairobi. He took them to Johannesburg and ushered them into the airport. There would be AliYusuf people waiting for them on the other side. He has not had contact with them since.

Only a handful of South Africans ever spoke to Asad or Foosiya about Kaafi's death. They would do so discreetly, in lowered tones, when nobody else was in earshot. As for Asad's landlady and her friends, they did not offer to do Foosiya's hair anymore. They still bought from the shop. They greeted, thanked, and that was all. The same with the many members of Madoda's and Aubrey's families. They came to the shop to buy as usual, but they did not stay to chat.


Asad's accounts of the next two months are no more than a series of vignettes. I have had trouble trying to order them chronologically and have supplemented what he has said with my own visit to Sterkstroom's police station and to the regional court in Grahamstown. I think that things happened like this:

Madoda was released. All charges against him had been dropped. Asad went to the police station to talk to the investigating officer about what had happened. On his third trip, he was received by a thin, wiry man, his countenance nakedly impatient. Neither suspect would talk, he said, and there were no witnesses. Aubrey was still inside because of the blood on his shirt, but Madoda had no blood on him; there was no clear evidence against him. But against Aubrey they surely had a good case. His shirt had been taken to the DNA lab in Pretoria, as had a sample of Kaafi's blood. If the two matched, the case would be easy. It was simply a question of awaiting the results.

A rumor coursed through the township: Asad was going to kill Madoda. That is what Somalis did, it was said. If you killed a member of their family, they would come and kill you in revenge. It was written in Somali law.

When the rumor reached Madoda, he took fright and went to the police station. He reported that Asad and three Somalis he did not know had come to his house in a white car. The car just stood there outside the house. The people inside did not get out. He believed that they had come to kill him.

Later that day, Asad received a visit from three uniformed police officers. They emerged from their car with Madoda in tow.

"When I saw Madoda with the cops I got very angry," Asad recalls. "Here was the man who killed Kaafi. He was not only free, but he was being escorted by the police.

"The cops were very aggressive. They pointed their fingers at me: 'You went to his house? You want to kill him?'

"I got very upset. I got very angry. I could feel I was not in control. I began to shout there in the street at the top of my voice. 'He is the one who killed my brother! Even if he was fired, he had no reason to kill Kaafi!'

"It all came out, brother.

"'When Kaafi was taken to the clinic, Madoda was already there, waiting.'

"The police tried to shut me up: 'This is our investigation. Do not tell us how to do our work.'

"I kept shouting: 'The clinic is far away, in the white town. Why did he go all that way? And why was he crying in the clinic?'

"While I was saying this to the police, Madoda began to shake all over and to cry.

"The police said, 'Look how frightened you have made this man. We cannot allow you to intimidate somebody like this.'"

Asad was issued with a restraining order. He was not permitted to walk on the street where Madoda lived, nor the next street; he had to give Madoda's home a two-block berth. And were he to see Madoda on the streets, he must remain outside a ten-meter radius of Madoda. Were he to break the conditions of this order, he would be arrested. Conspiracy to commit murder was a very serious charge, he was told. It would be best for him to obey the restraining order.

Foosiya had watched the altercation between Asad and the police. She had looked on when the restraining order was read to him.

"We cannot stay here," she said. "By the time my baby is born I will be with my family in Somaliland. With or without you."

Much of what Asad heard during the following weeks came to him in the form of rumor: South Africans discreetly whispering something in his ear; a phone call from a Somali who had heard something from someone.

Among these rumors was news of a hearing for Aubrey in Grahamstown. Asad did not know whether this was a bail application or a trial or an inquiry. He phoned the investigating officer, the man who had assured him that the DNA on Aubrey's shirt would match Kaafi's. He now said that the DNA lab was taking much longer than expected but that, yes, Aubrey was going to appear in court in Grahamstown. Asad asked whether it was not a problem that the DNA evidence might not be done in time for the hearing. The detective told Asad not to worry, that everything was running smoothly, and that he would phone Asad a few days before the hearing so that Asad could attend.

When he went to Big Daddy's in Queenstown, the Somalis he met there advised him to stay away from the hearing.

"They were all telling me that if I went to court Aubrey's family would recognize me and kill me," Asad recalls. "They kept warning me: Aubrey was from an old, old Sterkstroom family. His cousin was the elected representative of the township. The pastor of the township church was also a relative of his. They were saying, 'Asad, this town belongs to these people. If you fight, you will get hurt.'"

The investigating officer did not inform Asad about the hearing. One evening, Asad heard that it had been held that morning and that Aubrey was back in the township. Whether he was out on bail or had in fact been found not guilty, Asad did not know. He heard conflicting stories about this. He phoned the investigating officer and left messages on his voice mail. He received no reply.

The following morning, at about eleven o'clock, pretty much the time when Kaafi had died, Aubrey walked into Asad's shop and asked for a single cigarette.

"I said nothing," Asad recalls. "I did nothing. I just stood there. He put his money down on the table. I just remained still.

"'Asad,' he said. 'There is nothing you can do. I have been here since my birth in 1984. You came only yesterday.'"

By the time Aubrey left his shop, Asad had resolved to leave Sterkstroom. To wake every morning and know that your brother's killer may breeze into your shop, may put his hands on your merchandise and his money on your counter, as if he were a stranger, as if he had never done anything to you—to be treated like that was to be treated like a goat. One slaughters a beast and then throws feed to his brother. One does not do that to a human being.

That very afternoon, he put word out that he was selling his shop. He would leave the moment he was offered a reasonable price. The question was where to go. It was November now. Kaafi had been killed in early August. He had thought that Foosiya's desire to return to her home would diminish with time. It had not.

"If we stay, they will kill you," he recalls her saying. "If we stay, Khalid will one day crawl around in your blood while I cup your head in my hands. I am not staying for that."

Asad pleaded. The whole of South Africa was not dangerous, he said. It was a big country. Parts were both safe and lucrative.

"You want to run from the dangerous place to the safe place," he recalls her saying. "The people do not want us here, Asad. One day, the country will decide that it has had enough of us. And then there will be no safe place. Wherever we go, the people will want to kill us."

Asad remembers growing angry. "You have just arrived in this country," he shouted. "And already you think you are an expert. There are Somalis who have been here since 1995. They are still alive. They are rich. And they are safe."

"Things change, Asad," she shot back. "Nineteen ninety-five is not 2006. Things change."

From deep in his bones, he resisted the prospect of going to Somaliland. For one, he did not know how an Ogadeni man would be received there. In the late 1980s, during the final years of Siad Barre's rule, when Somaliland was still part of Somalia, terrible things had been done to the Isaaq people up north. He was Daarood and was thus associated with the old regime. And he was Ogadeni; the Isaaq had a long and complicated history with his kind. He would be on foreign turf. He would not have a place there.

But more than that, returning to the Horn of Africa would signal a defeat of the deepest kind.

"I knew life there," he tells me. "I knew that if I went back there life would be the same, the same, the same, until I die. To be able to wake up in the morning one must know that one day life can be different. To stay in South Africa is to keep that possibility of something different alive. Maybe if I applied again I could get a refugee card. Then I could travel.

It is easy to get an invitation to visit Europe. You have an invitation, you can get a visa. You get a visa, you can go and never come back."

He looks at me carefully to see that I have understood.

"You are only on this earth a few years," he says. "How long? Sixty years? Maybe eighty years? For many of those years you are a child. For many of those years you are an old person. The years in between: it is a small time, really; it goes fast. If you do not make something then, you have lost your opportunity. You die without having lived."

He sold the shop to a Somali man who owned a string of businesses in Eastern Cape. He got seventy thousand rand; it was a good price. And why should he not get a good price? His was still the only shop in the black township next to Sterkstroom. There was a lot of money to be made. And the new owner would employ a shopkeeper to run it; if someone were again slaughtered it would only be a hired hand.

Aside from the seventy thousand rand, Asad had saved a fair amount of money during his time in Sterkstroom. He and Kaafi had done well. He was flush.

On an afternoon in mid-November, Asad, Khalid, and a heavily pregnant Foosiya left Sterkstroom for Port Elizabeth. Early the following morning, they queued outside Home Affairs. When they finally got to the front of the queue, they asked for "go-home" papers for Foosiya and Khalid.

"Why do you want go-home papers?" they were asked. "Your country is very dangerous. You cannot go there."

"Here is dangerous," Asad replied.

Foosiya's and Khalid's applications were refused.

Asad made some calls. Among others, he phoned AbdiNoor, the man who had once been so efficient at getting the papers Asad needed from Home Affairs. He was told that one could not buy go-home papers, but there was a way to acquire them without buying them. He was given a phone number and an address for a refugee-support organization in Johannesburg. These people knew how to get go-home papers, he was told.

They left Port Elizabeth that very afternoon on an intercity bus. In the morning, they checked into a lodge in Mayfair, washed, changed, and headed for the offices of the organization they had been advised to visit.

"They ask Foosiya why she wants to go home," Asad tells me. "Foosiya says, 'My grandmother died. I must go for the funeral.' They write a letter. We go to the Home Affairs office in Johannesburg and show them the letter. She is given permission. Khalid is given permission. There is nothing to stop them now.

"From there on, brother, it happens quickly. I find a flight to Nairobi. I buy two tickets. She phones some Isaaq people in Islii. They will meet her. They will make arrangements for her to travel from there to Hargeisa and from Hargeisa to her father's home. From the time we got to Johannesburg to the time she left, it was just a few days.

"When we said good-bye, we said it was not for forever. We would find a way. We would be together in a place that could make us both happy.

"I parked at the airport and walked inside with them. All the time, I was holding Khalid. I stood with them in the queue to check in. I was still holding Khalid. Then it was time for them to walk where I could not walk. I handed Khalid to Foosiya, and I turned around."

She called him the following morning. She was in Eastleigh. She was safe. Arrangements had been made. She was going home. She would phone again once she had given birth. She would tell Asad whether it was a boy or a girl.

He put down the phone. He was once again a young man in a travelers' lodge in an African city.

He never did find out whether the hearing in Grahamstown was just for bail or a trial proper. He does not know whether Aubrey was ever punished for his crime.


That very afternoon, he got to work. He had a lot of money from the sale of his business. He would not invest in another South African venture. He would use what he had to get to Europe or to America. He had to move fast. Every day in South Africa his savings would diminish. By the end of the year, he wanted to be gone.

There were several options. The first was to go again to Home Affairs to get a refugee card. With a refugee card, he could get a refugee passport. With a refugee passport, he could travel. He knew of a dozen people who had gotten to Europe this way.

He went to the same Home Affairs office that had granted Foosiya her go-home papers. He was told, once again, that there was no record of his ever having applied for a refugee card, and that he would have to do so yet again.

He did not have time to wait. He turned his mind to a second option: the United States.

"You pay a smuggler a lot of money to get you a good passport," he tells me. "You fly to São Paulo. Next, you must get through Venezuela and Ecuador, en route to Mexico. We had heard that it is not difficult. They give you transit visas. They do not care whether your passport is fake. They know you are on your way elsewhere and they do not care.

"But next is Mexico. For that, you need a visa. You need an illegal transporter to get you into Mexico.

"I had heard of people who had done it. A cousin of mine had done it from Nairobi. I also heard of two others who had done it successfully. They all flew to Brazil; they walked across the border into America. They were arrested there.

"Brother, in America, they do not deport you to Somalia because Somalia is at war. They do not deport you back to Mexico because Mexico does not want you; you were not there legally in the first place. So they lock you away for a long time. One person I heard of spent two years in the cells. Another was in the cells three and a quarter years. Another for only one year.

"While you are in prison, they are finding out who you really are: Are you militia? Have you received military training? Have you been involved in terrorist activity? When they are happy that you are truly a refugee, they give you documentation. You leave prison. You go and live in America.

"Brother, my plan was to spend twenty-four months in jail. Then I would bring my wife and children."

"Would Foosiya have followed you?" I ask.

"Who knows? Maybe she would have married someone else in the meantime."

In Mayfair, he got the cell-phone numbers of three smugglers.

"I phone the first one. He asks me where I am. I say Mayfair.

"*'Ai,'* he says. 'I am in Pretoria. I will call you when I have time to come to Johannesburg.'

"But he doesn't call. Finally, after I have phoned him three, four times, he says, 'We meet tonight at eight p.m. at a restaurant called Al Jazeera in Mayfair.'

"We meet. We drink tea. He says he must pay eight thousand rand to the man who brings the fake South African passport. This man will also put a history of visas into the passport; an unused passport is suspicious. Another eight thousand rand go to the officials at the airport who must be bribed. Then another eight thousand for the ticket to São Paulo. Plus another twenty thousand for the smuggler himself. Altogether, it is forty-four thousand. I must pay the whole thing up front.

"I tell him I will think about it.

"The second smuggler I phone offers to meet me immediately. He was too rushed. I did not trust him. He wanted thirty thousand rand up front for everything. It was too simple. He said everything was guaranteed. Nothing could go wrong. I did not like it. I walked away.

"The third smuggler was always too busy to see me. I waited two weeks. Finally, he picks me up, takes me to where he lives in Mayfair, tells me the options available: 'UK, nonstop flight. But probably they will send you back when you get to Heathrow.'

"America: he can get me as far as Brazil. No guarantee after that. He says, 'In Brazil, maybe they can catch you and bring you back. Who knows?'

"As for the price: twenty thousand rand, which you pay up front. It gets you the passport and the ticket and the instructions about what to do at the airport. Another twenty thousand for the smuggler. But you only pay once you are safely in Brazil. If you do not get there, the smuggler forfeits his fee.

"I go with this one. I trust him. He is talking straight. I pay him twenty thousand rand. The other twenty thousand I give to an Ogadeni man called Ahmed, a shopkeeper. He is trustworthy. I give him the money in front of the smuggler. I know that if I do not make it, Ahmed will keep the money for me. Or he will use it to get me out of whatever trouble I am in.

"The smuggler comes back with a passport. It has a few visas, visa stamps. He gives me an air ticket. I do not remember for how long I waited for this. A week, maybe? I am not sure.

"I begin spending time with the other people he is smuggling. There are fourteen of us. Eight will go in one shift. The following night, I will go with five others. We agree that all fourteen of us will join together again in Brazil. For once we are in Brazil, we are on our own. It will be difficult there, we know. We are vulnerable. We can be robbed. We can be arrested. Even small things are bothering us. We will have to change our South African rand. Where do you do that in Brazil? Do they take South African rand? And what if I am robbed at the airport? I will have thirty thousand rand in cash with me. That is the money I will need to get from Brazil to America. What if I lose it all on day one and I am in Brazil with no money? We are all asking ourselves this question. We must stick together in São Paulo.

"A couple of days before it is time to leave, the smuggler tells us what is going to happen. On the day of our departure, he will tell us what time we must be at the airport. He will hire us a taxi. While we wait for the taxi, he will speak on the phone to a manager at the airport. He is the one who is being bribed. He will tell the smuggler at the last minute: 'Your people must go to check-in counter number forty-seven.' The smuggler puts you in the taxi. You never see him again.

"The first batch, the eight, left the night before us. They said they would turn off their phones when they got to the airport. If the phones remained off, they have flown. One guy said to me, 'If we do not get through, you are the first person I will phone.'

"I got a missed call from him at eleven thirty. I thought this meant that he had passed through. We got another call at twelve thirty, this one from the smuggler. 'They are in the cells.'

"Actually, six of them were in the cells. Two hid in the toilets. They locked themselves in. They only came out at midday the next day. They had seen the people in front of them being arrested. They had turned and walked.

"The smuggler met with us the next day. People were very angry with him. They were shouting at him. They wanted their money back. I was not one of the people shouting. The smuggler had told us from the start that we were gambling. He had told us that he could not control everything. That is why I went with him. He was honest.

"He tried to talk nicely to the other people. 'We wait,' he said. 'We try again. But it will take time.'"

# PART IV

# Cape Town

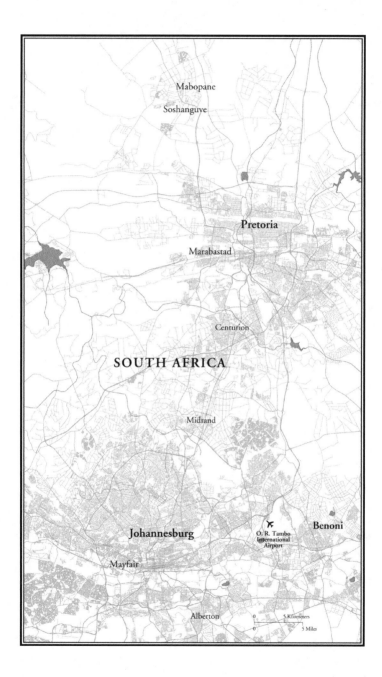

# Abris

At first, Asad did not understand that he had aborted his American plans. He thought that he was simply marking time.

"When the smuggler told us that we must be patient, that he would reconnect the line, I thought, Okay, that's fine. But I cannot eat my money while I wait."

He had blown twenty thousand rand on his attempt to get to America, but he still had fifty thousand change from the sale of his Sterkstroom business.

For twenty-eight thousand rand he bought a pickup truck and spread word that he could deliver stock to *spaza* shops throughout the province of Gauteng.

"My thinking was: I buy the car. I use it to make money. When it is time to go to America, I sell the car and get the twenty-eight thousand back."

The way he remembers it now, his new business was successful from the start. Mayfair is a hub connecting every Somali throughout the north of the country; from there, it does not take much time for word to spread. And within an hour's drive, there were literally hundreds of Somali shop owners without their own transport.

His phone started ringing the day after he took possession of the pickup. Within a week, he was declining work. The rent at his lodge in Mayfair was six hundred rand a month. He calculated that if business remained good he would be making that in ten days; the rest of each month's takings would be profit. In his daily prayers, he found himself both thanking and berating his God. "You make things so easy for me now," he muttered. "While my family was still here, nothing was possible."

He understood now that Somalis in South Africa lived in two zones. There was Mayfair in Johannesburg, Marabastad in Pretoria, the town center of Uitenhage: each of the country's urban centers had a Somali space. These pockets of the world were safe. There would be no guns pointed at one's head here, no worrying about the private thoughts of one's neighbors.

But unless one was already rich or well connected or lucky enough to find a good job, living in these spaces kept one poor. To make money one had to venture into the townships or the shacklands or to rural hamlets like Sterkstroom and take one's chances among black South Africans. With hard work, their money would find its way to your pockets. But in exchange for your riches, you lived in fear. Anyone could kill you, not just strangers who come with gun in hand, but also your neighbor, the quiet man whose car you took the trouble to repair. He, too, could come and slaughter you, and the people you thought you had come to know would look away.

Asad was reaping the benefits of both worlds. He bedded down each night in the security of Mayfair. But he was also making a little money. Yes, he spent his days outside the Somali bubble, driving from *spaza* shop to wholesale store. But the very fact that he was on the move kept him safe. He would come to a shop, help carry the stock from his pickup into the store, and then leave. There were no Madodas in his life now. No sitting behind cash registers worrying about the money above one's knees. No listening to the noise of the corrugated-iron roof in the night.

He slept well in Mayfair. South Africa was not going to take his life. Less than a month after she left, Foosiya sent word that she had given birth to a son. There were now three people in the world who made him what he was: a father and a husband.

Several of Asad's new customers owned shops in the townships around Pretoria—Mabopane, Soshanguve, Mamelodi, Atteridgeville. Once or twice a week, when his last delivery of the day was in one of these places, he would drive to the Somali section of Marabastad, Pretoria's equivalent of Mayfair, and spend the night in a Somali lodge.

That is where he met an AliYusuf store owner called AbdiKadir.

Abdi was a man of ritual. When the sun set each day, he would turn his store in Mabopane over to his shopkeeper, drive to Marabastad, and eat his dinner in the Somali restaurant across the street from the Home Affairs office. Asad would take his dinner in the same restaurant. It did not take long before the two AliYusuf men were eating together.

On the third or fourth evening of their acquaintance, Abdi tossed a proposal into Asad's lap. His business was thriving, Abdi said, but he had no car, and the costs of hiring transport irked him. If Asad were to bring his car into the business, Abdi said, he would get 50 percent equity in return.

Owning another shop had not figured in Asad's plans. He was happy with his mobile life. And he had it in his mind that one day soon he would up and leave. A car could be sold in a day. Half of a business was another story.

It was too tempting an offer to turn down flat. He chewed on it for a day or two and tried to absorb what it might mean to put down roots again. He told himself that he would put aside time to go and see Abdi's business. But he was always busy, and work did not take him to Mabopane; the idea soon drifted from his mind.

Two or three weeks later, his cell phone rang, and it was Abdi, asking if Asad had thought about the offer. Asad was in a Pretoria township when he took the call, less than half an hour away. He hung up and drove straight to Mabopane.

Abdi was a man of easy laughter and light spirit; his rapport with his customers seemed comfortable. His shop was ordered, his stock clearly tailored to a customer base he knew well. There seemed to be a serenity about the place.

Asad visited two or three more times before offering Abdi a proposition of his own.

"I told him I liked the deal," Asad recalls, "but that I did not want ever to sleep in the shop. I did not want ever to spend more than an hour or two in the shop. He said fine, but I must be reasonable. If there are times when there is nobody available to manage the shop, I must help out."

In January 2007, the two men went into business. Asad moved his base from Mayfair to a lodge in Marabastad. He was happy there; it was a small version of Mayfair, a pure Somali world. When one slept, one could close the eyes in the back of one's head.

The shop was even more successful than Asad had calculated. By the end of March, his share of the profit was more than twenty thousand rand. The business partners hired a young man to drive Asad's pickup, and Asad used his profits to buy a sedan and start a taxi business, ferrying Somalis between Pretoria and Johannesburg. He charged some 15 percent less than the minibus taxis that traded on the same route and took grim pleasure in the fact that, whatever business he entered, undercutting South Africans' prices was easy.

What were his thoughts about Foosiya and his children at this time? I frame it as a question because I'm not sure that he is able truly to reinhabit this moment in his life. Given all that has happened since, too much is at stake.

The first time I ask, he tells me that for each second of each day he was thinking of Foosiya and the children and of the future. But when I ask him again several weeks later, his answer is different.

"I forgot the other thing," he says.

"What other thing?"

"I forgot the plan to go to Brazil and kept working."

Months later, when I remind him of his words, he shows a flash of impatience.

"I was thinking of the future every fucking day," he snaps.

In the moment of his rebuke, I feel duly chastised. I sit with pen in hand, looking out over the Blikkiesdorp street, and avoid his eyes. Who on earth am I to second-guess a man's feelings about the woman and children he has just lost? How can I presume to see that far into a person's inner world?

But in the afternoon, sitting alone in my office, the heat of that moment now cooled, I know that it is himself he is rebuking, not me. I have brought to the surface a feeling of discomfort with which it isn't easy to live.

He had more than enough money to head north. He could have rejoined Foosiya anytime. And if the idea of living among the Isaaq in Somaliland was unbearable, he might have twisted her arm into settling elsewhere in East Africa, perhaps in Addis again.

I drew his ire, I think, because I had asked what it was he wanted, and the answer lay beyond any words he might wish to utter. He desired more than anything to be a husband and a father, but not in the world he knew. He would have to burst through a wall and into another world. Only there, on the other side, could he build a family. His planned trip to São Paulo had failed. He did not know how else to burst through that wall. Perhaps if he began making money again, another way would come.

. . .

Soon after he bought into the Mabopane business, Foosiya phoned him with an ultimatum.

"I left South Africa on November 18, 2006," she said, her voice icily formal. "If you have not joined me by November 18, 2007, we will be divorced and I will look for another man and he will be father to my children."

It was February 2007. He had nine months. He resolved that he would be with Foosiya by then. Whether he believed his resolution, neither of us knows.

He spent more time at the shop in Mabopane than he would have liked. It is hard to judge what is going to happen in a business day by day. A family member of Abdi's falls ill, and he must take her to the hospital, and the shop ought not stand empty. Or the shopkeeper they have hired part-time has urgent business in Johannesburg. There were always reasons for Asad to be called.

He soon became familiar with some of the regulars. As in Sterkstroom, and in Kirkwood before that, he took comfort in old people. He enjoyed their slowness, their evenness of temper. They smiled with their eyes, not just their mouths. They took time to greet.

Two people in particular warmed his heart. One was a woman called Evelyn. When he looks back now, he recalls that she was not especially old—fifty, perhaps—but at the time he thought of her as a woman of seventy. She was alone and she was poor; perhaps that is what made him think of her as a pensioner. There were days when she lingered at the storefront without buying, and Asad knew that she had no money. He would slip her a loaf of bread and make sure not to make eye contact, saving her the shame of acknowledging his charity.

Then there was an old man named Bra Sam. He was positively ancient, in his late eighties at least. From Asad's place behind the counter, he had a clear line of vision to Bra Sam's front door, some fifty yards down the street. He would watch the old man's progress from home to shop, his stick stretched out before him like an antenna, feeling the gravel surface for the stone or ditch that might trip him. Upon his arrival, Bra Sam's eyes would flash with triumph. He, too, would get a free loaf of bread, Asad's acknowledgment of the feat of the journey.

In the feelings he harbored for these old people, I wonder whether he was not searching for a bond, one strong enough to keep him in South Africa. Way below consciousness, I suspect he knew that he was to stay a long while.

On the afternoon of April 21, 2007, Asad and his driver went to Pretoria to buy stock. They returned to Mabopane in the twilight and parked at the rear of the shop. Asad lifted a box from the back of the pickup, walked into the shop, and greeted Abdi.

From outside the back door, he heard a scream. It was not the scream of somebody who had dropped a heavy load on his foot or stepped into a ditch and sprained his ankle. It was a yawning, existential scream. Yindy came instantly to his mind—the terrible sounds she emitted when she was shot in the leg under the shade of her *balbalo.* He put the box down and made for the door.

The moment Asad appeared in the doorway, one of the three men surrounding Asad's driver lifted his gun, pointed it at Asad, and fired. Above his head, the wooden doorframe shattered, and a shower of splinters hit the back of his neck. As he turned to take cover inside, he heard another shot. His sweater tugged against him, as if some fleeting demon had tried briefly to tear it off. Later, when it was all over, he would find a neat round bullet hole in his sweater's hood.

A single thought filled his mind: he must save his precious pickup; he must hide the keys. To his irritation, he could not recall where he had put them down.

"The keys!" he shouted to Abdi once he was back in the shop.

"What?"

"Where are they?"

"What keys?"

Out of the corner of his eye, he saw them. They were lying in plain sight, on a table behind the counter. Where to put them? He could throw them in the dustbin, but that was so obvious a place. He stood there frozen—at the time it seemed for some minutes, but it could only have been for a second or two—staring over the counter into the faces of the customers in front of the shop. They stared back at him, their faces quite inscrutable. Did they understand what was happening? Why did they not run away? He dropped the keys onto the floor and kicked them under the counter, the sounds of the robbers' footfalls in his ears.

The three men were in the shop now, and the one who had shot at Asad told him to turn around and put his hands in the air. The moment he did so, he heard the thud of a pistol butt against the back of his head. He felt curiously distant from the part of him that had just been attacked, as if it were the tabletop or the wall that had come in for a beating.

"I told you to lie on your stomach."

Asad dropped to his knees, then stretched himself flat against the bags of mealie-meal that lay on the floor. Soon, he was joined by the driver, Abdi, and the shopkeeper, whom the robbers had dragged from the toilet.

"Brother, the four of us were lying there side by side on the bags of mealie-meal," Asad tells me. "And our customers were standing in front of the shop watching. I could hear them talking quietly to each other. The robbers picked up the shopkeeper, took him to the other side of the shop, and asked him where the money was. He said there was no money here, aside from what was in the till. They hit him very badly, brother. They hit him in the face with a bottle. Then they kicked his teeth out. I was lying facedown. I could not see. But I could hear. The sound of a person's face breaking, brother. It is something I do not know how to describe.

"They left the shopkeeper on the floor. He was quiet. He must have been unconscious. They came back to us. They wanted to know where the money was, where the safe was. They checked our pockets.

"One of them grabbed my sweater and turned me around onto my back. He kept shouting, 'Don't look at me, Somali! Don't look at my face!'

"He asked me for the key to the pickup. I said I didn't know. He picked up a bottle and raised it above his head.

"Brother, here in the Western Cape, bottles are plastic. Up in Gauteng, they are glass. Thick glass. I used my arm to protect my face. I heard a crack. I knew that my arm was broken. I did not need an X-ray to know."

Asad found his assailant's eyes. It was an instinctive thing to do. A man has just smashed your arm as if you are a carcass. You show him your humanity; you do not even know you are doing it.

"The second our eyes met," Asad says, "he grew very, very angry.

"'What the fuck did I tell you? I fucking told you not to look! Turn around! Turn the fuck around!'

"He dragged me by my feet away from the mealie-meal bags onto the cold floor. Then he started hitting me on the back of the head with his feet. My head bounced off the floor and he hit it again. Hit, up, hit, up, hit, up, like my head was a ball. I felt dizzy. I started losing my vision.

"But, brother, the thing I must share with you from that time is my mood. I felt no fear. Even as my head was being bashed in, the thought that I might die did not come to me. I was worried about the pickup."

From outside the storefront, he heard a voice. It was Evelyn's. Unmistakably. It was scratched and gnarled, as if her throat had dried out many years ago, and the words had to scrape their way out.

"Look under the counter," she said in Pedi. "He kicked them under the counter."

Asad heard footsteps and then the jangle of keys. And with that, the mood in the shop changed. The voices of the robbers grew light, almost cheerful.

"One of them went to the front of the shop and addressed the customers.

"'Does anyone want anything?' he asked.

"He told them to come around the back. Then he opened the door for them.

"The four of us lay facedown on the floor listening to our customers walk around our bodies. They were helping themselves to bags of mealie-meal, to frozen chickens, to airtime. Some of them took cartons of cigarettes."

The robbers left. Asad heard his pickup's engine rev. The Somalis lay silently on the floor. Then Asad staggered to his feet and stumbled through the back door.

"Where are you going?" Abdi asked.

"To save my pickup," Asad replied.

It was as if he had cracked a whip. Abdi and the driver jumped to their feet and followed Asad, and the three men sprinted through the darkening streets. They had not even checked to see if their shopkeeper was still alive.

They found the pickup abandoned three blocks away.

"If you start the car with the alarm on," Asad explains, "the engine cuts out in a few minutes. And the button to disarm it is in a place you would not think to look; it is right above the driver's head."

An hour or so later the police arrived. The Somalis were taken to the station, where they made statements, and then the police took them to the hospital. The shopkeeper was badly hurt; his jaw was broken, and one of his cheekbones was cracked. He was missing several teeth.

As for Asad, his arm was X-rayed and set in plaster, as he had expected. But it was his right eye that bothered him most. It had throbbed throughout his police interview, and when he closed his left eye he realized that the injured one was almost blind. He raised his hand to touch it and felt a thick, rubbery swelling. He pressed gently against it to feel if it was as soft and liquid as it felt; a spear of pain shot deep into the inside of his head.

"Something there was broken," Asad says, "something around my eye. As the evening went on I felt it closing. By the time I woke up the next morning, it was closed shut like it had been stuck with glue. I went to the mirror. I did not recognize myself, brother."


The following morning, Abdi and Asad opened the shop for business at about nine o'clock, some two hours later than usual. Asad stood at the counter and, with his good eye, looked out onto the street. Bra Sam's door opened, and the old man stepped unsteadily out of his home. Asad looked at his watch. A couple of weeks earlier, he had started to time the old man's journey to the shop. Now it had become a habit. While he waited, a young woman came to buy milk. Two men who were strolling past stopped and bought loose cigarettes. Each time another person stepped up to the counter, Asad went cold. He could not recall seeing any of them during the robbery. But each surely knew what had happened. Why did they not say something? Why did they not comment on the state of Asad's eye? Why could they not at least say that they were sorry that the people from whom they bought food every day had been hurt?

He imagined the days ahead. He imagined life just going on as if yesterday's events had never happened. He could not stand the thought. The robbery would soon be swallowed up by the passage of time. Would he require a permanent injury to remind himself that it had happened at all?

At about ten o'clock, Evelyn appeared. With downcast eyes, she asked for half a liter of milk and half a loaf of bread. The end of a crumpled ten-rand note spilled out of her closed fist.

Asad stared at her in disbelief. He was frozen. He could not move.

Evelyn looked up at him quizzically and asked again for milk and bread. He examined her a moment longer, then turned to fetch her purchases.

He placed the bread and milk carefully on the counter.

"You are *abris*," he said softly.

"What is that?" she asked. "Why are you talking to me in your language?"

"*Abris* is a kind of snake," Asad replied. As he spoke, he heard the pitch of his voice rise. He struggled to contain it. He did not want to lose his cool. "Most snakes have a head and a tail. They can bite from only one side. An *abris* has two mouths, one in the head, the other in the tail. It bites when you think there is no danger."

As he spoke, he watched her indignation form at the sides of her mouth and climb into her eyes. She began shouting at him in a stream of Pedi that he did not understand.

"Brother," Asad recalls, "she wanted to fight me. There and then on the streets of Mabopane, she wanted the two of us to fight each other with our fists."

Asad left the shop in disgust. With his good arm and his good eye, he drove himself to the hospital in Pretoria and asked to see an ophthalmologist. After waiting two or three hours he was seen by an elderly man who appeared incapable of communication. He gave Asad two injections but could not say what they were for. He also gave Asad tablets to take home with him but did not explain what they might do.

When Asad woke the following morning, the puss around his eye had crusted. He ran a finger over the space where his eye had once been, and it felt like cracked, grainy earth. He found the name and number of an ophthalmologist in Mayfair and got his driver to take him to Johannesburg.

On the journey, Evelyn's image infested his thoughts. The more he tried to shake her free, the more tenaciously she clung. He hated her as much as he had hated anyone. As much as he had hated Yindy's father when the old man decided to leave him in Wardheer.

His eye throbbed. He kept touching the swollen ball above it. It felt enormous, as if it were protruding several feet from his face, as if his arm would soon be too short to reach the end of it. The idea of Evelyn and the pain in his eye swirled together and became inseparable. It seemed that Evelyn herself was the pain; she had taken residence in the side of his face and was beating him with her fists from the inside.

In what had happened the previous morning there was a darkness more insidious than anything he had experienced; more insidious, even, than the aftermath of Kaafi's murder. As grim as it was, one could understand that Madoda's people wanted to protect him. In their treachery there was something to which Asad could relate.

But this was something else. To watch the Somalis being tortured and then walk over them and steal their stock; to arrive the following morning and behave as if yesterday had not happened. He felt a surge of hatred. For Evelyn, for Bra Sam, for every single South African with a black skin. They were something less than human. He did not know much of the history of southern Africa, but he guessed that for generation upon generation, their ancestors had been slaves. Their masters had beaten them into a new shape, a subhuman shape. They had become submissive, treacherous slave-beings, beings without self-worth, without honor. And then the whites had come and made them slaves again. Now they had been freed, but such beings could not handle freedom.

The ophthalmologist in Mayfair told him that there was nothing wrong with the eye itself. It would get better once the wound above it healed. He injected an anti-inflammatory into the area above the eye and gave Asad a cream and some tablets to take home. He also wanted payment up front. When Asad saw the bill he swallowed hard. This robbery was going to cost him, he thought to himself. In the following days and weeks and months, he would keep paying for this robbery.

On the highway back to Pretoria, he found that his hands were shaking. At first, he was not sure why. He tilted his neck, pushed his head back into the seat, and listened to the sound of his breathing. Once it came to him, it was obvious. He was shaking because he was on his way back to Mabopane. He did not want ever to see that shop again. It was an evil place. Going back there would make him ill.

That afternoon he told Abdi that he could not work in the shop anymore. Abdi said nothing, but his eyes pleaded.

"I felt very sorry for him," Asad tells me. "His savings were all in the shop. His life was in the shop. He felt he had to keep going. I was leaving him to face Mabopane alone.

"I told him honestly, 'I can't stay. Those people can turn against you anytime. If one is your friend, they are all your friend. If one is your enemy, they are all your enemy. If I stay I will die.'"

Abdi struggled on alone for a while. Asad busied himself with his taxi business, ferrying people between Pretoria and Johannesburg. He did not set foot in Mabopane or in any other township. He lived his life in Marabastad, in Mayfair, and on the highway in between.

Within a couple of weeks, Abdi lost heart. He and Asad sold the shop, together with the pickup, for eighty thousand rand. Asad sold the car he had been using as a taxi for sixteen thousand. The income from the taxi alone was not sufficient to sustain him; he would have to look for something new.

The man to whom he sold the car didn't have nearly enough money to buy it. But he was married with children and had no shop of his own and desperately needed to earn money. Asad took six thousand rand from him and deferred the remainder of the payment.

He went back to Mayfair and looked for work.

"I wanted to drive a truck. I went to the big Somali businessmen, the ones who live in very nice houses and have chains of shops and buy in bulk. If I could drive a truck, I would never have to go to a township again. You pick up your load, you take it to Mayfair, to Marabastad, to the Somali places in Cape Town, in Durban. You are a hundred percent safe.

"But it was difficult. You need a code-fourteen license to drive a truck, and you can't get one without a South African ID. I thought that maybe one of the big Somalis would give me a job anyway. But they said it was not worth their while for their drivers to keep getting caught by the police.

"I went back to Pretoria. Nobody would employ me to drive a truck if I did not have a license. So I packed my bags and went to Cape Town."

"Why Cape Town?" I ask.

"If you are stuck in one city, you move to another," he replies.

"Yes, but why Cape Town?"

He shifts in his seat. "We had heard rumors about Cape Town," he says.

I wait for him to continue, but he remains silent.

"What rumors?"

He says it rapidly, as if to get it over with as soon as possible. "Cape Town was run by white people. Therefore it was safe."

I write down what he has said in my notebook, my face quite solemn. Then I look at him and laugh. He turns his head from me, rests his chin on his elbow, and stares out into the Blikkiesdorp street.

# The Month of May

He took a bus to Cape Town. It was June 2007. In the contacts file on his SIM card was the cell-phone number of a man called Jbene and the word "Bellville." Jbene and Asad had played pool together in Uitenhage three years before, when Asad had first come to South Africa. They had been in touch ever since.

He took a taxi from the Cape Town railway station to Bellville Town Centre, where Jbene was waiting for him. The following morning, they hired a Somali driver to take them on a long, circular drive through the townships that fanned from the southeastern periphery of the city, an introduction for Asad.

As he took in the scenes, his heart became lead. It was a new city, to be sure: some of the faces were much lighter, the houses stubbier and flatter. The spaces seemed more open. On the sides of the streets there was beach sand. But these differences were skin deep. The underlying structure was the same.

Cape Town had two Mayfairs: Bellville Town Centre and Mitchells Plain Town Centre. These places were thick with Somalis and with commerce. There were travelers' lodges and supermarkets and cell-phone shops and shops selling contraband designer clothing. In the residential flats above the commercial areas, Somali faces stared out of the windows.

Around these oases stretched mile upon mile of township. Just like in Johannesburg, in Pretoria, in Port Elizabeth. He recalled that first bus journey from Johannesburg to his uncle Abdicuur in Uitenhage. He remembered staring out of the window as the bus passed one town after

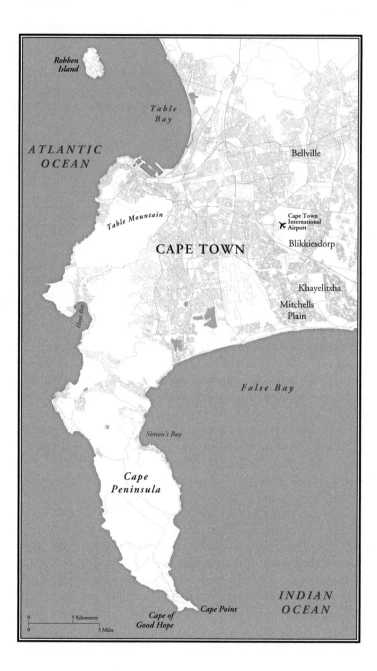

Robben
Island

Table
Bay

ATLANTIC
OCEAN

Table Mountain

CAPE TOWN

Bellville

Cape Town
International
Airport

Blikkiesdorp

Khayelitsha

Mitchells
Plain

Hout Bay

False Bay

Simon's Bay

Cape
Peninsula

Cape Point

INDIAN
OCEAN

Cape of
Good Hope

0          5 Kilometers
0                    5 Miles

another. How peculiar they seemed at the time: each town divided into an outer and an inner world, the outer consisting of rows of identical houses, the inner full of old trees and church steeples and history. Now this geography seemed his prison. He was an able-bodied man; his two feet could carry him wherever he commanded. And yet all paths led to the outer world, to the township, where he was going to die.

Again, he plowed his energy into the quest to drive a truck. As in Johannesburg, he hit a brick wall. Without a South African identity document, he could not get a code-14 license. And without the right license, nobody would employ him to drive a truck.

He returned each night to Jbene's home in Bellville and unloaded his frustration on his friend.

"Jbene told me I was wasting my time and my money," Asad recalls. "He said it was obvious: in this country you had to make business, and to make business you must go to the township. I told him I would die in the township. I could feel it in my bones. He said Allah had decided long ago when I was going to die. It was not for a bunch of South Africans to decide. But I knew he was wrong. If I went to live there again, I would die there."

"You have also said that Allah wrote your future while you were in the womb," I say.

"I know," he replies. "I have thought about that a lot. It is a difficult question."

He looks at me closely. "Why do you ask that question?"

He does not wait for me to reply. "Look at it this way," he says. "If you want to have a child, you cannot say, 'I don't need to do anything; Allah has willed that I will have a child.' You need to have sex to have a child.

"If you want to make money, you cannot say, 'I can sit back; Allah has already decided how much money I will make.' You need to go out and make business.

"So it is the same with deciding to go to live in a township. Because of that decision, you may get paralyzed or burned alive or killed."

But as his third week in Cape Town came and went, and the prospect of driving a truck remained as remote as ever, he realized that he was once again walking the road to the township. He was living off his savings, and that was intolerable. He had to invest, and there was nowhere to do so but in the place he most feared.

"You might have left altogether," I say. "You could have headed north. You could have gone to Addis again."

He says nothing; he merely sighs. As if what I have said is a barbed comment tossed from a gallery of spectators.

"I forgot to leave South Africa," he says finally, his voice tinged with sarcasm.


In the end, he chose the biggest township of all, Khayelitsha. A settlement of more than a million people, some twenty-five kilometers from the center of Cape Town, it was a place of Xhosa-speaking migrants. Almost everyone over the age of fifteen had been born in Eastern Cape and had come to Cape Town to look for work. From the first day, Asad found himself looking for women with nine and a half fingers. Most young people from Sterkstroom went to Cape Town at one time or another. Many ended up in Khayelitsha. It was as if there were a foul-smelling creature inside him searching for the very worst of the past.

He had a new business partner, yet another AliYusuf man. His name was Hassan.

They were both old hands, Asad and Hassan, and they went about establishing a shop with methodical precision. They walked the streets of Khayelitsha, day in and day out, looking for an empty shack, a vacant prefabricated hut, or a stand on which they might construct a building themselves. Once they found something promising, they examined the surrounds. It had to be on a thoroughfare people used to get to or from work. Just a street or two away, and there would not be enough passing trade. Then they would look for the nearest Somali *spaza* shop. Did it feed off the same commuters somewhere upstream? Or did it service other people on their way to other places?

On their third day, they found an empty shack on Mew Way, one of the two arteries linking Khayelitsha to the N2 motorway. Thousands of people streamed past this point every day. The nearest Somali shop was five blocks away, far enough. They knocked on neighboring doors and asked who owned the property. Within an hour, they were negotiating with the owner, a well-off, middle-aged Xhosa man keen to do business.

The following day, they spoke to the neighbors once more, this time asking for people in the construction business. By the end of the week, they had entered into an agreement with local builders who demolished the shack and erected a prefabricated wooden structure tailored to the Somalis' needs. It was small. The two men would share a two-by-three-meter bedroom at the back.

Slowly, they began to gather stock. With their first two days' proceeds they bought more stock and then more. Business was steady on bad days, brisk on good days. Within a month, they had a full-fledged *spaza* shop. Asad was back in business.

I ask him what he thought of the people of Khayelitsha, and his answers are careful and judicious.

"Different people had different attitudes," he says. "Some made friends with us. They looked us in the eye, and when they smiled at us you could see that they were smiling with their hearts. But most people were saying, 'You are Somali, you don't belong. You are *makwerekwere*. You are making money in our country. We will kill you.'

"Some of the people who said these things were our customers. They bought bread from us, they bought cigarettes from us. And they said they were going to kill us. I got used to it. Maybe it is because we were making good money. Maybe it is that we prayed five times a day. Five times is a lot, brother. You turn your back on these people, and you face your God. It fills you. It makes you strong.

"But then something happens and suddenly you realize you are not okay. One day, my colleague arrived at the shop with stock. The door was open. Two guys wanted to help unload. We said no. We knew, if they just touch our stuff, they will want a lot of money. Whether it is a man, a woman, or a child, they must not touch our stuff. It will cause a problem. We said: We don't want your help.

"One of them went to pick up our box. I pushed him. He said, 'Why are you pushing me?' He took a gun from his waistband. I ran behind a car. He shot at me twice. Some taxi drivers were standing in front of the shop. They shouted, 'Hey, put your gun away, for fuck's sake, this is a public road, there are people walking past.'

"These two young guys just walked away. Slowly. Taking their time. Down the street.

"When you lie in bed on the night after something like that has happened you start to think: I could have been dead. One of those bullets could have hit me and killed me, and those boys would still have just walked down the street. Maybe they would have been arrested. But they would not be in jail for long. No witness would come forward. The case would die.

"So you lie in bed and you think: This is crazy; I can't live like this. But the next morning you open your shop and everything is normal and the money is coming in. You forget."

Now, he says, when he looks back he sees such obvious signs.

"Like what?" I ask.

"There were some schoolgirls who'd come to us every day asking for sweets. They were little: maybe six years old, seven years old. They would hold out their hands and say, 'Sweets. Sweets. Sweets.' We would say: 'Tomorrow.' What we meant was that every day was tomorrow.

"Once, I think maybe it was in March or April 2008, I said to a little girl, 'Tomorrow.' And she said, 'Tomorrow *uzohamba* [you will be leaving].' She knew what the adults had been talking about. She knew what they wanted to do."

On a Sunday evening in the early winter of 2008, an old man stumbled up to the counter and asked for a loose cigarette. His breath reeked of brandy, and his eyes were shot with blood. He had clearly been drinking all weekend.

"Somali," he said as Asad passed him his cigarette. "Have you seen what they are doing to your brothers in Alexandra?"

"What are they doing to my brothers?"

"They are slaughtering them, Somali. There is *makwerekwere* blood flowing on the streets."

Asad watched the old man stagger back into the street and wondered whether what he had offered was a drunken hallucination or a rumor he had picked up from a drinking partner. But the words stayed with him. He made a mental note to watch the seven o'clock news.

It was the first item. A mob in Alexandra, a densely populated township of several hundred thousand people in Johannesburg, had marauded through the streets chasing foreigners from their homes. Many hundreds of shacks had been looted. Many hundreds more had been burned to the ground. It was believed that thousands of foreign nationals had fled their homes.

The news did not surprise Asad. But it also shocked him to his core. These were precisely the scenes he kept sweeping from his mind. Such sweeping was the daily labor that made life in South Africa possible. A tremor worked its way through his body, a faint echo of the convulsions that had gripped him on the night of Uncle Abdicuur's murder. It was as if a thin facsimile of that time had returned.

He did not know anybody who lived in Alexandra. He felt pity for these souls who had lost their homes. And then he went to sleep.

Over the following two days, what had happened in Alexandra settled into the recesses of his skull and began tapping away, softly, as if a tiny sponge-headed hammer was at work in his head. Occasionally, customers would mention it, an ominous excitement in their voices. He asked Hassan if he knew anyone who lived in Alexandra. He did not.

Two nights later, there was another news story. The violence had spread. There had been incidents around the Jeppe Hostel in central Johannesburg and in one or two townships on the East Rand. More people had fled their homes.

"Now, the seven o'clock news was a daily terror," Asad tells me. "All of the next day, it would sit in our minds: What are we going to find out at seven o'clock?

"Each night, the news was worse. The violence was spreading, spreading, spreading. They were calling it 'the xenophobic violence.' We watched, brother. There is this place on the East Rand in Johannesburg called Ramaphosa. In Ramaphosa, a Mozambican man burned. They put a tire around his head and burned him to death.

"We phoned people in Mayfair. They said Mayfair is safe. The blacks will not dare to come there. But the townships. All the Somalis in the townships. We need to do something for them. People in Mayfair were spending the whole day on the phone talking to people in their tribes who were living out there. People were making space in their homes. 'Pack up your stock,' they'd say. 'Leave behind what will not fit into your car. Your stock will be useless to you if you are dead.'

"The next thing we knew, it was spreading beyond Johannesburg. It was in Durban. It was somewhere in Mpumalanga we had never heard of. Some were saying it was in Knysna. We were taking out our maps, brother. We were marking with an *X* where it was happening. We were praying to our God that the *X*s do not drop too far south.

"Every night, now, we are closing the shop at seven to watch the news. The leaders of the country are being interviewed. We are listening to them carefully. What are they going to do to stop it?

"Then one night the premier of the Western Cape, Ebrahim Rasool, was on the television. He had just met with a lot of foreign nationals, mainly with Somalis. He and the provincial police commissioner made a press conference after their meeting. They said it was not going to happen here. They guaranteed it. From the way they were speaking, I believed them. It gave me confidence.

"The moment the news was over, my phone started ringing. Hassan's phone started ringing. As soon as we put down our phones, they would ring again. By nine o'clock every Somali in the Western Cape had joined the debate. Can we believe the South African politicians? I and others said that the mayor and the police would stop it, the premier would stop it. Those who opposed us said no, it is unstoppable.

"The day after the meeting with the premier, the police came.

" 'Close the shop,' they said.

"I asked why.

" 'Because the people are going to attack you.'

"I said, 'At the meeting yesterday, the premier promised it will not happen.'

" 'This is exactly what we are doing to stop it from happening,' the policeman said.

"I closed the shop. The police left. I opened it again. I phoned other Somalis. 'What are you doing? Opening or closing?' Others phoned to ask me. That time was the time of the cell phone, brother. Every Somali had his phone to his ear listening to other Somalis predict the future.

"On the seven o'clock news that night, we saw that it was happening in Dunoon. Dunoon is a shack settlement just outside Cape Town, brother. Now my position changed: I realized that nobody could stop this.

"It was early evening. The streets were full of people. It seemed that they were talking louder than usual, moving faster than usual. I thought maybe people were staring at us more than they usually do. But I thought maybe it was just my fear making me see these things. I closed the shop. I start phoning other Somalis. At seven thirty, I got a phone call: 'It has started in Khayelitsha, at Makhaza.' I get on the phone to the Somali who owns the shop just a little farther down Mew Way: 'What should we do?' "

"At eight p.m., a group formed outside our shop, singing, shouting, throwing stones.

" '*Makwere*, you are leaving. *Hamba!*'

"Hassan and I locked the shop. We double bolted the door. We could not see well, but from the voices it sounded like everyone was there: young, old, men, women. These were just people on their way home. They would form a little group and shout for a while and throw stones. Then they would go on their way. Then another group came and shouted as it passed. Then another.

"I phoned the police many times, starting from when they began to throw stones. No response. Holding, holding, holding. Finally, someone answers. 'What is your name? Your cell-phone number?' You hold some more. They say, 'This is happening everywhere. We are busy.' I hear them talking to the patrol car while I hold the phone: 'A Somali is being attacked on Mew Way.' Answer: 'I can't help. I am busy with another Somali.'

"At nine thirty p.m. we heard thumping on our walls, on our door. We heard what we thought were people marching in the street. We tried to phone this Xhosa guy, a community representative. He was always asking us for free airtime and free chicken because he was representing the community. We phoned him.

" 'Hey, my friend,' he said. 'I can't do anything.'

" 'Just tell them not to kill us.'

"But he clearly could not stop this thing.

"I phoned the landlord.

" 'You must save our lives,' I said to him. 'The police won't come. The community representative won't come. You are all we have left.'

"He was silent. He did not know what to do.

"Things were now happening back to back. They arrived. They broke down the door. I put airtime in one sock, cash in the other. I tried to break a hole in the zinc in the back door with a panga. I thought maybe we could get out of the back and run away. We couldn't do it. They came quick. One minute the door was there, the next it was lying flat on the floor. I tried to run through the door. They held me. Hassan, too. The shop was full. A big crowd. Most of them were men, but some mamas, too. Children, also.

"They started beating me with their hands, with sticks.

" 'Where is the money? Where is the money? Where is the money?'

"Hassan had also put money and airtime in his socks. The coins were all in a bin outside. There was not a single cent anywhere in the shop.

"An old man started to speak. He said to the guy holding me, 'Let him go. Don't kill him.'

"The one holding me was carrying an iron pole. He hit me on the back, then let me go. I ran. Another person threw a stone. It hit me very hard on the back. Still, today, I feel it, when I turn sharply. I fell when the stone hit me. I got up. I kept running. After I'd crossed Mew Way, I turned and looked. I could not see Hassan. When I last saw him he had been sitting next to the fridge.

"I did not know what to do. I was trying to hide myself, but I was also trying to see what had happened to Hassan. I kept on walking back to the shop, then running away again.

"Ten minutes later, Hassan came out. His head was bleeding.

" 'Why did you take so long?' I asked.

" 'Because whenever I tried to get up and leave, they beat me. So I stayed still.'

"His cell phone had been stolen. Mine was still working. We phoned the nearest Somali neighbor. No reply. We went to his shop; it had been looted. We saw a police car driving down Mew Way and waved it down. They drove us to Mitchells Plain police station. They wanted our names, our phone numbers. They wanted us to make statements.

"I said, 'No statement. We are bleeding.'

"We walked across the road to Mitchells Plain Town Centre. Thousands of Somalis were there. There were pickups full of groceries people had saved from the looters. Every new person who arrived was questioned.

" 'What happened? Let us see your injuries.'

"Some were sleeping in their cars. Some were walking up and down. The first-comers got a place in the lodge.

"It was safe here. It was Mitchells Plain Town Centre, a Somali place. The only South Africans here were colored. It was Xhosas who attacked us.

"With the feeling of safety, brother, came anger. The ones walking up and down, they were shouting. They were shouting at the tops of their voices about the terrible things they were going to do to South Africans. They were going to get automatic weapons. They were going to walk into Khayelitsha shooting from the hip. I just looked at them, brother.

"I could not sleep. I sat. I walked around. In the morning, I went to the police. The station was full, full. White people were coming and asking, 'What do you want? You want to open a case? A safe place? Do you want a lift back to your shop?'

" 'A safe place,' I said.

" 'Go and sit over there. We will arrange it.'

"But none of the Somalis would sit. We wandered. We talked loudly. Nobody was doing as he was told. This happened for a long time, brother, until late afternoon—the Somalis walking around and shouting and not doing as they had been told. The white people kept saying, 'You want a safe place, sit here. You want to stay at the police station, sit here.' Nobody listened.

"Hassan and I got into a truck taking people to a safe place. They dropped us at a military base in Ottery called Youngsfield. The place was full. It was raining. It was full of water. There were few tents. Inside the tents, men were sitting. Outside, women were standing in the rain.

"There were many nationalities there: Somalis, Congolese, Ethiopians. The Somalis had a meeting. We must come out of the tents. The women and children must have shelter first. The meeting agreed to this and broke up, but nobody listened. The women remained outside in the rain. There was water on the ground. They had to stand. It was cold and raining. There were no blankets.

"Somalis were coming and going in cars. But once night fell, the authorities did not allow anyone to come or to leave. I spent the whole night sitting around a fire we had made. There were many Somalis waiting outside the gate. They stood the whole night in the rain.

"Early, early in the morning, before it was light, the Somalis started making trouble. Some wanted to go out of the camp because they were told that the ground was drier there. People were trying to jump the fence. Some were hungry and looking for food. Some were separated from their families and wanted to leave. Others, their wives were locked out, just on the other side of the fence. Some wanted to take baby food to their wives. As for me, I was fighting hunger. I had not eaten since Mitchells Plain.

"A Somali came to the gate with food. He said, 'Please give this to a woman called Ayaan. She is just in that tent there. I have just spoken to her on her cell phone.'

"A man took the food, but he did not give it to Ayaan; he shared it with his family. Us Somalis, we were fighting one another, we were fighting the authorities. We were fighting, fighting."

"On the second day after the attack, in the afternoon, we heard that they had opened a refugee camp for us. It was at a place called Soetwater. We heard that it was dry. It was near Kommetjie, on the sea, far away from any township. Pickups full of Somalis were going there. My own car, it was being fixed in a garage in Mitchells Plain. There was a problem with the gearbox. I was still with Hassan. We were making decisions together. We thought we should go to Soetwater. We arrived there in the late afternoon. It was a quiet place, far away. On either side was beach and bush.

"Each Somali who arrived was tagged around the wrist with a number. There was a book at the gate. They wrote down your name in that book. Next to your name, they wrote the number that was put around your wrist.

"By the time that was done, the sun was setting. We walked in and found that there were too few tents. Much too few. There was not enough space for people to sleep. But it was much, much better than Youngsfield because it was dry and people were making tea.

"There was no food, though; we had come too late. I was very hungry, brother. How long had it been since I had eaten? A day and a half by now, I think.

"The next morning, they started building tents. You needed to join a group to grab a tent, otherwise you would be left outside. If the group threw you out, you fought.

"I joined a group. We chose some people, threw others out."

"How did you choose?" I ask.

"You make a few quick judgments. First, will this person make trouble? Second, are they your tribe? My group was mainly Daarood, all sorts of Daarood. Just a minority of us were Ogadeni. There were some others, too, who were not Daarood. Like I say, we were making quick judgments. If this one looks calm, relaxed, if he looks like he will be useful, if you like the way he looks at you, even if he is not Daarood, you take him."

"How did you decide whether somebody was Daarood?" I asked.

"First, they are taller. Second, you tell by their accent. Third, they are lighter. Anyone who seemed maybe to be Hawiye, we said no. Anyone thinner, shorter, with softer hair, or darker, you said no."

"I slept very deeply that night, brother. It was the sort of sleep where you do not dream, and when you wake up you do not know for how long you have been sleeping. We walked out of the tent, and there were people giving out clothes and socks and blankets. There was food, also, but the queue was very long. Hassan and I decided to walk to Kommetjie, the village next to Soetwater, to buy food. We had stuffed a lot of money into our socks. Between us we had three thousand six hundred rand. We decided to pool it and use it to make business. The Somalis in that camp needed to talk to people, brother. They needed to know where their family was. We bought a lot of airtime in Kommetjie. And when we got back to Soetwater, we started selling it."

# *Carnival*

When the troubles began, I was in the middle of a two-year visit to New York. I went online each morning and watched the violence spread day by day, first from Alexandra into eastern Johannesburg, then across a radius of smaller towns, then into other provinces. When it reached the Western Cape I called a photographer I knew, and we bought ourselves an air ticket each and flew home.

Our plane touched down on the morning of May 23. By late afternoon, we were in a shack settlement on the eastern periphery of Johannesburg called Ramaphosa, where, six days earlier, a crowd had doused a tire with petrol, put it around the neck of a Mozambican man, and set him alight.

In a square that had once been lined with the vegetable stalls and *spaza* shops of foreign nationals, we found a tense scene—a dozen or so young men at one end of the square, a group of police in body armor at the other. From the clump of young men arose a string of curses and insults and, every now and then, a stone.

My photographer friend is a big, beefy man, six feet three inches at least, and without fear. He muscled his way into the circle of young men, literally pushing their scrawny frames out of his way. Once he had their attention, he barked out his questions.

"What are you feeling? Who are you angry with? What are your thoughts about the Mozambican man who was killed?"

They all began shouting at once, and he raised his arms over his head and called for quiet and suggested that they choose a spokesperson.

One of them began to speak. "They are gone now," he said. "South

Africans can breathe again. All these empty stalls"—he raised his hand above his head and swirled an invisible sketch of the square—"they will soon be filled with South African businessmen. Now, when our mothers buy their tomatoes and their spinach, the money they spend will stay in South Africa instead of leaking, leaking, leaking. The wealth of this country is leaking away across the border."

May 23 happened to be the very day on which Asad and Hassan fled their shop in Khayelitsha, some fourteen hundred kilometers from the ground on which we stood. Our discussion with the young men took place at about 5:00 p.m., I think, just when Asad boarded up his shop and began peering at the crowds through the cracks in the door.

I had returned from New York because the events unfolding were so obviously significant. It was as if South Africa had reeled back in time and was replaying a story long past, but a little differently now, the protagonists not quite the same. The last time people across the country had taken to the streets and burned tires and buildings and other human beings was in the mid-1980s during a two-year-long insurrection against apartheid. The crowds back then had sung freedom songs that spoke of heroes returning from exile with weapons and resolve and a taste for power. Now, more than two decades later, those old freedom songs were dusted off once more. But the words were different. Instead of condemning apartheid, they condemned foreigners for the jobs and houses and women they were stealing.

South Africa's middle class, and especially its white minority, watched the violence spread with grave unease. The image of an anarchic black crowd, unhinged and bent on destruction, is among the very oldest in white South African consciousness. When democracy came, and Nelson Mandela opened his arms and forgave, the worst white fear was that the moment of vengeance had merely been postponed.

And now, here these black crowds were, as if conjured by white fear, clearly unhappy with their lot since the dawning of democracy. But their anger was not aimed at white people, nor at the government they had voted into power, but at black African foreigners. Middle-class volunteers poured into the police stations and churches where foreign nationals had taken refuge, eager to help. They understood the victims as proxies of themselves; it was all too close to the bone.

From where did this xenophobia arise? After all, black Africans had been coming to South Africa for generations. Hundreds and thousands of Mozambicans worked underground in South Africa's gold mines during the course of the twentieth century. And countless others, from Zimba-bwe, Malawi, and Zambia, came illegally and worked without documents. They lived among black South Africans, largely at peace. Many of them learned to speak Zulu or Pedi, married local men and women, and bore South African children. Today, in Soweto, in Alexandra, in all of the country's large urban townships, born-and-bred South Africans walk the streets with their Malawian and Zambian surnames, testimony to a time when nationality counted for less.

Back then, the fact that everyone in the townships was black mattered a great deal. That some were not South African mattered less. These were times, after all, when millions of black South Africans had no right to walk the streets of their own cities and could be rounded up and expelled at any moment. South African, Zambian, Malawian—everyone was in the same boat.

Perversely, xenophobia is a product of citizenship, the claiming of a new birthright. Finally, we belong here, and that means that you do not.

Some say that the perversion runs deep, that black South Africans are reenacting the rules of the old apartheid state. Apartheid, after all, was an endless system of measuring and categorizing. All human beings had to be sorted into those who belonged in South Africa's cities and those who did not. Behind this frenetic sorting lay a persistent fear: that the cities were too full, too dangerous, that there were always people walking the streets who did not belong. Everyone must thus be measured and counted and put in his allotted place, for if all were to merge into an indistinguishable mass there would be no control.

This is precisely what the crowds of May 2008 were doing, some say. As they rampaged through South Africa's informal settlements, they were sorting, categorizing, differentiating. Those deemed not to belong were expelled. Apartheid thinking had finally reached its nadir, fourteen years after its demise. For now it was in the souls of black folk, and they were executing its logic with fervor.

There is truth in all of this, no doubt. But there is something else, something largely new. And that is Asad and his ilk.

White South Africans have wielded immense power. During the course of the twentieth century, they used black labor to build the edifice of a modern society. But they seldom encountered black South Africa unguarded. They have always protected themselves: behind walls; through a welter of laws; via a powerful and well-armed state; by building schools and churches and sports clubs and professions to which black people were not admitted.

With Asad and his kind—the thousands of lone entrepreneurs who have crossed South Africa's borders since the end of apartheid—it is different. They have walked naked into the settlements of the South African poor.

They come neither with weapons nor with the protections of citizenship. There may be a police force, but it does not bother to answer their calls. Nor do they come with pretenses or with artful stories. They do not want to make friends. They do not want to make South Africa their home. They want to make money.

And that is what they do. Night and day. Without rest. They leave their shops to defecate and to restock. Otherwise, they work.

They watch you closely. They learn never to run out of what you most want to buy. And they are always cheaper than their South African rivals. There is something magical, something insidious and relentless, about this moneymaking. Something less than human.

They can be killed, for the law is unlikely to catch the ones who murder them. And yet killing them does not take them away. The wife of the murdered one will simply sell to another. And if he is killed, his widow will sell to another yet. They are ineradicable. When one of them dies, they come from miles for the funeral, hundreds of them. They are grief-stricken. They are crying. They bury the dead one, and they cry some more. And then they come back.

Soon it seems that they are made to be hurt, that it is a part of who they are. Drawing their blood becomes a fashion. It starts because it is possible, and it keeps happening because nobody stops it.

During those weeks in May, the fashion became a carnival. One hundred thousand people were chased from their homes. When the last one had left, the crowds went home.

And then they started coming back, first the bravest, then the more cautious. They began selling again. People shook their hands and said sorry. And the game resumed.

# Sadicya

Soetwater looks out over the Atlantic Ocean. To the south, swaths of beach and scrubland stretch away for miles. It is a beautiful place.

When the rain stopped and the clouds dissolved, the sea appeared. It was a deep blue, and it was alive and full of force, and as he walked through Soetwater, Asad felt himself splitting in two. He was in a makeshift camp of the homeless, forging alliances and selling airtime—he was falling backward into his own past.

At first, his predominant feeling was regret.

"I wished that I could have gone back in time," he recalls. "I wished I had another chance to be in Ethiopia with Rooda. I was so close to my father. I kept asking myself: Why did I not look for him? Why did I forget myself? Why did I forget my family? It was as if my head was empty. Look at me now. I am in this terrible place because I lost myself."

Soetwater faces due west. On the first evening after the skies cleared, he watched the sun sink into the ocean. As he remembers it now, he had found a quiet spot, somewhere outside the camp, on the rocks. He was alone—or, in any event, he had sealed himself off from the people around him. The sun scattered its orange across the water, and as he watched he thought of Foosiya.

"I remembered her saying, 'If you stay in this country, there will come a time when there is no place to run.'"

She was a prophetess, he thought. Truly, she was. He marveled at her wisdom. From where did such insight come? Why did she see things so clearly? He had no idea. None at all. He could not even begin to imagine what it might mean to be wise.

Was his current fate not deserved? he wondered. Yindy had contempt for him, and her father had contempt for him, and he understood their feelings. A person who forgets his family has emptied himself of his worth. He is ripe for contempt. He is the sort who gets chased from his home by a mob, his cash in one sock, his airtime in another. A human being who loses himself will be kicked around.

On their seventh morning in Soetwater, Asad and Hassan caught a bus to Mitchells Plain.

"We had no problem going there," Asad tells me. "There are only coloreds in Mitchells Plain."

He went to the mechanic in whose care he had left his car, paid seven hundred rand for the repairs, and drove back to Soetwater.

"I started making business with my car, brother. People at Soetwater needed to travel. I start loading the people. I charged ten rand to go to Kommetjie, twenty rand to Fish Hoek, thirty rand to Mitchells Plain or Bellville."

In the evenings, in their tent of Daarood, Asad and Hassan spoke to people who had begun venturing back into Khayelitsha. They had encountered no hostility there, only apology and regret. They had returned to Soetwater in one piece.

Hassan suggested that they visit their shop. The very idea made Asad's limbs tingle. He was frightened, and not only at the prospect of what the people of Khayelitsha might do to him. He suspected, too, that walking on Mew Way would let loose dangerous feelings. That his thoughts were steering him at every moment back into his childhood disturbed him. It had never happened before, never with this bald insistence. Asad the man and Asad the boy were mingling, blurring. He knew that the violence of Khayelitsha had mixed this strange cocktail of adult and child, but he did not know why.

And yet as much as he feared Mew Way, he knew that he would go. He had to see. He had to know in what state the people of Khayelitsha had left his shop. It was of the utmost importance to him.

They took a taxi. It seemed safer than driving their own car; they could slip in and out anonymously, they thought.

To Asad's dismay, the taxi dropped them directly outside their landlord's house on Mew Way. He was not prepared for this. In his mind, he had it that the taxi would let them off several blocks away, that he and

Hassan would approach the site of their shop gradually, on foot. To be disgorged right here, at the scene of his flight, quickened his heart.

It was a weekday morning. There were few people about.

"The first ones who came to us were our landlord's wife and her friends," Asad recalls. "They said shame. They said sorry. One of them wanted to touch us. More people came. They also said how sorry they were. They shook their heads.

"We were polite. We greeted them. We smiled. We said thank you. From there, we went to pay our respects to the landlord. We greeted him. We shook his hand. We did not even raise any question of compensation.

"Then we went to our shop. Brother, I had not expected to see what I saw. On the way to Khayelitsha, I had thought maybe it was possible to go back, to start again. But now I stared at where our shop had been, and there was nothing. Only the cement floor remained. Brother, I did not think that they would destroy the walls."

He took the image of this burned-out nothingness back with him to Soetwater. He resolved never again to go to Khayelitsha. In that will to destroy, that will to see an empty space where once there had been a shop, was something too personal. He lay awake that night. To sleep would have been to court trouble.


At about the time that Asad and Hassan visited the site of their old shop, Somalis began returning to the places from which they had fled. People who had owned *spaza* shops in Dunoon went back to Dunoon. People who had had businesses in Khayelitsha went back. Their South African neighbors did not attack them. Their South African neighbors said they were sorry.

Hassan was among those advocating a return.

"He said that we must go back and rebuild," Asad recalls. "Our old neighbor in Khayelitsha was looking for a tenant. She had a structure she wanted to rent to a shopkeeper. She was a Xhosa woman.

"I did not agree. I said to Hassan, 'It is too risky; we survived once, we will not survive again.'

"'Everyone is going back,' he said. 'You take your luck.'

"Hassan left Soetwater and went back to Khayelitsha. He rented the neighbor's place, he rebuilt, he stocked. He called me many times and asked me to join him. I said no."

Asad sold his pickup for seventeen thousand rand. With that money he would chart a future. He was not sure yet what he wanted to do. He knew only that he did not want to return to Khayelitsha.

Besides, by the end of May there was something else keeping Asad at Soetwater.

Inside the campgrounds was a parking lot. In a lane between two rows of cars, a young woman sat on a short stool making tea over a gas flame. Each afternoon she was there, and each afternoon a small boy sat alongside her. The boy was very young, maybe three or four years old, and in his eyes was a vacancy that caught Asad's attention. Those eyes, Asad thought to himself, belong to a child who does not expect anyone to see him.

The third or fourth time he passed them, Asad felt a chill rise up the length of his spine. It struck him that this mother and child were dying. Not literally: they were not mortally ill. But in their future lay death. To be all alone here in this godforsaken camp trying to make a living selling tea was surely no way to survive. Women were being treated very badly here. Men were pouncing on single women and proposing marriage in order to get a dry place inside a tent. Most of these women had somebody to protect them, somebody to help them to say no. But a woman alone: she would be used, and she would be discarded.

"I asked myself: Why does she have nobody? She is not very pretty, it is true. But she is also not ugly. For her to be alone, there must be something wrong."

He began to buy tea from her. As he drank, he lingered. He asked her questions.

Her name was Sadicya, pronounced "Sadia." Her son's name was Musharaf. At first, she looked away when Asad spoke to her, and her replies to his questions were blown away by the wind. But he was insistent. He held her eyes and asked her to repeat her answers. She looked back into his eyes and spoke in a clearer voice.

When the violence came, she said, she and Musharaf had been living alone in Strand, a small town some fifty kilometers southeast of Cape Town. She made a living selling odds and ends at a table outside a supermarket. Hers was an isolated life, she told Asad. She avoided other people. She neither offered nor received news. And so the violence had flung itself upon her without warning. One moment, she was standing behind her table selling loose cigarettes and fruit and crisps. The next, a mob had descended upon her. It was only as she was fleeing, her son plastered to her back, that she understood the anger to be trained on her—she was running for her life.

As he listened, Asad remembered all the cell-phone calls he had made and received in the prelude to the violence. Being connected to other Somalis—listening, advising, predicting—was so much a part of his experience of what had happened. It would take a great labor of imagination to put himself in the shoes of this woman as she ran.

At some point during her flight, she told Asad, she had had to cross a storm-water drain. She lowered herself into it easily enough, the child still on her back. But when she tried to climb out the other side, she lost her footing. That is where the police found her and Musharaf, she said, in a pool of water at the floor of the drain, their clothes sodden.

"I asked her why she was alone, brother, and when she told me I felt a terrible sadness. I looked at her, and I saw myself as a child. I thought: We are the same. What is happening to her happened to me."

"What did she tell you?" I ask.

"The name of her tribe."

"Her tribe?"

"She is Nuuh Mahamud. But there is also a terrible name for them: Galgale."

At first, he wants to tell me the story of the Galgale. But before he has begun speaking, he has changed his mind.

"You are good at reading about the Somalis," he says. "Go and read about the people who are called Galgale."

He is flagging. Throughout our association, he has sat with me in my car and with unwavering diligence has trawled his memories. But in the last few days, things have begun to change. I am giving him draft chapters of the book, and he is reading them, and the reading has drawn unexpected feelings. It is one thing to fish for memories and present them to me in my car; he can anesthetize each recollection as he speaks it, and thus go on talking forever. But to see himself on the page, from a distance, to see this boy kicked through life like a stone: the reading strips him of his guard. He stands before his childhood stark naked, clutching blindly for something with which to cover himself.

Seeing his life in this way is breaking his heart, he reports. He is afraid to read further, lest the lost boy on the page creep inside him and install himself forever.

And so he will not tell me about the people called Galgale, and, in this refusal, he is signaling a more general shutting down.

I go and I read. I read through the night, in fact. When I next see Asad, I look at him anew.

Nobody knows for certain how many Somalis fall into the category of "Saab"; even if there were peace in Somalia, it is the sort of category that would be awkward to count. Long ago, in the 1970s, scholars settled on a proportion: fewer than 1 percent of Somalis were Saab, it was said, and that is the figure that has been quoted ever since.

The Saab are outcasts of a sort, for although they speak Somali and know of no other home but Somalia, and although they are physically indistinguishable from their countrymen and -women, they have no place in Somali genealogy. The six Somali clan families that compose the nation—Daarood, Dir, Isaaq, Hawiye, Digil, and Rahanwiin—trace their respective histories to two founding ancestors. The Saab cannot do so. They are thus a negative; they are defined by what they lack.

Saab blood has for generations been considered by many to be impure. The 99 percent who can locate themselves in Somali clan history ought not marry them, procreate with them, or, indeed, break bread with them. Nor work with them, for that matter. Historically, the Saab have been confined to specific occupations, passed from one generation to the next. Some have been shoemakers, others barbers. Some among the barbers have also performed circumcisions. Others are craftspeople. One Saab group, the Migdan, were hunters in past times.

Without territory or genealogy, how, you might ask, do the Saab acquire legal standing and physical protection? They borrow all of these from others by finding patrons among the Somali clan families. For generations at a time, a Saab group will attach itself to a clan. It will offer its patron clan labor and in exchange will be permitted to settle and to go about life in peace. But it will live forever at the edge of a history that it cannot claim. Its members cannot own land. Paths of upward mobility are blocked to them. They are excluded from councils of elders. And should one of them be killed by a Somali of pure blood, they can claim no right to compensation, except through the patron clan to which they are attached.

It is said that the Saab are not to be trusted because they are known to wear masks. They come to understand the clan history of their patrons intimately and are thus skilled at passing as people they are not. Some are said to speak a secret dialect so foreign to Somali that others cannot follow it. They have a reputation, too, for witchcraft and magic. One should not, it is said, turn one's back for too long on a Saab.


When Asad fled Mogadishu in 1991 in his uncle's care, their first stop was the town of Afgooye. He may well have come across members of a small Saab group called the Galgale, for some of them were there at the time. For generations, the Galgale had lived under the patronage of a Hawiye clan called the Abgal. They were shoemakers and butchers and some of them were craftspeople who worked with wood.

Sometime in the late 1980s, the elders of the Galgale made a decision they would soon regret. Somalia's president, Siad Barre, had for some years been courting Saab groups and using them as bodyguards, drivers, soldiers, and spies. Because they had no independent base of their own, Barre considered the Saab to be excellent clients.

During his last years in office, Barre convinced the Galgale elders to turn against their Abgal clients. As hard as I have looked, I cannot find any detailed account of the treachery, but it appears that many Abgal people were butchered by young Galgale men. It seems, too, that in exchange for turning on their old patrons, the Galgale were given a place in Daarood genealogy. It was said that they were Nuuh Mahamud, a lineage that falls within the Majerten, a famous Daarood clan.

In January 1991, when Mogadishu was overrun by Hawiye militias, Siad Barre, the Galgale's new patron, fled his own capital. At the very moment that Asad was robbed of his home and his childhood, the Galgale lost all protection in the world. Dominant among the Hawiye militia who took control of Mogadishu were Abgal people. They were quick to wreak vengeance. At some point in early 1991, many hundreds of Galgale were herded into Mogadishu's football stadium and slaughtered.

In the two decades since, news of the Galgale's fate surfaces periodically, usually in the course of asylum applications somewhere in the developed world. The Galgale have suffered twenty-one years of war without protection. Despised by Hawiye people for their betrayal, they are despised, too, among the Daarood, for having been Hawiye clients for so many years. That is probably why Asad sets so much store by their name. To call them Galgale is to invoke a history in which they are fickle clients and traitors. To call them Nuuh Mahamud is to give them a place in a lineage.

Defenseless, most were driven from the towns in which they had lived for generations. It is said that some five thousand of them are now in a camp for internally displaced people in Kismayo in southern Somalia. The rest, whether in Somalia itself or among the diaspora, are doubly branded as Saab and as traitors. They are people without a home on this earth.

Asad tells me of Sadicya's history only in the briefest terms. I am not sure that he knows much of the detail himself. She was born in Mogadishu, it seems; many Galgale settled there during the latter years of the Barre regime. In the early stages of the war she was orphaned; she will not say how or why, only that her parents were no more. She is Asad's age, perhaps a little younger; from early in her life she was without family to mind her.

At some point in her late teens, she no longer recalls exactly when, she fled Mogadishu to Kismayo because she had heard that that was the one place in Somalia where Galgale were safe. But she never made it to the camp where her kinspeople had settled. She was taken in by a Daarood man who married her and with whom she had Musharaf. When the boy was still an infant, her husband had kicked her and the child out of his home. Apparently, he had miscalculated when he wed her; the shame of having married a Galgale was too much. He cut her lose.

That she came to South Africa was a matter of pure chance. After her abandonment by her husband, a strange woman took pity on her. This woman was going to South Africa. Sadicya had never heard of South Africa. She knew only what she was told on the journey: that it was a place of refuge, that one could be at peace there. She arrived in May 2007, precisely a year before the onset of the violence that would deposit her and her son in a pool of water at the bottom of a storm-water drain.

Asad met Sadicya in the last week of May 2008. Three months later, on August 24, he married her.

When news got out that Asad was to marry a Galgale, an impromptu group of Ogadeni elders met to discuss the matter. It was his first taste of the fact that his impending marriage was more than a personal matter, that his choosing to sully his Ogadeni blood was considered by many to be communal business. As he remembers it now, the elders were split. Some said that it was a disgrace to marry a Saab and that it could not be countenanced. Others said that he was saving a woman and child from certain death and that Allah would reward him in the next life.

Asad did not care what the elders said. His will to marry her was as strong as his spine.

After she had told him her story, he had finished his tea and walked away in a state of bewilderment. At first, he did not understand why she had moved him so. He knew only that something of great profundity had transpired, something too powerful to grasp.

That night, lying on a mat in his tent of Daarood people, he was able to think about it more clearly. Standing before her, listening to her story, it was as if his childhood, his whole childhood, from his days in Mogadishu to his wanderings in the Ogaden, had taken residence in her body and was now talking to him. Sadicya and the young Asad were one and the same. That is what had so confused him as he had walked away.

It was such a strange thought, and yet it was possibly the most powerful thought he had ever had. He resolved to sleep and to see in the morning whether the power of what had happened remained.

Over the coming days and weeks, he bought tea from her. He would give her small sums of money with which she bought raw food to cook and to sell. And so he began to take his meals with her. He spoke to her softly, quietly. He let her see that he was just showing kindness, that he wanted nothing in return.

On the second or third day, he placed his hands over the boy Musharaf's head and ran his fingernails through the boy's hair. Then he stretched out his hands and cupped the boy's skull. He felt a great tension pressing against his palms, as if the terror of that day in Strand had sunk into the boy's being and was now banging and thumping on the inside of his head. His bones must be thick, Asad thought, or else we would all hear the racket going on inside.

Sitting and eating with these people each day felt good. The terrible things that had happened to all three of them were now spread out and shared. Being with them was so very healing. He could hardly tear himself away.

After a week or two of these daily meals, the idea of marrying her passed from fleeting idea to imperative. Not to marry her would be to abandon her and the boy to their fate, and that was intolerable.

He cast an eye back over his past and fingered all the people who might have saved him: Yindy, her father, the AliYusuf at the Hotel Taleh. How many people had observed Asad, took in his situation, surmised his fate, and then walked on? How many knew full well what was to befall him and yet cast him out of their minds?

He could not do the same to Sadicya. He could not expel her from his thoughts. Were he to walk away, she would remain with him nonetheless, a rotting wound in his soul. He must marry her. He must take in her son. With her he must have children of his own. A child from her womb would be a good child.

I put it to him that his love for Sadicya was pragmatic.

He looks at me closely.

"The violence in Khayelitsha had made you a child again," I say. "You couldn't get rid of this horrible child, and he was preventing you from functioning as a man. It was better to put the child into somebody else and look after him there. You were in search of a wounded person."

I ought to have put it differently. The words did not come out quite right; some things are very difficult to say.

"Sadicya is the price you are paying for everything that has happened to you" is what I wanted to tell him. "All your life, you have treasured your nimbleness. You have dreamed big dreams and taken crazy risks. Heading south from Addis with twelve hundred dollars in your sock; staying in South Africa despite the Abdullahi blood that had spilled, despite the loss of your wife and child, because you refused to stop dreaming. Now you have given up your nimbleness. You have shackled yourself to two helpless people. You have done so because the violence in Khayelitsha brought back the lost and scorned and broken Asad-child, and you have no choice but to carry him around with you. He is Sadicya; he is Musharaf. They are the wounds of your history opened up anew."

He listens closely to the words I *did* utter, and I can see that he wants to quarrel with me. But he checks himself and smiles instead.

"I know I only married her because life was hard," he says. "But I don't regret it. Just like I don't regret anything."

"Did she like you back then?" I ask.

"She was very happy that I wanted to marry her," he says.

"I'm sure that she was happy that you were saving her, but did she like you?"

"I will never ask her that," he replies. "There are some things a person does not ask; whatever the answer, it can only bring trouble."

Sitting here at my desk, writing, I think of Asad returning to Mew Way and staring at the space where his shop once stood. The walls are gone; only the concrete floor remains. He gasps when he takes this in. Around him is evidence of a will to obliterate him, to scorch and burn him until he no longer has a presence on this earth. It is in his history to be obliterated. It is in Sadicya's history.

## Blue Waters, America

What would Asad do now that he was bound to a woman and child? Here inside the camp, they were safe. But out there was South Africa. He would not take them there.

His idea was to leapfrog from the camp to America. He would refuse to leave until this wish was granted. He would hold himself and his wife and child hostage.

He was not the only one thinking this way.

The violence reached the Western Cape on May 22. Within forty-eight hours, more than twenty thousand foreign nationals in the province had fled their homes. The provincial and city governments had never before had to deal with such a large and sudden uprooting of human beings. What to do with all these people?

The city of Cape Town hastily established more than eighty make-shift emergency centers to house those who had fled. These ranged from mosques to police stations to community halls. People could not stay in such places long. They did not have the proper facilities. And, besides, these institutions had other purposes and needed to return to normal.

On May 28, the city announced that the displaced would be moved from the places in which they had found shelter to six temporary sites, one of which was Soetwater, a camping site that in normal times served tourists. Midwinter was approaching and the camp was closed. By the time the spring trade arrived in early September it was assumed that the displaced people would be long gone.

Asad had arrived in Soetwater on May 24. It was on about May 30 or 31 that he first laid eyes on Sadicya and Musharaf.

By mid-June, most of the people who had been placed in Soetwater were leaving. They were making their way back to the townships from which they had fled. Or they were looking for new ground, places where there had been no violence, places rumor deemed to be safe.

As far as Asad was concerned, there were no such places in South Africa. Foosiya had been right. One could run from province to province, from town to town. South African violence would find you.

Those who remained in Soetwater talked and talked and talked. They soon bound themselves around a common purpose. They swore to one another that they would never return to South Africa; they would simply refuse. If the authorities wanted them to be among South Africans again, they would have to slaughter them and dump their bodies in Khayelit-sha. That was the only way they would go back.

Officials from South Africa's Department of Home Affairs met repre-sentatives of the United Nations High Commission for Refugees. It was in nobody's interests that these people be classified as refugees. If news were to spread that the ones in the camps were to get tickets to the First World, every undocumented person in the country would surely descend upon the camps. And besides, recognizing foreign nationals within its borders as refugees would be intolerably humiliating for the South Afri-can government. The buzzword of the time was "reintegration." People must go back to live among South Africans again.

After much debate, the UNHCR advised that the people in the camps be classified as internally displaced persons. They were given three options. They could opt for repatriation to their countries of origin. With monetary assistance from the UNHCR and the South African gov-ernment, they could reintegrate into the communities that had thrown them out. Or they would be helped to relocate to another part of South Africa, somewhere that had remained peaceful during the disturbances.

For those from Somalia and the Democratic Republic of Congo, the first option was void. The UNHCR would not repatriate them to coun-tries that were at war. And so the last two options remained: Khayelitsha or somewhere else in South Africa. Asad and Sadicya, together with sev-eral hundred others, declined all options given to them. They would stay in the camp until another country accepted them as refugees.

·  ·  ·

At the end of August, just a few days after Asad and Sadicya were married, the city of Cape Town closed Soetwater in time for the tourist season. The newlyweds and their child were moved to yet another camping site. This one was called Blue Waters. It was less than two kilometers due south from Mitchells Plain Town Centre, a windswept place looking out over the middle of False Bay. Asad did not like it much.

"It was worse than Soetwater," he recalls. "It was less safe because it was close to a small township where people were selling drugs and illegal firearms. Between Blue Waters and Mitchells Plain, it was very dangerous to walk. You did not want to do it. Also, the toilets and showers were not permanent structures. They were mobile facilities."

In any event, Asad and Sadicya had been in Blue Waters less than two months when the authorities announced that they were closing it down and that its residents must accept assistance to reintegrate. Asad and Sadicya were among several hundred people who still refused to leave. At the end of October, the electricity was cut. The water supply was turned off. All services ceased. Still, the occupants of Blue Waters held their ground. The city of Cape Town went to court seeking an eviction order. By now, a host of nongovernmental organizations, including South Africa's venerable nonprofit litigation service, the Legal Resources Centre, had come to the aid of the displaced ones. Counsel was hired on their behalf. The matter went to court.


Asad had never before in his life been involved in politics. Wherever he had lived, the Somali diaspora had been awash in political talk. His interest had only ever been pragmatic: he wanted to know what had become of Mogadishu, and that was all.

But with Sadicya and Musharaf beside him, he was someone else now. He was the outer shell of a tender and wounded being. He needed quickly to learn to be very hard.

He will not talk to me much about the activism he undertook after moving to Blue Waters. He tells me in the sparest terms that he became a spokesperson for the refugees. That is all. I suspect that he considers the persona he presented and the tactics he adopted as bitter necessities; one does not speak of them, for they are not a part of one's true self. The real substance of his being was turned inward, to Sadicya and Musharaf. When he sees himself in the camp, that is what he chooses to see.

I have spoken to others who encountered Asad during that time. I have interviewed government officials who faced him and other camp representatives across the table. They speak unhappily of their experiences.

"The Somalis lacked basic civility," one of them said. "We understood that they were in a condition of terrible distress. We tried to offer them humanity. We wanted to listen. We wanted to resettle them as gently and as thoughtfully as possible. We were prepared to put a lot of money and care into the process. They rebuffed us without grace. 'We want nothing to do with you,' they said. 'The only people we want to talk to are the Americans. You can go to hell.'

"They had talked themselves into a frenzy. They believed that they had a right to go to America. They believed that in trying to help them find homes in Cape Town, we were violating their rights. They treated us like we were representing the devil. Whenever I walked out of a meeting with them I felt indignant, insulted, and dirty.

"I am not sure where they got it into their heads that they had a right to resettle in a third country. I think it is because some of them had been in refugee camps in Kenya, where third-country resettlement was an option. They took this Kenyan experience and insisted that it was universal law."

For the people in Blue Waters, South Africa was considerably more dangerous than Kenya had ever been. If being in Kenya warranted repatriation to a third country, why on earth not South Africa?

Asad is prepared to share the details of one altercation he had with officialdom during this time.

On a morning in mid-September he received a call from a friend to tell him that Hassan had been shot. It had happened just as Asad feared—behind the counter in his *spaza* shop on Mew Way. He was lying in a hospital bed in Mitchells Plain.

"I went straight to the hospital," Asad says. "He was not critically injured. He had been shot in the chest but the bullet went straight out of the back without touching organs or bones. He was very lucky.

"The next day I went back and discharged him and brought him to Blue Waters. I kept him inside my tent. But the very first time he went to the toilet, the coordinator of the camp, a man called Cecil, saw him and started to shout at him.

"'What are you doing here? You are not a member of the camp. Leave.'

"I said to Cecil, 'He is my brother. He has been shot.'

"Cecil said, 'You cannot bring him here. This is not a lodge.'

"He brought in law enforcement. Hassan was removed. He went to live in a lodge in Mitchells Plain. He healed there. Then he returned to Somalia.

"It was a sign to me, brother. For once, I had made the correct decision. If I had gone back to Khayelitsha with Hassan it would maybe have been me shot through the chest. Maybe the bullet would have hit my heart and I would have died. What would Sadicya and Musharaf have done then? Brother, the thought of them being alone in Khayelitsha . . . It was not going to happen. I was not going to leave that camp."

During his time in Blue Waters, Asad befriended whomever he felt might help him get to America. All sorts of people were coming into the camp: nongovernmental organization workers, lawyers, officials from the UNHCR, volunteers of various descriptions. He was especially interested in anybody who had an inside track at the UNHCR or who had knowledge of the American refugee-admission process.

The most valued connection he made was with a man called Gabriel, a young American student working for the UNHCR.

"I met him after I had cried in a meeting with the UNHCR and the government," Asad tells me. "I was a spokesperson for the joint refugee leaders. They told us at that meeting that for Somalis and Congolese there was no choice: we must reintegrate. When they said that I tried to speak, but instead I cried. I was thinking of Foosiya's prophesy, of my son crawling around in my blood. I thought that her prophecy was now going to come true, only it would be Musharaf walking in my blood.

"We were desperate, brother. Straight after that meeting, we called a press conference. We wanted to explain to the world what it meant to be a Somali in South Africa. We sat in that press conference and tried to explain. We tried to put them in our shoes.

"After the press conference, the UNHCR sent investigators to document who was being killed. They wanted to find out what was happening to us in South Africa. That is how I met Gabriel. The UNHCR employed him as an interviewer. None of the interpreters could understand his accent. I was the only one. So I spent many, many hours with Gabriel. We talked. I told him my story."

A bond between the two men formed. They grew to like each other very much. Gabriel became his inside track, a person who both under-stood the inscrutable world of the law and had Asad's true interests at heart.

"Gabriel told me that there was no way, absolutely no way, ever, that I would get to America if I stayed in the camp. He said that it was a rule that would never ever be broken: 'These people cannot be rewarded for staying here against the law.' The city was offering to move us to Blikkies-dorp. Gabriel said that if I moved, there was a very good chance I would get to America. He had spoken to UNHCR people. He had spoken to American people. He was clever. He knew how the system worked. He said that those interviews the UNHCR had done with us were enough to get us to America. My family and some others would be officially classi-fied as 'vulnerable' and that would get us to America. But only if we went to Blikkiesdorp—that was the route to America.

"Brother, I said no. I was not going to take Sadicya and Musharaf out into South Africa. Especially not a place like Blikkiesdorp. I was not leaving."

He shut out Gabriel's words. He refused to absorb them: You can go to America if you like, but to get there you must sit it out in a shack settlement littered with guns and gangs. It will take maybe a year, maybe two or three years. If you can survive Blikkiesdorp for that long, you can go to America.

He kept fighting. He kept talking of defiance. He told all sorts of people that he would be the very last one to leave. They would have to kill him and drag his body away. Around him were dozens of assenting voices—it was their right to go to America. If the South Africans wanted them to leave, they would have to bring in soldiers to slaughter them.

Asad kept talking like this, but slowly, barely consciously, he started to wonder whether he believed what he was saying. Sometimes, it would come to him with a shock that he had been listening to his own voice as if another person were speaking, a person who was becoming less and less useful. Gabriel had authority. Gabriel knew.

Inside, two voices mingled. One spoke to the world. It was as defiant as ever. The other spoke quietly and privately. It coaxed. It explained. It was preparing Asad for what he desperately did not want.


Asad and his family arrived at Blue Waters in early September 2008. It was only on February 24, 2010, sixteen months after all services at Blue

Waters had ceased, that the Cape High Court handed down judgment. The people of Blue Waters were ordered to leave by March 31. They were to receive a relocation payment as well as the option of skills training, which would include a course in life skills and another in English language instruction, and trauma counseling. If they did not take the training and the counseling, they would get additional money instead.

Thirty-four of the Blue Waters families had been classified by the UNHCR as "vulnerable." These families, the court ordered, would be settled in Blikkiesdorp, each family in a separate abode. The homes to which they were to be moved were described as "18-square-metre insulated wooden and metal framework structures including a roof and windows, erected on a concrete slab, situated on a site serviced with electricity, water and sanitation." They would pay no rent.

Asad, Sadicya, and Musharaf were among several families who abided by the settlement. On March 31, 2010, they looked on as their possessions were loaded onto a truck. Then they themselves climbed aboard; they made their way to their new home.

The rest of the Blue Waters people, more than four hundred of them, defied. They believed to the depths of their bones that if they made hostages of themselves they would go to America. The task of removing them was messy and prolonged. On April 15, a large contingent of police pushed them out of the campsite grounds. Most simply relocated to a parking lot across the road, where they remained for another week. The women and children among them spent each night in a public toilet next to the parking lot. The men slept under the stars.

By the end of April, thirty-seven people had been arrested for trespassing. The remainder dissolved into the townships of Cape Town.

As for Asad, he was back in a South African township with a wife and a child, precisely his situation on the eve of Foosiya's departure three and a half years earlier. Whatever choices he made, it seemed, his life went around in a circle.

# Blikkiesdorp

I first visited Asad in Blikkiesdorp on September 24, 2010. He had been living there a week shy of six months.

It was on my third visit, I think, that I watched him watch three hooded young men approach us in my rearview mirror. His fear crossed a boundary right then and inhabited me. I saw what he saw and felt what he felt. It was a gift. In that moment he gave me the ink with which I have written this book.

Today, as I write, Christmas is approaching. It is late December 2012. I feel obliged to document, baldly and without adornment, some of what Asad has experienced in the two-and-a-bit years I have known him.

On an evening in November 2010, about three dozen people surrounded his place. They sang and danced. The lyrics to their song demanded that he close his doors and leave Blikkiesdorp. They threw stones. They sang of setting his shop alight. Sadicya and Musharaf fled to a South African community leader's place elsewhere in the settlement. Asad phoned the Delft police station. The police did not come. He then phoned Pearlie Joubert, the journalist who had introduced us; she called the provincial police spokesperson. This time, a police patrol arrived.

The crowd had a ringleader, a middle-aged South African man who ran a *spaza* shop several blocks from Asad's place. When the police came, he switched roles; with large and exaggerated gestures, he began to shield Asad from his attackers. It took the police just a few minutes to ascertain that this man had in fact mobilized the crowd. They arrested him and took him away, but he was back later that night. No docket had been opened. When Asad went to the police station the next day to lay a charge, he was told that this was not possible.

Most of Asad's neighbors came to sympathize.

"They told me the *toyi-toyiers* were full of shit," he recalls. "I said, 'Thanks, brother, thanks, sister.' But I have learned that people can change their minds very quickly."

And, indeed, two weeks later, a packed community meeting in Blikkiesdorp resolved unanimously to demand that the City Council remove Somalis from Blikkiesdorp. It was said that they ran too many businesses and that they were making people poor.

The UNHCR encouraged the people they had resettled in Blikkiesdorp to leave. They offered a resettlement payment if the Somalis and Congolese would find homes for themselves elsewhere. But Asad's business was in Blikkiesdorp. It was feeding his family. He began searching the colored township of Belhar for an open space on which he might erect a shop. He could not find one. He resolved to sit it out in Blikkiesdorp.

The following month, two young men came to Asad's shop to buy. Asad knew one of them well. His name was Fayek. He lived in Blikkiesdorp Section 23, just a few hundred meters from Asad's place. He bought cigarettes, chips, and a small bag of sugar. In front of Asad, he dropped his purchases on the ground and accused Asad of having taken his money without giving him his order in return. He said he wanted cigarettes and chips and a small bag of sugar. Asad shook his head and asked Fayek to leave. Fayek and his friend began to shout. They would come back. They would kill Asad. They would kill his wife. They would kill his boy. They stepped back a few paces, and then began stoning Asad's walls. Then they turned and left.

Six weeks or so later, Asad walked past a group of young men playing dice. One of them was Fayek. When he saw Asad, he stood up, drew a gun from his waistband, crouched and aimed. As Asad bolted, he heard Fayek laugh. "Run, Somali, run!" Fayek shouted after him.

Early the following year, on January 13, 2011, Asad visited a Somali household in Blikkiesdorp in the early evening. His hosts invited him to chew *mira* with them. He accepted the invitation. Including Asad there were five men in all sitting in front of a shack chewing *mira*.

Two police vans screeched to a halt outside the shack, and four cops jumped out and told the men that they were under arrest for possession of drugs. They began confiscating wallets and cell phones. They were clearly there to rob the Somalis, rather than to arrest them. Their plan was to show up in force, shout, threaten, and then leave with their loot.

Sadicya arrived with Musharaf. In her broken English, she began to shout at the police. "It is not illegal to eat *mira,*" she told them. "It is in our culture. It is what we do."

One of the police officers smacked her across the face with an open hand. Now Asad began shouting, "She is a pregnant woman! You cannot hit her."

A policeman stormed Asad and sprayed his eyes with pepper spray. When Asad doubled over, the cop smacked him across the face. Then he went back to his van and retrieved a rifle. He pointed it in Sadicya's face and asked her if she would like to be shot. The police officers then hand-cuffed the five men and took them to the police cells. The Somalis never saw their wallets or cell phones again.

The cells were full, and the Somalis soon discovered that they were run by members of South Africa's infamous Number gangs: the 26s, 27s, and 28s. The gangsters instructed the Somalis to empty their pockets. The police had taken what they had, but from a sense of pride the Somalis refused. The gangsters began pushing and punching. The Somalis fought back. It seems that the gangsters were surprised by the Somalis' resolve and were not in the mood for a fight. They backed off.

Somebody on the outside paid seven hundred and fifty rand to get the Somalis a lawyer, who applied for police bail. The cops would not release them. As they were Somalis, the lawyer was told, they were not eligible for bail. They ended up staying four days. They appeared before a magistrate and were released on bail of one thousand rand each. The case dragged on until April when the charges were dropped.

On a Saturday evening in April 2011, Asad left home to visit a friend at the other end of Blikkiesdorp. It was about quarter past six. A block from his home, he passed five young men playing dice. He knew them well; they were, indeed, among his daily customers.

Once he had turned the corner and was out of sight, they went to his home, broke the lock on the back door, and kicked it down. Musharaf was in the toilet at this time. He stayed there and hid.

The intruders ignored Sadicya, who was by now heavily pregnant. They turned their attention instead to an old Somali man Asad had asked to look after the shop in his absence. They beat him in the face with a hard object. The old man said later that it was a monkey wrench, but Asad reckoned that a monkey wrench would have left a narrow, deep wound, whereas the old man's wound was wide and shallow, suggesting that the object was a rock.

Asad called the Delft police station, but nobody came until lunchtime the following day. The shack was dusted for fingerprints and photographs were taken. Asad was driven around Blikkiesdorp in a van looking for the culprits. Then a more senior detective arrived on the scene and said that no docket could be opened until the old man had signed a witness statement. But the old man was not there; he was being treated for his wounds at a clinic. The police left without opening a docket. They never returned.

A week later, two of the culprits came to the shop to buy cigarettes. Sadicya ran to Asad to tell him. Asad called the investigating officer, the one who said that no docket could be opened without the old man's testimony. He said he would come immediately, but he did not come at all.

Blikkiesdorp's street committees, staffed and run by South Africans, were also involved in the case. When the police arrived, the street committees sent a representative who followed them around and showed great concern.

Asad smiled to himself.

"The street committees could find the culprits in a few seconds if they wanted," he tells me. "But their job is not to snitch on people who rob Somalis."

On July 27, 2011, there was shooting throughout the night in Blikkiesdorp. Two rival gangs were fighting it out over drug turf. The police stayed away during the hours of darkness. Once light broke, they came in numbers and swarmed Blikkiesdorp. They raided shack after shack, picking more than a dozen young men off the street and throwing them into the backs of their vans.

At the very time that the police were all over Blikkiesdorp, a Somali child, aged ten, was found hanging from the clothesline by her own jersey in her parents' yard. She had gone out in the morning to buy a cold drink. Her mother, who had begun to worry because her daughter had been gone a long time, walked out of the shack into the yard and saw her swinging.

Two detectives were called to the scene. They were there for about twenty minutes. The investigating officer opened a suicide inquest, saying that no foul play was suspected. How he could determine this after such a short investigation, especially when the parents suspected foul play, one does not know.

During the course of the afternoon, the Somalis of Blikkiesdorp began to grow hysterical with fear. They had just been through a night of gunfire, the walls of their homes thin and frail; they had watched an army of men swarm their neighborhood; and now one of them, a young child, to boot, had died in the strangest circumstances, and the police had summarily determined that there was no case to investigate. They resolved to take their children out of school. If the young ones are now being targeted, they said, we do not want them to leave home in the mornings.

The twenty-seventh of July turned out to be Musharaf's last day of school in 2011. He stayed at home the remainder of the year and resumed school only in January 2012.

On July 28, I took a radio journalist to Blikkiesdorp. She interviewed the parents of the dead girl and watched the Somalis stand around her body in a small room at the local clinic. She interviewed the investigating officer. That evening, I listened to her report. A Somali girl was found hanging in her parents' yard in a settlement on the edge of Delft, she said. The parents suspect foul play. The police disagree and have opened a suicide inquest.

As I listened, I was struck by the deep inadequacy of news. How does one convey the enormity of what had happened? Thousands of listeners, in the bubbles of their cars, made their way home in the rush-hour traffic. Somewhere on the edge of the city, locals had a go at foreigners. The police were not terribly interested. That is how it is.


This is but a sample of what Asad experienced personally. Then there are his vicarious experiences—the stories that circulated, the funerals he attended, the burned, shot, and wounded people to whose aid he came.

In September 2010, two Somalis came under attack in their shop in Philippi. The intruders shot one of them through the heart, tied the other to a chair, poured petrol over him, and set him alight.

I went with Asad to visit him in the hospital. His face was a mummy of white bandages, his eyes staring out at us from deep sockets.

Earlier in 2010, a Somali man Asad knew who ran a shop in Khayelitsha was robbed at gunpoint by two regular customers. He filed a complaint, and they were charged with robbery with aggravating circumstances. A court date was set. On the evening before the Somali was due to testify in court, the father of one of the accused walked into the shop and asked to buy a liter of milk. The Somali told him to leave. The man pulled out a pistol and shot the Somali in the stomach. He survived, but decided that it was better not to lay charges against the father. He also told prosecutors that he would no longer give testimony in the son's trial.

In October 2010, a gang in Khayelitsha had gone from one Somali shop to another robbing and executing the owners: in a single night, they killed three people in three separate incidents. The fourth shop owner they attacked shot back, wounding one of his assailants. In response, the police raided more than a dozen Somali shops in the Khayelitsha area looking for illegal weapons. Five Somalis were picked up. They were all denied bail on the grounds that they were planning revenge.

On the last day of the Soccer World Cup in July 2010, a mob surrounded the shop of a Somali retailer in Philippi. He called the police. The officers who arrived on the scene insisted on taking his fridge and his television set for safekeeping, lest the mob come back later to loot. When the Somali went to the police station to retrieve his possessions, he was told that officers wanted to buy his electronic goods. He declined the offer and was threatened with arrest and thrown out of the police station. He hired a lawyer and pressed charges against the officers who had taken his possessions. That night, he received a death threat on his cell phone.

In February 2011, three armed men entered a Somali-owned *spaza* shop in a section of Delft about two kilometers from Asad's place. The shop was owned by two men. One was staffing the counter, the other was taking a nap upstairs. The robbers shot and killed the man behind the counter. His colleague was woken by the gunfire and jumped from the second floor of the house and ran away. The robbers doused the shop in petrol, lit a match, and watched the shop and the corpse burn.

Asad rushed to the scene along with several other Blikkiesdorp Somalis. They arrived long before the fire department and walked into the burning shop; they wanted to save their compatriot's body from the flames for his burial. Asad found the corpse and knelt down over it and touched it on the forearm. It was so hot that he flinched. When he looked at his fingers they were scalded. After he had returned home that evening he sank his hand into a bowl of ice. In the weeks that they took to heal he acquired a fascination with the burn marks. He would open his hand every so often and stare at them.

# Texas News

A couple of months after they had settled in Blikkiesdorp, the Blue Waters families were interviewed by the Americans. In a marathon session that lasted an afternoon, Asad told a carefully crafted story about his life. He did not lie; he described faithfully and in great detail the incidents of violence to which he had been subject since coming to South Africa. The power of his memory surprised him; it was as if he had recorded each act of violence and was replaying the very worst of his life in slow motion.

But nor did he really tell the truth. For the fuel that burned inside him and that made him Asad Hirsi Abdullahi was drained from the story he related. He did not, for instance, tell his interviewers that life in Addis had been pretty good when he chose to leave, that what took him to South Africa was a soaring dream. He did not tell of his choice to remain in South Africa when Foosiya left with their toddler and their unborn child. And he certainly did not speak of his false passport or of his air ticket to Brazil. The story he crafted whittled away at the flesh of his being, leaving only a stick figure, a hapless refugee.

That was what was expected, after all. What would an American immigration official do with information about his soul?

A few weeks later, the Blikkiesdorp families began receiving news. Some were informed that their applications to become refugees in the United States had been rejected. Asad was told that he, Sadicya, and Musharaf would be resettled in America.

Six weeks later, three of the Blikkiesdorp families were summoned for medical tests. After that, nobody heard a word for a long time. Six months later, the same three families were told that their medical certificates had expired and that they must be examined again. They waited some more. Then, out of the blue, they received word on a Monday morning that they were leaving for the United States. By the following Thursday evening, they were gone.

Asad waited. He did not ever turn off his cell phone. Who knows? The Americans might phone at three o'clock in the morning. It was unlikely, but it was best to be sure. Would it not be especially cruel, he asked me, were South Africa to kill him now, after all he had survived, on the brink of being whisked away to a safe life, simply because he had turned off his phone?

The race was on, he said. Who would get to him first: the Americans or a South African with a gun in his hand?

In November 2011, more than eighteen months after he had been told that his family would be resettled in the United States, Asad was summoned to an interview "to check that I am not a terrorist," he said. In February 2012, he and his family were called for medical examinations. They did not have any infections that would prevent them from entering America. They waited.

Just less than six months later, two families who had received their medical examinations on the same day as Asad were summoned to retake theirs. Asad and his family were not called to retake their tests. So he knew that he was somewhere at the back of the queue. He visited the office where he had been interviewed and asked when he might be leaving. He was told that nobody could tell him and that he must not inquire again.

From others he knew that it was possible to wait for as long as three years.

On the first day that I met Asad in Blikkiesdorp there was a visitor in his yard, a young man called Omar. About a year later, Asad and I were driving across the southeastern perimeter of Cape Town when I suddenly thought of Omar; I am not sure why.

"Do you still see him?" I asked.

"He is in America," Asad replied. "About a month after you met him, he got a call. It was a Thursday afternoon, I think. He left the following Monday night."

"Have you been in contact with him?"

"He has phoned a few times. He is in a place called Texas. He said that he is living in paradise. He said that you do not realize how much of a prison you are living in South Africa until you are free. He said he looks at himself in the mirror each morning and he is getting lighter every day."

"Why lighter?"

"Because he is becoming healthier. Healthy skin is light."

"Do you know where in Texas?" I asked.

"He did not say."

"Did he tell you whether he is in a city or in the countryside?"

"I did not ask him that. I don't know."

We drove into Mitchells Plain, parked the car, and walked through the shopping mall across the way from Mitchells Plain Town Centre. It was late afternoon. The mall was very busy. We had to dodge the streams of people walking into us.

I had recently spent two years in New York. I commuted every day to a street in a housing project where a couple of thousand Liberian refugees lived. I knew from intimate experience that to be black and foreign and undereducated in America was very hard. I had seen New York hollow out people's souls.

Asad knew that I had lived in the United States. He knew that I had worked among African refugees. He had never asked me what I had seen there.

I told him, as we walked through the shopping mall, that America was big and varied, and that while some parts may be the heaven Omar had described, others were difficult and violent. It was possible, I told him, that the place to which he was to be relocated would not be suitable. If this was so, he should not despair. He should move. I told him that many of the more successful and well-adjusted refugees I had met in America had chosen to move soon after arriving. It seemed that the very act of choosing to go somewhere else had given them strength.

He stopped and looked at me. A person walking in the opposite direction bumped against his shoulder and quietly cursed him.

"I'm sorry, sister," Asad called out. Then he walked again.

"I am so very tired of violence, brother," he said as we left the mall. "There is so much violence for as far back as I can remember. If I am relocated to a violent place, I will definitely move. We have been getting orientation courses from an NGO. They say that we should not move. They say we must make the best of wherever the program settles us. But if it is violent, I will move."

Then he wiped the subject from his mind. I could see it in his face.

His eyes were smiling, and he was pointing at a cell-phone shop we had just passed, and he began telling me a long story about the troubles Somalis had when they bought cell phones. He was babbling compulsively, like a person playing with worry beads. He was babbling away the things I had said about America.

I regretted having raised it. I cannot prepare him for life there. It is not my business.

# *Father*

When I first walked into Asad's shack I took in the cloth that covered the walls and the muted colors of the duvet under which the family slept and the pots and pans sticking out from under the bed. And then I saw with a start that a woman was sitting on a stool in the dim light in the corner of the room.

It was Sadicya's will that I not see her. She would respond curtly to my greetings whenever I visited, her words short and clipped. She would turn her face away as she spoke, showing me the side of her head shawl. Many months passed before she met my eyes.

Negotiating with South Africa and South Africans, it seems, was Asad's business. I wondered how she had survived a year in this country before she met him. She had been without friends among Somalis and without a language to talk to South Africans.

Once, several months after I had started coming regularly to Blik-kiesdorp, I arrived to find only Sadicya and Musharaf at home. I phoned Asad, but his cell phone went to voice mail; I smiled to myself and hoped that this would not be the morning on which the Americans called.

Sadicya greeted me as stiffly as usual. She carried a chair out into the yard, put it down in the shade, and gestured for me to sit. I thanked her. Then she gathered Musharaf and left, bolting the door to her yard behind her, locking me inside.

I made some calls. I took out a book and read. An hour passed. I phoned Asad but got his voice mail again. I read some more. Then I dragged my chair to the edge of the yard and stood on it. On tiptoes, my arms stretched above my head, the top of the wall was still out of reach. I would have to jump from the chair and scramble over. I acknowledged defeat, retreated into the shade and read some more.

Sitting, waiting, I grew annoyed with poor Sadicya. Propelled by my irritation, my thoughts began to wander. Was the urgency with which Asad had married her circumstantial? The violence had awoken his child self, injured and rejected and tossed around; he had needed to look after this child and had found a repository for it in Sadicya.

Is that still what he needed now? Had their relationship in the meantime evolved into something else, something less tied to that desperate moment? How much did he dwell upon Foosiya? As I asked myself these questions, I knew that I could not put them to Asad. He would be unlikely to respond with candor, at any rate.

Some three hours later, he finally answered his phone. I told him that I was locked in his yard alone and had already missed a meeting in town. He called Sadicya and a few minutes later I heard her keys clink and the bolt unlock.

She stood in the doorway and pointed at me sitting on my chair and threw her head back and laughed. It was a full, unguarded laugh, on the edge of raucous. She cupped her chin in her hand and chuckled and shook her head, then dropped her arms and laughed more loudly than ever, her shoulders heaving. I looked at her, astonished, and an image formed in my mind: I saw her in front of a television set, watching a cartoon in which a creature keeps running into walls and getting shot to bits and falling down cliff faces.

"I forget you," she said. "Sorry, sorry, sorry. I forget you."

From that day forth, she was unvaryingly warm. Each time I came to her home she greeted me and looked into my eyes, and her own eyes smiled. When I had been traveling, she said that she was pleased that I had returned safely. She would ask after my family. The idea of me sitting all those hours in her yard had made me human.

I considered asking her whether she would think about the prospect of talking to me about her past. I would have to use Asad as an interpreter. But it was a foolish idea and I abandoned it. Asad had studiously left many questions about Sadicya unasked. He did not want to know everything that had happened to her. Such silences, it seemed to me, were among the foundation stones of their marriage.

I could perhaps ask somebody else to interpret for me, and maybe

Sadicya would tell me something of substance about her experiences. But then Asad would read on the page what he did not want to know. And so I left it.

I was away when Sadicya gave birth to a baby girl. When I first laid eyes on the child she was in her father's arms. He stared down at her with an intensity I had not seen on his face before. She was six weeks old now, and she had been ill for five of them.

To be born in winter and go home from the hospital to a shack in Cape Town, Asad complained, what chances does a child have?

"When I wake up in the mornings," he said, "there is dew on the rafters above me. My lungs are developed. Hers are still tiny. They cannot handle all this wet."

They struggled to get the child adequate medical attention. The nurses at the local clinic at Delft said that there was nothing wrong with her and sent her away. Asad took her to Red Cross War Memorial Children's Hospital, where he was told that she could only be admitted if she was referred by a clinic. He refused to leave. He sat with his baby in a waiting room for more than twelve hours before she was admitted.

She was diagnosed with pneumonia, prescribed antibiotics, and discharged after four days. Asad was told that once the course of medication was complete she would be fine. But she was not. She kept coughing from somewhere deep inside her. He took her back to the clinic and was once again told that there was nothing wrong. And so he returned to Red Cross Hospital and again refused to leave until she was admitted.

She was three months old before she was seen by a doctor who cared enough to examine her thoroughly. The doctor explained to Asad that his daughter had coughed so much in her first weeks that her stomach had been damaged and she could not properly digest her food. He told Asad that with proper attention she would be fine, that Asad must bring her back once a week without fail. At four months old, she stopped coughing. She began digesting all her food. The visits to the hospital ceased.

Her name was Rahma.

"Do you remember that name?" Asad asked me.

"Yes. It is the name of one of your sisters."

He nodded. "My other sister was Khadra. But I did not know her as well. Khadra was taken by my aunt before we left Mogadishu. It was Rahma I was with when we fled with my uncle. It was Rahma who was beside my uncle when the truck drove off with me on it. I called my daughter Rahma after the sister I knew better."

That evening, I returned to the notes I had taken about his flight from Mogadishu. They recorded all sorts of observations about his uncle, about the people around them, about fear. But there was just one passing reference to his sister. It occurred to me, once again, that if I had spoken to him about that time on another morning, a morning on which different thoughts were passing through his mind, a morning after a night during which he had dreamed different dreams, he would have told me another version of the story of his flight from Mogadishu, a version connected to the one he did tell me, but different; a version that included his sister Rahma and what her presence alongside him in the days after his flight meant to him now.

If I began to interview him again from scratch, I thought, this book would be very different. It would be connected to the book I have written here, but it would not be the same book at all.

It came to me that I ought not finish writing about Asad before talking to Foosiya. I wanted to ask her about insulting Asad in the car after the wedding, about marrying him and having to manage his wild friends, about her journey to South Africa, about Sterkstroom.

It would not be difficult. Were Asad to give me the name of her subclan and her lineage, and the nicknames of her father and her grandfather, I could find them in Somaliland. After all, I had found members of Asad's family in this way. I could fly to Addis and from Addis to Hargeisa. I could be with her in less than a week.

I was in the United Kingdom when this desire descended upon me. I would not come to Cape Town again for at least three months. And so I talked to Asad about my plans on the phone. I asked him to think about it over the next few days and then to let me know whether it was okay.

He e-mailed three days later. He said it was fine. I wrote back thanking him and asking for the details of Foosiya's family. He did not reply.

I called him a week later. He said that the idea of my going to see Foosiya had been sitting with him for days and that he did not like it.

"Why not?" I asked.

"At first it was because I worried that you would be in danger in Somaliland," he said. "But then I realized that was not it. It is just sitting badly in my gut. I do not want you to look for her."

I abandoned the idea and moved on. We had never discussed the rules I ought to obey as I went about my research. But to rummage through his intimate history when he had forbidden me to go there was clearly unthinkable.

Months later, we met one morning in Bellville. He was tired. For a fee he had driven a carload of people to Swellendam and back the previous night. He had had only two or three hours' sleep.

We sat in my car outside the Bellville police station and talked. There was so much to say. This was the first time I had seen him since discovering that his parents were refugees from the Ogaden. Today, I had to let him know that when he moved through Qorahay he was in the place where his parents had grown up and were married.

Blow by blow, I told him of my journey to his relations in London and of everything they had said. I gave him names and phone numbers. I told him that these London Abdullahis had kept track of some of his siblings; they would tell him where some of them were.

He listened. He said that the story of his parents made him sad. To think that they, like him, were refugees, that they also had to run from place to place, knowing no home—such thoughts were very sad.

We went for a long walk through Bellville, then returned to my car to talk some more. I asked him why he did not want me to meet Foosiya.

"My first thought was your safety," he replied. "I worried that in Somaliland you would get hurt or even killed. But then I sat with that and I realized that was not the reason. I was having a second thought. It had not been clear at the beginning.

"If you do this before I go to America I could have a big problem. What if you find that my children are in trouble and I am not in a position to help them? Brother, that is not something that can happen. I must wait until I am settled in America. I must wait until I am established. If I succeed there, the first thing I will do is contact them.

"I don't hate Foosiya. I am in fact still in love with Foosiya. I thought that she was standing in the wrong position. But I realized later that she was actually standing in the right position. She was so stubborn. But she was right. We were being slaughtered in this country. She was right to leave.

"We abuse the women. We do not take their ideas, even when they are right."

It is the strangest moment. Listening to these words, I have glimpsed, for the first time, an imaginary Asad lodged deep inside him. It is the

Asad that preserves his dignity and his pride, the Asad that allows the flesh-and-blood Asad to rise each morning.

The words with which one might describe this Asad are so deceptively simple. He is a breadwinner, a head of a family, a provider for his children. He is shepherding his kids into lives profoundly different from his own.

This Asad has a wife. She is beautiful and willful and also unknowable; he cannot anticipate what she will decide next.

I try to imagine when this Asad is at his most alive. I guess that it is early in the morning, when the real Asad is not quite awake but no longer asleep. In this transitional moment, while the censors are distracted and the real day has yet to take hold, the fantasy is free to grow.

Were I to see his actual children in Somaliland, and were they to need something from him, the imaginary Asad would shatter. For he knows very well that it is the flesh-and-blood Asad who will be asked to provide and that he is not in a position to do so. The imaginary Asad and the corporeal Asad will become one and the same in America, this place about which he will hear nothing but good.

## Epilogue

Jet-lagged and without enough sleep, a transatlantic journey in my bones, I board a flight from Newark International to Kansas City, Missouri. I am going to visit Asad in his new home. He has been there five and a half months.

It happened very fast. In mid-March 2013, without warning, he received the call for which he had waited almost three years. He and Sadicya and the two children would fly to Johannesburg one afternoon the following week, he was told, just in time to board the evening flight to New York. The following day, they would get a transfer to Kansas City, Missouri, their new home.

No sooner had Asad put down his phone than it signaled an incoming text message. On his screen was the street address and zip code of his apartment in Kansas City. He stared at it a long time. Then he forwarded it to me.

I was in Johannesburg at the time.

"The kids don't have new clothes for America," he said to me on the phone later that day. "There are so many things we must buy."

Several times over the last year, I had offered him a loan. It would be deducted from his portion of the royalty advance we would receive once I had finished writing this book. He had always declined it. Until this moment.

He had been banking his side of our deal. He did not want to spill a drop of it on South African soil. It was for America.

We have struggled to communicate since he left. Our relationship was destined to be played out in a car, it seems. Robbed of this proximity, there is no traction between us. His voice at the other end of the line is thin, whatever life it once possessed left somewhere in the ocean between us. I try to compensate by enthusing my own voice with energy, but it comes out all tin and zinc.

And so I know that the family lived rent-free for three months and was given food stamps, but that by the time this grace period ended, Asad had not found a job. He was offered work cleaning corridors and bathrooms in the middle of the night but had refused it. Sadicya had been going off each morning for English lessons, leaving Asad to look after Rahma. "I have become a housewife," he told me, giggling. Finally, just a week ago, he found work at the airport, parking rental cars.

I know these things, but I cannot imagine them. I have no idea what they might mean for Asad's spirit.

Looking down at New Jersey's rusted colors, I race ahead of the aircraft and fly low and fast above Missouri's wide farmland. I catch sight of Asad at the end of my journey, wandering around his kitchen in a purple *macawi,* in an apartment I cannot properly imagine. In the months since I saw him last I have thought and written about him more than I have done anything else, and my sense of him has changed.

It has taken this long to see him properly, I think, because the language with which he describes himself is misleading.

When he told me his story he did so in the words of a refugee, for these are the words he must use, always, at every border post he approaches, at every government office outside which he queues.

A refugee has lost control. Great historical forces have upended him and he no longer has a place in the world. He has become an in-between sort of being, suspended between a past in which he belonged somewhere and a future in which he might belong somewhere once more. But for now he is in abeyance; he is swept this way and that, like flotsam in a tide.

I no longer think this a useful way to understand Asad. He is in America now, I have concluded, because he is a person with an enormous appetite for risk. If I look at the course his life has taken, it is simply not adequate to say that he has been kicked around like a stone. His trajectory has been shaped by his propensity to plunge, again and again, into the unknown. He is a man who stuffs twelve hundred dollars in his pocket and heads south, without a clue how he will reach his destination or what he will find there, all because a traveler once showed him a suitcase full of money. He is a man who returns to South Africa's townships, again and again, to open a cash business, in full knowledge that his course of action will probably kill him. He is a person prepared to say good-bye to his beloved children and wife because he will not go back to the past.

I have come to understand that Asad and I are very different. He is prepared to court death in ways that I am not.

I do not mean by this that he has some dark proclivity I cannot understand, nor that he is insane. At the back of all of our thoughts and our actions, I think, stands an image of a completed life, a sense of who we will have been at the moment of our deaths. For Asad, to have lived a fully human life is to have altered radically the course of his family's history, so that his children and their children and their children in turn live lives nobody in Somalia at the time of his own birth could have imagined.

If this is indeed Asad's idea of a worthwhile life then it must by definition entail plunging into the unknown. For there is no bridge from the world of his parents to the one he imagines for his children. Getting there requires jumping over a void in the hope that he will land on his feet on the other side.


It is a Tuesday, which is fortuitous, for Tuesday is his day off, and he has set several hours aside for me. I have told him that my flight lands a little after 11 a.m., that I will come to him shortly thereafter.

But the GPS in my rented car will not accept my hotel's address, and the one-page city map I have been given is awfully schematic, and I get lost and drive around for ages. By the time I call Asad from my hotel room to tell him I am on my way it is two in the afternoon.

"I have been waiting for you since eleven thirty," he says sharply. "If I had known that you were only coming in the afternoon, I would have worked a half-shift overtime this morning."

I am silent for a moment. In the three years I have known him he has been gracious to a fault. I have come to see it has a kind of a trademark.

"I was in fact meant to do two overtime shifts today," he continues. "Now I am missing the morning and the afternoon."

"I'm sorry," I say. "I will pay you what you have lost."

"That's good," he replies, in a much lighter tone. "But even if you hadn't offered, if I'd been given the choice between earning extra money and seeing Jonny, I would see Jonny."

If this is a retraction, or an attempt to backtrack, it is halfhearted and lazy. He hangs up the phone.

Driving to his apartment, I wonder whence his rudeness comes. What has he been thinking about me in the months we've been apart?

Perhaps my doggedness has simply become too weird for him. Hour upon hour I sat him down in the passenger seat of my car and twisted and tugged at every last memory inside him. All the while, he kept an eye in the rearview mirror for the violent death he believed that my presence might court. Then I went to Kenya and to Ethiopia to trace his footsteps and then to London to find his family; there was nothing, it seemed, that I would not do, nowhere I would not go. I had come back brandishing the rewards of my travels—news of some tender and difficult family history. And, now, it still isn't over. I have followed him all the way to America to probe and fiddle some more, like some cartoon character who is always waiting around the next corner.

This book was never his, after all. I wedged him between the seven thousand rand I paid to start his business and the promise of a share of royalties. He cooperated in part out of gratitude for what I had done and in part for the prospect of future reward.

But it is more than that. I know that he abandoned the book shortly after starting it and has been unable to pick it up again. We have not yet discussed in any depth why he reacted this way. The book has upset him. His upset, I think, has become anger.

When I arrive at the apartment, his irritation is gone. He is walking around barefoot, in an undershirt and jeans, and is breezy and full of laughter. Sadicya greets me in an English she did not possess when I last saw her, and Rahma grabs a fistful of Asad's jeans and stares at me from between his legs. They are the happy immigrant family, pleased to see the guest who has come from so far.

The apartment is sparsely furnished, but not unpleasant. Sadicya sits at the end of a very long couch, long enough for her lanky husband to stretch out on, I surmise, and the floor is strewn with Rahma's toys. The two bedrooms at the back are roomy and high-ceilinged and furnished with good beds. It strikes me that this is the first time Asad has ever had a home shared with nobody but his own family. There was the shack in Blikkiesdorp, of course, but that was barely longer than his couch.

In Cape Town, our customary space was the inside of a car. Now, in Kansas City, we begin another custom—we walk long distances through the stifling heat. It starts on our first afternoon together. He tells me that the family has just moved to the apartment in which we are sitting, and I ask if we can walk to the one to which they arrived.

"Walk?" he asks. "It's quite far. Let's take the car."

"No," I say. "Let's walk."

We stroll through a neighborhood of freestanding clapboard houses, each surrounded by a square of garden. Every so often, the houses are interrupted by brown apartment blocks like the one in which I found Asad and his family. Kansas City is so very neat, so green and manicured, even the poorer parts, like Asad's neighborhood. And it is so mysteriously empty. There is nobody on the front porches and nobody on the sidewalks.

We cross a bridge. Beneath us on the left, rich, matted parkland stretches into the distance. A little farther on is a large lake surrounded by a landscaped garden and then forest. Like everything else in Kansas City, all this space is empty.

"When I arrived," Asad says, "the trees were bare. Now, this whole city is thick with green. It is as if there are two Kansas Cities, one for winter and the other for summer. It is amazing to me."

We cross a small, handsome park with fountains and symmetrical paths and carefully cut grass, and Asad tells me that during their first weeks in Kansas City he would take Rahma and Musharaf here every morning. Rahma would put her finger in the fountain, he says, as if the finger were a person and the fountain a massive waterfall. The moment the water hit her hand she would shriek.

I picture them in this pretty American park, these three Africans trailing their crazy history, and for a split second, I see the whole thing: Asad's and Musharaf's odysseys from East Africa to Cape Town, Rahma's birth in Blikkiesdorp, their trip across the Atlantic. Their pasts are attached to them like long, smoky tails, and I am momentarily overcome with emotion.

"Asad," I say. "It is amazing that you are here. I can barely believe it."

"It was very hard for a while, brother," he tells me. "For the first few weeks, I was not so sure about this place."

An organization called Jewish Vocational Service was responsible for resettling them. They were fetched from the airport and delivered to an apartment with a fridge full of fresh food and a check for just sixty-eight dollars. The following weeks were filled with the bureaucracy of becoming American residents: applications for Social Security numbers, for food stamps, for Medicaid.

The primary function of Jewish Vocational Service, it seemed, was to place refugees in employment. Asad did not like the way they went about it.

"They only wanted us to work downtown," he tells me. "They would get very upset if we wanted to work anywhere else. And they only wanted us to do bullshit work. They wanted me to clean toilets, brother, to wash floors in some empty building at three o'clock in the morning. And for this, they take a dollar an hour of your pay for the first three months."

He got online and looked for work.

"Everything requires a high school certificate," he tells me. "Everything requires this or that or something I don't have. Every day, I would walk to the Somali shop, I would get online and search for jobs. There was nothing for me. Then I would walk to Jewish Vocational Service and see if they needed an interpreter that day. Brother, I walked for hours and hours and hours. I walked this whole city. I would come home every evening with nothing."

A couple of months after he arrived, the first advance on royalties for this book came through, and Asad immediately bought a car.

"A Toyota," he tells me. "They have Fords and Chevrolets in this country, but what I know to be reliable are Toyotas."

It was this, a car, registered in his name, a driver's license in his wallet, that took him truly inside America. For with these things, he discovered that America was watching him and that it remembered what it saw.

"Brother," he says, "you commit a traffic offense in this country and it goes into a system and the system remembers. After your third offense, your fourth offense, they take away your license."

It was a revelation. In this city of half a million people, everyone was clocked and monitored and bound to a sprawling filigree of rules. And when you were caught breaking one of them, your violation was marked, and the mark did not go away.

At first, it frightened him. Not only did this place want certificates and qualifications he could not possibly acquire. It also circled above him like a hunting bird ready to swoop. He was locked out, incessantly watched, ready to be devoured.

And then something happened that changed his perspective. Sadicya had gotten pregnant again before they left Cape Town; on an evening in late July, four months to the week after their arrival in Kansas City, she went into labor.

"We phone for the ambulance," Asad recalls, "and the woman on the phone starts talking. 'Do not allow her to cross her legs. Position her like this. Do not allow her to do that.' While she is still talking, I hear the siren. It has taken maybe four minutes. And I realize: there is a whole machine in this city waiting for the ladies to go into labor. You pick up the phone and it comes to you. Before I had hung up, I said to myself: When I get a job, I want to pay taxes in this country.

"The day after Sadicya and our daughter Rayan came home, there is a knock at the door. It is two social workers. They come in. They start telling us what to do with our child. She must not lie this way at night; she must lie that way. You must not feed her like this; you must feed her like that. Brother, at the hospital, they record every death of a small baby, and they ask why that baby has died. And they realize that many die because the parents are doing things wrong, and they send these social workers out to make sure that the babies do not die.

"I can't believe it. I am staring at this social worker. She sees me staring, and she says, 'This is your American daughter.'

"It sounded so strange to me. I said, 'No, she is not my American daughter. She is my daughter.'

"The social worker laughed. She said, 'Yes, she is your daughter. But she is your *American* daughter.'

"I didn't like it when she said it. But she is right. Where is home? Somalia? I cannot even go to Somalia. How can you call a place you cannot go 'home'? Home is where the Social Security is, brother. Home is where the social workers knock on the door because they do not want you to kill your baby by mistake."

During his first weeks in Kansas City, when he had no car and walked the city, he would pass groups of homeless men early each morning on the outskirts of downtown. Their clothes were dirty, their faces rough like leather, their worldly possessions stuffed into giant backpacks that they wore like astronauts stepping onto the moon. They never met his eyes when he passed. They would huddle together and speak to one another intently, but the rest of the city seemed not to exist for them.

They sent a chill through him. Why people might stumble and fall in a place like this was beyond his imagination.

"It took me a while to find out," he tells me. "Sometime in the past, when they were younger, they made a mistake. They were arrested for something. Maybe they fought in a bar and someone got badly hurt. When you are found guilty of doing something serious, they take away your Social Security."

"You mean your food stamps and your Medicaid?" I ask.

"Yes, but everything else, too. You cannot sign a rent contract, for example. The landlord will not sign. So you have nowhere to live."

"What if one of them wins the lottery and has ten million dollars?" I ask.

"You can have as much money as you like; you will not be allowed to buy a home. Nobody will employ you or sell you anything or buy anything from you. There are places for these people: shelters, food kitchens. They make sure that you do not starve to death, but that is all."

I say nothing. It seems churlish to quibble. In time, his picture of America will no doubt change. But for now what he sees are the terms of a grand contract. He lives in a country where everything he ever does leaves a trace, and every trace is judged. If he abides by the rules, America will care for him. If he does not, it will ruin him.

Whether he has asked himself if America will honor its side of the deal I am not sure. At this early stage, it is probably not a helpful question to ask.

The idea of this contract has freed him, he says. It has filled him with confidence. And with confidence, he has found work. It is only parking cars at a rental agency, but it pays $8.50 an hour, enough to pay the rent and feed and clothe his family; enough to stand back and ask what he is going to do next.

His idea is to drive a truck or, even better, to use his share of the royalties for this book as a down payment for a truck of his own. He has already taken the first of several exams to get a commercial permit.

"This is a good place," he says. "The future is close. If I reach out with my arm, I can almost touch it."

We are on our way home now, walking again across the pretty square park where he used to take his children. I do not think that his immigrant's zeal is illusory. He is an immensely competent man. His capacity to read a place for ways it might secrete money is now hardwired into his being. If it is possible for a stranger with no formal education to earn a good living here, he will do it.

And then what? As soon as he is able, he says, he will go to Somaliland and find his two lost children. He will bring them here.

"And Foosiya?" I ask.

"She is their mother. I will offer to find a way for her to come, too."

"What if she is married to another man and has children with him?"

"They must all come."

We walk on in silence, but he can hear my skepticism in the sound of my gait.

"Brother," he says, "I cannot know the details. I cannot plan the whole thing from A to Z. I can only deal with each problem as it comes to me."

Perhaps it is the heat: walking beside him, my thoughts about Asad take on a corporeal form. From his neck to his midriff, I see extending before him a translucent bubble, visible only when the light hits it from the right angle. It is here that he lives most fiercely, not in his flesh and bones. He is a paterfamilias. He is gathering the children he has spawned around his new American life. It is a long, slow project. It may take forever.

During my time in Kansas City, I make myself useful. Asad works eight or nine hours a day. While he is gone, Musharaf needs to be fetched from school, Rahma to attend doctors' appointments, Sadicya to shop. Public transportation in this city is patchy, and Sadicya does not drive. So I come each morning, and Asad and I take our daily walk. Then he leaves for work and I stay and ferry various family members to wherever they need to go.

His departure is always difficult for it draws from Rahma the most terrible grief. She sees the signs of his leaving early—a change of shirt, a search for shoes—and she sits herself down on the living room floor and wails. When he closes the door behind him, her crying gives way to screeching and I feel her rage and her lostness in my bones. She does not stop, sometimes for more than an hour.

She is two years and five months old, and she speaks neither Somali nor English, but her own invented language. On the first day, Asad puts an arm around me, pokes a finger into my chest, and says, "This is Jonny."

She looks me over skeptically, from head to toe.

"In twenty minutes," Asad says, "she will have her own name for you."

And so she does. Later in the day, she begins calling me "Guffer," and that is what I remain. Her brother, Musharaf, is "Mick," her bed is "misser," to sleep is to "ssssshz," a car is a "bleeper."

She and Asad have long conversations, he in Somali, she in her gobbledygook. They are always eye to eye when they talk; she stands on her father's thighs and holds his face, feeling for the vibrations of his voice in his jaws.

She will not take her eyes off him, will not stop touching him. When he is walking around the house, she is wrapped around his back. When he is talking to me, she is curled up in his lap. When we eat a meal, she sits on his knee and eats from his plate.

Once, on a trip to the supermarket with the two of them, I turn into an aisle and come upon the oddest scene. She is sitting on the floor weeping, her legs stretched out in front of her. He has crouched down very low, his mouth over her ear. He is whispering to her. His eyes are downcast, his face full of care, full of love. As I walk past them, I am, momentarily, close enough to hear: "Sorry," he says, over and over again. "I am so, so sorry."

In the car, I ask what has upset her.

"She pooed in her pants," he replies mildly. "It is her worst experience. It humiliates her."

On my third day in Kansas City, Rahma has a doctor's appointment half an hour before Asad starts work; time is tight. He bundles her and Sadicya into his car, and I follow to the hospital. It is only once we are there that I see how little Sadicya can do. Asad must find the doctor's room, for Sadicya could never do so on her own. He must answer the nurse's simple questions—Rahma's age, the family's address, their Medicaid details—for Sadicya cannot. Asad is now late for work. I rush out with him so that we can swap Rahma's baby seat from his car to mine. He disappears into the traffic, and I walk slowly back inside.

I hear Rahma screaming from a hundred yards away. By the time I reach the doctor's waiting room, it is deafening. She is lying on her back howling for all she's worth. Asad has been gone twenty minutes now, and still, she is enraged. A group of three ladies, all of them elderly and large, have gathered around her. They are charming and lovely, and they are trying to cheer her up.

"Any minute now, you're gonna set me to cryin', child," one them says. "You're gonna set me to cryin' and that ain't something you want to see. No, ma'am, you do not wanna set me to cryin'."

Sadicya is on the couch next to Rahma. Her body is turned from her daughter, her chin is lifted, and her gaze is fixed on something in another world. She is here but not here. The howls that fill the room are background noise.

I saw Sadicya so often in Cape Town, but I did not know her at all. We shared almost no language. She expressed no desire to communicate with me. And, besides, Asad and I sat always in my car, and she was thus forever out of sight.

It is only now that I see the extent of her disability and thus the full weight of Asad's burden. It is for him to earn a living, to see that Musharaf attends the after-school programs necessary for him to catch up, that he has the right equipment for baseball and soccer, that Rahma sees the doctor, that there are linens on the beds and food in the fridge.

And it is for him to love the children.

Perhaps I misinterpreted his irritation when I arrived late. Moving his family from one day to the next is a multipronged campaign requiring more limbs than he has. The tasks that stack up waiting for Tuesday, his precious day off, must be longer than his arm. To set aside the day to see me is already a sacrifice; I had not appreciated what it might mean for me to come three hours late.

During my time in Kansas City, I meet Somali women who drive cars, who work in offices, who run their households. I meet Somali women who play with their children. When Asad came across Sadicya and Musharaf in the wake of the violence, the mother hunched over a gas burner, the child looking lost, his judgment had been right. They would have died without his help; Sadicya was no longer able to make her way in the world.

When I ask Asad about it, he is philosophical.

"You cannot change a person's nature," he says quietly.

"And if she never learns to drive?" I ask. "If she is never able to shop for food or talk to a doctor about her daughter's illness?"

"Brother, I hope she gets to learn these things," he says.

He is far more concerned by something else. Of Kansas City's small Somali population, more than half are Ogadeni. People have been giving him trouble about Sadicya. With contempt in their voices, they ask why he stooped to marry a Galgale.

"I tell them that who I marry is my business. 'No,' they say. 'When you stoop, we all stoop. When you bury your face in shit, our faces stink too.'"

"There were many Ogadeni in Cape Town," I say. "Did they not say things like that?"

"In Cape Town," he replies, "you fight people who insult you. Here, if you fight, you go to jail and you lose your Social Security. One of the problems of living in this country is that people can say what they like to your face."

There is a hint of irony in his voice, as if the whole matter can be brushed aside with a little humor. But his face is dark and furrowed. He is not telling me the full story, I think. He is holding in reserve some of the pain that throbs from the stigmata on his skin.

"When I told you the story about Sadicya," he asks, "and you went away and read about the people they call the Galgale, what did you learn?"

I tell him that they have no place in Somali genealogy; they are not among the six great clans that constitute the Somali nation and are thus found in Somali history only as negatives, as people who are not.

"What do you mean, they cannot be found in Somali history?" he asks. "They are nothing but Somali. They were always there. How can you say that they were there, but they were also not there? Who has the right to tell them: 'My forebears were there; yours were not'? Whoever says that is an idiot."

He is speaking in no more than a murmur. We are in his sitting room, Sadicya is in the kitchen, and he does not want her to overhear. But even in these quiet tones I sense the force of his rage.

He may be an immensely competent man, I think to myself, but the violence in his past still hobbles him. It has taken corporeal form—it is the burden of Sadicya and Musharaf. He was reeling when he met them. The pogroms had slashed at the flesh of his being. He had become half man, half child. It was only by taking these scorned people under his wing that he could escape their fate and become an adult again. They are the scars of his past and price of his restoration.

On my fourth day in Kansas City, a sudden burst of communication from Sadicya.

"I must find work," she says. "It is a very big something. That I get money."

She is sitting in the backseat of my car with her daughters. I have just taken her to an appointment at the other end of the city. We are almost home. I eye her in the rearview mirror.

"Why?" I ask.

"My grandmother. She in refugee camp in Kenya. I must bring her. My sister. My sister in Kismayo. She suffer. I must bring her."

"What work will you do?" I ask.

"Any work. Any. Whatever. Cleaning. Whatever."

Neither of us says anything more. We get home, and I watch her and her children make their way indoors. She turns and waves from the front door, her cheeks bulging from under her head scarf. I have glanced for no more than an instant through a tiny crack in the door to her world. That is enough to have learned a great deal. It will cost Asad all his worth to track down his children, to bring them here, to settle them. It may take him the rest of his life. Her family, I surmise, is far from his thoughts. She is powerless to enforce her will upon this world. Between her and Asad lies a chasm.

"Why are you unable to read the book?" I ask.

He glances at me briefly, on his face a look of apology, I think. I am not sure.

It is early evening. Although the whole family is home there is a stillness about the house. He is staring out of the window. Rahma has fallen asleep in his lap, and he cups her head in his open palm.

"I am not demanding that you read it," I continue. "If it is too upsetting, then of course you mustn't. But I worry. What if I've said things that will hurt you or offend you? What if I've said things that are just wrong?"

"When you said a book," he begins, "I thought you would ask ten questions and then go and write. I never thought . . ." He throws his head back and laughs. "You came back and back and back. You went deeper and deeper and deeper."

"I went to Ethiopia—"

"That was fine. I was happy for you to go there, to see for yourself. But when you said you want to come here to Kansas City and it was for *more book*. Man!"

I smile to myself. Right at the beginning, a few weeks after I began interviewing him, he asked to see a book I had written about South Africa's prison gangs. He had just spent a weekend in the cells of a police station, and had had his first rude encounter with the fearsome 28s. He had wanted to know more.

I gave him the book, and when we saw each other next he told me that he'd spent several days dipping in and out of it. From then on, during the sessions in my car, I thought I detected a change in the way he told stories. He was much more attentive to the particular; he was straining, I thought, to capture the woof of his childhood days. He froze moments and described them with care; he began speaking of objects, of things. I was so appreciative. From his reading, I imagined, he had imbibed what it meant to fashion a book from a conversation. He was helping me in my task.

It is amazing how we—I—listen for what we most want to hear. For months I had walked around with this idea of a collaboration between us, one we both fully understood. I try to remember when I started doubting this story. I do not recall.

"What is it that upsets you when you read it?" I ask.

"It is two things," he says crisply. "The one is the loss, loss, loss. First I lose my mother. Then I lose my home. Then I lose Yindy. Then the Ali-Yusuf in Nairobi. Then I lose Yindy's family in Wardheer. Then Rooda. Then I lose my uncle, then my cousin, then Foosiya and my children. Everywhere, it is loss, loss, loss."

His raised voice has woken Rahma. She crawls out of the fetal position in which she had been sleeping and lies on her back. She is watchful, her eyes on her father's face.

I am on the brink of telling him that he did in fact lose all these things, but I check myself. The import of what he has conveyed is so obvious that there is nothing to say.

I have spent the last couple of years memorializing his life. But there is no intrinsic value in remembering. He has in fact just told me that he cannot afford to take in the sweep of his life. To remember in this way is crippling. It is better for him, I think, to see his past as a series of sparks or flashes, a selection of moments when he was the one who decided what would happen next. That is what he must see in his past in order to craft a future.

This book is for me and for those who read it. It is of no value to him but for the money that will come his way. He will buy a truck with that money, or a part of a truck. From this book he will fashion another moment when he is the one who decides.

"What is the second thing that upset you?" I ask.

"The business with her," he says, pointing his chin at the kitchen, where Sadicya is preparing dinner. "I think of Abdullahi people reading this book and feeling shameful. They will be angry."

He stares out of the window. I stare at him.

"Are you asking me to take Sadicya's origins out of the book?" I ask eventually.

"No," he says quietly. "It is shameful for them to feel shameful. I don't care."

I could push the point, but it is in my interests to hold my tongue. I cast an eye into the future and see a time when he regrets having answered my question thus.

Rahma has crawled up in his lap again. Her thumb is in her mouth, her nose pressed up against his side. From the kitchen comes the smell of chicken and the crackling of meat in a pan. Sadicya is calling Musharaf to the table. We will eat in a moment. And after dinner I will say good-bye.

# Acknowledgments

First thanks go to Pearlie Joubert, who introduced me to Asad Abdullahi and vouched for my trustworthiness. I am enormously grateful.

When I began working with Asad in September 2010 I was a senior researcher at the Institute for the Humanities in Africa (Huma) at the University of Cape Town. In exchange for a monthly salary, I was obliged only to research and write what I liked, an inordinately privileged position. Many thanks to my former colleagues Deborah Posel, Shamil Jeppie, Natasha Distiller, and Heather Maytham.

Halfway through this project, I moved to the African Studies Centre at Oxford University. The formidable cohort of doctoral students who ran the Horn of Africa Seminar gave me the induction I needed to the politics of Somalia and Ethiopia. I am especially indebted to Emma Lochery who so generously shared both her deep knowledge and her circle of Ethiopian friends.

Many thanks to Hiruy Gossaye, who helped me get inside Bole Mikhael.

I was blessed to visit Dire Dawa and Harar in the company of Khalid Yousuph who, with grace and without inhibition, showed me so much of his own life.

I am also immensely grateful to Mohamed Mohamud, without whom I would not have discovered the life histories of Asad's parents.

Many thanks to David Godwin, Jeremy Boraine, and Dan Franklin. Special thanks to Dan Frank and Betsy Sallee, with whom it has been such a pleasure to work.

I am grateful, as ever, to Mark Gevisser for his shrewd eye, and to Tony Hamburger who helped me better to understand Asad's relationship with Sadicya.

Thank you, again, to Lomin Saayman, for more than I can possibly say here. And to Carol Steinberg and David Jammy, my bedrock.

# Further Reading

The following books and articles helped shape aspects of *A Man of Good Hope*. They also serve as a guide to those who wish to read further about some of the many episodes, themes, and events covered in these pages.

Why a country whose citizens share a common language, religion, and long-standing heritage has torn itself to pieces is the great question that hangs over Somalia. It is the subject of an ongoing and sometimes ill-tempered debate. On one side are those who see the civil war of the 1990s as the expression of an ancient Somali proclivity to fight. The best proponent of this position is I. M. Lewis, the grand old ethnographer of northern Somali society. His ethnography of the Somali clan system, *A Pastoral Democracy* (Oxford: Oxford University Press, 1961), was the bible of Somali scholarship until the 1990s, when younger scholars finally rose to challenge it. The latest edition of his *A Modern History of the Somali* (Oxford and Athens, Ohio: James Currey and Ohio University Press, 2002) contains his fullest account of the origins of the civil war. His take on the war is in part an expression of personal disappointment; he was an ardent supporter of anticolonial Somali movements in the 1940s and 1950s and a great friend to many of the Somali nationalists who dreamed of building a progressive African nation from the ruins of empire.

Pitted against Lewis are a host of younger scholars who take umbrage at the idea that the roots of the war are primordial and are offended by the implication that Somalis are born to violence. These scholars find the roots of the war not in the ancient clan system, but in modern inequities of race and class, in the political economy of avarice and greed, and in the global politics of the Cold War. For an account of Somali society that differs sharply with Lewis's, see Catherine Besteman, *Unraveling Somalia: Race, Violence and the Legacy of Slavery* (Philadelphia: University of Pennsylvania Press, 1999). And for an interpretation of the causes of the war that challenges Lewis's account, see the articles collected in Catherine

Besteman and Lee V. Cassanelli, eds., *The Struggle for Land in Southern Somalia: The War Behind the War* (London and New Brunswick: Haan and Transaction, 1996).

In the late 1990s, Besteman and Lewis had an abrasive exchange in the pages of a prestigious anthropology journal: Catherine Besteman, "Representing Violence and 'Othering' Somalia," *Cultural Anthropology* 11, no. 1 (1996): 120–33; I. M. Lewis, "Doing Violence to Ethnography: A Response to Catherine Besteman's 'Representing Violence and "Othering" Somalia,'" *Cultural Anthropology* 13, no. 1 (1998): 100–108; Catherine Besteman, "Primordialist Blinders: A Reply to I. M. Lewis," *Cultural Anthropology* 13, no. 1 (1998): 109–20.

In recent years, the debate has moderated somewhat and has become better for it. Now that scholars are no longer shouting one another down, more serious attention is being paid to the obvious complexity of the place of history in the Somali present. See, for instance, Jutta Bakonyi, "Moral Economies of Mass Violence: Somalia, 1988–1991," *Civil Wars* 11, no. 4 (2009): 434–54.

Looking at Asad's life, you can see that questions about ancient times are strikingly close to the surface and yet no less mercurial for that. It never occurred to Asad to ask Rooda, the most important benefactor of his childhood and youth, his clan. And yet, when Asad accounts for the behavior of black South Africans, he refers to what he believes happened to their ancestors in the mists of time. And his decision to marry Sadicya is at once a defiance of genealogical chauvinism and an acknowledgment of its continuing power.

For a penetrating account of the condition of Asad's home city of Mogadishu a decade after he fled, see Roland Marchal, *A Survey of Mogadishu's Economy* (Nairobi: European Commission, 2002). For a brief and incisive account of Somali politics during two decades of war, see Ken Menkhaus, "Somalia at the Tipping Point," *Current History* (May 2012).

Anyone interested in Somalia would do well to read the novels of Nuruddin Farah. Readers of *A Man of Good Hope* might be especially interested in his trilogy made up of *Maps* (New York: Pantheon, 1986), *Secrets* (New York: Penguin, 1999), and *Gifts* (New York: Penguin, 2000) for its attention to the Ogadeni war and its aftermath, which, unbeknownst to Asad, did so much to shape his fate.

For a portrait of the Dadaab refugee camps where Asad and Yindy lived, see Cindy Horst, *Transnational Nomads* (New York and Oxford:

Berghahn, 2006). An excellent book on how money moves around the Somali diaspora, which includes an interesting portrait of Somalis in Eastleigh, Nairobi, is Anna Lindley, *The Early Morning Call: Somali Refugees' Remittances* (New York and Oxford: Berghahn, 2010). An essay-length history of Somalis in Eastleigh is Neil Carrier and Emma Lochery, "Missing States? Somali Trade Networks and the Eastleigh Transformation," *Journal of East African Studies* 7, no. 2 (2013): 334–52.

Precious little has been written on Somalis in Addis Ababa or in Dire Dawa. There is, though, a very fine doctoral dissertation on young hustlers who work the streets of inner-city Addis, the world Asad managed to crack and in which he earned a good living. See Marco DiNunzio, "'The Arada Have Been Eaten': Living Through Marginality in Addis Ababa's Inner City" (Ph.D. diss., University of Oxford, 2012).

The most useful account of the Ogadeni war of 1977–78 I have read is Gebru Tareke, "The Ethiopia-Somalia War of 1977 Revisited," *International Journal of African Historical Studies* 33, no. 3 (2000): 635–67. On the Somali region of Ethiopia during the period when Asad lived there, see Tobias Hagmann, "Beyond Clannishness and Colonialism: Understanding Political Disorder in Ethiopia's Somali Region, 1991–2004," *Journal of Modern African Studies* 43, no. 4 (2005): 509–36; and Tobias Hagmann and Mohamud H. Khalif, "State and Politics in Ethiopia's Somali Region Since 1991," *Bildhaan: An International Journal of Somali Studies* 6 (2006): 25–49. On the complicated ethnic politics of Ethiopia and the nationalist movements in its borderlands, see Christopher Clapham, "Rewriting Ethiopian History," *Annales d'Ethiopie* 18 (2002): 37–54.

Asad's journey from the Horn of Africa to Johannesburg is well trodden. Thousands embark upon it each year. For an attempt to map this odyssey and to account for the various fates of those who undertake it, see Christopher Horwood, *In Pursuit of the Southern Dream: Victims of Necessity: Assessment of the Irregular Movement of Men from East Africa and the Horn to South Africa* (Geneva: International Organization for Migration, April 2009). There is also a perceptive and deeply intelligent doctoral dissertation on the subjective dimensions of the sort of journey Asad embarked upon, albeit the subjects of this study were moving north, toward Europe, rather than south. See Joris Schapendonk, "Turbulent Trajectories: Sub-Saharan African Migrants Heading North" (Ph.D. diss., Radboud Universiteit Nijmegen, 2011).

A small literature is beginning to emerge on the Somali traders who operate in the shacklands and townships on the southeastern periphery of Cape Town. See Andrew Charman and Laurence Piper, "From Township Survivalism to Foreign Entrepreneurship: The Transformation of the Spaza Sector in Delft, Cape Town," *Transformation* 78 (2012): 47–73; Andrew Charman and Laurence Piper, "Xenophobia, Criminality and Violent Entrepreneurship: Violence Against Somali Shopkeepers in Delft South, Cape Town, South Africa," *South African Review of Sociology* 13, no. 3 (2012): 81–105; Vanya Gastrow with Roni Amit, *Elusive Justice: Somali Traders' Access to Formal and Informal Justice Mechanisms in the Western Cape* (research report, African Centre for Migration and Society, Johannesburg, 2012).

Much has been written on the nationwide violence against foreign nationals that broke out across South Africa in May 2008. Of particular interest is a debate between two scholars from the University of Witwatersrand in Johannesburg. See Daryl Glaser, "[Dis]connection: Elite and Popular 'Common Sense' on the Matter of Foreigners," in *Go Home or Die Here: Violence, Xenophobia and the Reinvention of Difference in South Africa,* ed. Shireen Hassim, Tawana Kupe, and Eric Worby (Johannesburg: Wits University Press, 2008), pp. 53–64; and Loren Landau, "Loving the Alien? Law, Citizenship and the Future of South Africa's Demonic Society," *African Affairs* 109, no. 435 (2010): 213–30. See also Southern African Migration Project, "The Perfect Storm: The Realities of Xenophobia in Contemporary South Africa," Migration Policy Brief, no. 50 (Southern African Migration Project, 2008); Loren Landau, ed., *Exorcising the Demons Within: Xenophobia, Violence and Statecraft in Contemporary South Africa* (Johannesburg: Wits, 2011).

As for Sadicya's harrowing story, the most illuminating material I could find on Somali minority clans was by the scholar and human rights activist Virginia Luling, who died while this book was being written. Especially informative is the expert testimony she gave to the UK Asylum and Immigration Tribunal in 2006 on the fate of the Galgale during the civil war. See https://tribunalsdecisions.service.gov.uk/utiac/decisions/2006-ukait-73. See also a document prepared for Canada's immigration services by Lee Casanelli, *Victims and Vulnerable Groups in Southern Somalia* (Canada: Immigration and Refugee Board, 1995).

My understanding of the arc of Asad's life was influenced by the work of the wonderful anthropologist Michael Jackson. See, especially, *At Home in the World* (Durham, North Carolina, and London: Duke University Press, 1995); *The Politics of Storytelling: Violence, Transgres-*

*sion and Intersubjectivity* (Copenhagen: Museum Tusculanum Press); and *Existential Anthropology: Events, Exigencies and Effects* (New York and Oxford: Berghahn, 2008). It is from Jackson that I got the idea that Asad's journey was animated by the desire to effect a revolution in the history of his lineage. See Jackson, "The Shock of the New: On Migrant Imaginaries and Critical Transitions," *Ethnos: Journal of Anthropology* 73, no. 1 (2008): 57–72. Interestingly, when he republished this essay in his book *Lifeworlds: Essays in Existential Anthropology* (Chicago: University of Chicago Press, 2013), Jackson excised the word "revolution." Jackson has recently published a book on migration that I did not get to read before *A Man of Good Hope* went to press: *The Wherewithal of Life: Ethics, Migration and the Question of Well-Being* (Berkeley: University of California Press, 2013).

# Index

### WHAT IS THE WHAT
#### by Dave Eggers

*What Is the What* is the epic novel based on the life of Valentino Achak Deng who, along with thousands of other children—the so-called Lost Boys—was forced to leave his village in Sudan at the age of seven and trek hundreds of miles by foot, pursued by militias, government bombers, and wild animals, crossing the deserts of three countries to find freedom. When he finally is resettled in the United States, he finds a life full of promise, but also heartache and myriad new challenges. Moving, suspenseful, and unexpectedly funny, *What Is the What* is an astonishing novel that illuminates the lives of millions through one extraordinary man.

Fiction

### THE PIRATES OF SOMALIA
#### by Jay Bahadur

The first close-up look at the hidden world of Somali pirates by a young journalist who dared to make his way into their remote havens and spent a year infiltrating their lives. For centuries, stories of pirates have captured imaginations around the world. The recent ragtag bands of pirates off the coast of Somalia, hijacking multimillion-dollar tankers owned by international shipping conglomerates, have brought the scourge of piracy into the modern era. Jay Bahadur's riveting narrative exposé—the first of its kind— looks at who these men are, how they live, the forces that created piracy in Somalia, how the pirates spend the ransom money, how they deal with their hostages, among much, much more. It is a revelation of a dangerous world at the epicenter of political and natural disaster.

History

THE BOOK OF UNKNOWN AMERICANS
*by Christina Henríquez*

When fifteen-year-old Maribel Rivera sustains a terrible injury, the Riveras leave behind a comfortable life in Mexico and risk everything to come to the United States so that Maribel can have the care she needs. Once they arrive, it's not long before Maribel attracts the attention of Mayor Toro, the son of one of their new neighbors, who sees a kindred spirit in this beautiful, damaged outsider. Their love story sets in motion events that will have profound repercussions for everyone involved. Here Henríquez seamlessly interweaves the story of these star-crossed lovers, and of the Rivera and Toro families, with the testimonials of men and women who have come to the United States from all over Latin America. *The Book of Unknown Americans* is a stunning novel of hopes and dreams, guilt and love—a book that offers a resonant new definition of what it means to be American.

Fiction

VINTAGEBOOKS
Available wherever books are sold.
www.vintagebooks.com